Stephen and Pat's book is an absolute pleasure to read. It is just so timely to be looking at the real meaning of total inclusivity in all its dimensions, especially higher education. For too long we have known of and spoken of discrimination but have not been bold enough or organised enough to fully address it. This book will stimulate conversations – even uncomfortable conversations and that is what is needed.

Prof Deborah Eyre, *Executive Chair at High Performance Learning, UK*

This book is for anyone engaged with the question of what the University is for and asking how such institutions can achieve survival with integrity. Integrity, through the lens of Total Inclusion, refers to principled, respectful inclusion of all individuals pursuing their aspirations through Higher Education – and the avoidance of harm through systematic bias and prejudice – explicit or implicit. Such a responsibility attaches particularly to Universities, distinctive and powerful institutions in society that Whitehead and O'Connor argue should be exemplars of inclusive values and practice.

Whitehead and O'Connor start from basics; evidence and theory interwoven. The evidence is drawn with a global sweep, and the authors' comparative approach will broaden awareness. Throughout the book, they make their case with care, through a 'critical' lens that exposes the systematic injustices that result from many received practices. The analysis is neither sweeping, nor simplistic. Both authors have walked their talk. Both were what would now be termed 'non-traditional' entrants to HE; both have had long careers in Universities; and both are critical scholars with keen eyes for how structural and cultural injustices play out, and how they can be challenged. The book offers a credo; humanist, inclusive, and, in asking how to resolve rather than polarise issues of freedom and justice, appealing to our widest, collective interest.

Each chapter has a sharp summary and conclusion, but it's in the detail of the argument that the compelling value of the book is to be found. There's a lot to think about and a lot to do as the last two chapters reveal: Whitehead and O'Connor provide a powerful framework, and some useful practical moves to start the process of total inclusion.

Steve Cropper, *Emeritus Professor of Management, Keele University, UK*

T0373566

Whitehead and O'Connor have written a must-read primer for anyone concerned with the future of higher education. It is a book for students, leaders, lecturers, all who care to establish a university culture where individuals can bring their whole self to work and thrive in an environment in which people of all backgrounds are empowered and can contribute authentically and genuinely. The concept of Total Inclusivity is timely and powerful during this unprecedented time. Achieving diversity and equity in the workplace is a journey that never ends, but the most important thing is to start. The book is not only informed by contemporary research but also heavily embedded in organizational practices. Read this book – and learn both theoretical and practical knowledge to help you contribute to achieving Total Inclusivity in global higher education.

Dr Minh Nguyen, *Director of Education Services, Vinschool Education System, Vietnam*

Ever the voice of progressive clarity, Stephen Whitehead (with Pat O'Connor) explores the transient nature of identity in our world. No punches are pulled as the old, romantic notion of leadership is dispersed through a concise breakdown. *Creating a Totally Inclusive University* offers a clear path forward with a strong foundation of both research and morality, focusing on the implementation of true practice over lip service. Any stakeholders in the modern university system would do well to read and keep this one close at hand.

Alex Batten, *Head of Operations, Harrow Appi International School, Japan*

This is an important book, coming at an important time. Universities face critical scrutiny, not least of all from increasingly informed – and increasingly demanding – students and staff. Nothing short of 'total inclusivity' is enough. Relevant to managers and leaders in institutions of all shapes, sizes, and forms, *Creating a Totally Inclusive University* balances theory and actionable insight with powerful stories of lived experience (both where things went right and where things went wrong). Stephen and Pat add their authoritative and informed voices to the rising chorus demanding fully inclusive Universities.

Dr Denry Machin, *MD Pedagogue and International School Consultant*

This important book is emblematic of conversations happening across the education sector as a whole. In my work at a Russell Group UK university, I know first hand the importance placed on valuing, protecting, and nurturing diverse identities. This insightful book marries theory with practice, supporting universities with their current reflections and policy making in this area.

Nicholas McKie, *Assistant Professor, University of Warwick, UK*

This inspiring book confirms that universities must transform themselves in this new global era. Universities can no longer be exclusive; they must meet the changing needs of a global society. Universities have been based too much on specialization and elitism, with little concern for inclusivity and collaboration. Every aspect of this book and all the practical guidance given by the authors, leads us to co-rebuild a smarter total inclusive university.

Dr Chokchai Suttawet, *Thailand National Research Office and development activist*

As ever more intense scrutiny is placed on the capacity of Higher Education Institutions to create inclusive spaces, the authors offer accessible, non-judgemental pathways for HE communities to reframe approaches to Diversity, Equity, Inclusion and Justice. The book not only gives cause for a critical reassessment of HEI cultures (and the dominant hierarchies of value entrenched within it) but demonstrates how Totally Inclusive activism can impact positively on our lives – in education, and beyond. Aside from being a truly welcome addition to a flourishing literature on this subject, the book is notable for offering a framework for the creation of safe, intellectually stimulating, communities in which every individual belongs.

Dr Rob Power, *Founder, www.powerfulhistories.com*

Creating a Totally Inclusive University

This book introduces the concept and practices of Total Inclusivity to universities around the world. It is written to help universities contend with increasing public scrutiny and uncertainty around issues of diversity, equity, inclusion and justice now at the forefront of global higher education.

Providing a guide and template to higher education leaders, the book addresses such issues as work culture, free speech, student wellbeing, racism, LGBT+ identities, managerialism or 'simply' the ability of the institution to survive post-Covid. Whitehead and O'Connor argue that handling these issues can best be done in a university climate and system which is Totally Inclusive. This is the standard for any higher education institution to aim for, not only in its teaching but in its fundamental principles and everyday practices if it is to meet its obligations to its members and to wider society.

The book aims to support universities as well as challenge the status quo as they grapple with the different global and societal pressures confronting them. It is an essential read for anyone working in leadership in higher education institutions and those interested in creating inclusive practices within their institution.

Stephen Whitehead is a British sociologist and educationalist. He is an internationally recognised expert on men and masculinities, gender identity, and international education. This is his 16th book, and his third on Total Inclusivity. Stephen lives with his wife in Chiang Mai, Thailand. www.stephen-whitehead.com

Pat O'Connor is an Irish sociologist and feminist. She is an internationally recognised expert on gender equality, leadership, power and institutional resistance in higher education. An emeritus professor of sociology and social policy at the University of Limerick, she is a visiting professor at University College Dublin, Ireland. This is her ninth book. https://www.ul.ie/research/prof-pat-oconnor

STEPHEN WHITEHEAD WITH
PAT O'CONNOR

Creating a Totally Inclusive University

LONDON AND NEW YORK

Cover image: © Getty Images

First published 2023
by Routledge
4 Park Square, Milton Park, Abingdon, Oxon OX14 4RN

and by Routledge
605 Third Avenue, New York, NY 10158

Routledge is an imprint of the Taylor & Francis Group, an informa business

British Library Cataloguing-in-Publication Data
A catalogue record for this book is available from the British Library

Library of Congress Cataloging-in-Publication Data
Names: Whitehead, Stephen (Stephen M.) author. | O'Connor, Pat, author.
Title: Creating a totally inclusive university / Stephen Whitehead and Pat O'Connor.
Description: Abingdon, Oxon ; New York, NY : Routledge, 2023. | Includes bibliographical references.
Identifiers: LCCN 2022020753 (print) | LCCN 2022020754 (ebook) | ISBN 9781032234496 (hardback) | ISBN 9781032234489 (paperback) | ISBN 9781003277651 (ebook)
Subjects: LCSH: Inclusive education. | Education, Higher--Aims and objectives. | Educational equalization. | Academic freedom. | Universities and colleges--Social aspects.
Classification: LCC LC1200 .W52 2023 (print) | LCC LC1200 (ebook) | DDC 371.9/046--dc23/eng/20220718
LC record available at https://lccn.loc.gov/2022020753
LC ebook record available at https://lccn.loc.gov/2022020754

ISBN: 978-1-032-23449-6 (hbk)
ISBN: 978-1-032-23448-9 (pbk)
ISBN: 978-1-003-27765-1 (ebk)

DOI: 10.4324/9781003277651

Typeset in Joanna
by SPi Technologies India Pvt Ltd (Straive)

Contents

Acknowledgements xiii

Foreword xv

Introducing Total Inclusivity **One** 1

Stephen Whitehead

Defining total inclusivity 2

Total inclusive philosophy 3

Total inclusivity and universities 4

Solving problems? 8

So, who are we? 11

Pat: 'A mere woman...' 11

Stephen: a late starter 12

The structure 14

Part One: How inclusive are universities? 14

Part Two: You and 'your' university 15

Part Three: What next for universities? 15

Notes 16

How Inclusive are Universities? **Part One** 17

Pat O'Connor

Who Cares about Total Inclusivity? **Two** 19

Introduction 19

What are institutions of higher education for? 19

What do stakeholders see as the purpose of higher education? 20

The impact of neo-liberalism: the market as a key stakeholder 23

Is higher education not diverse today? 25

Possible levers to promote a TI agenda? 26

Summary 30

Academic Staff –
How Inclusive do Universities Look? Three **31**
Introduction 31
Higher education: gendered organisations 31
The evidence: gendered segregation in higher education 34
An alternative conceptualisation… 37
Summary and conclusions 41

How does Non-inclusion Work? – Key
Mechanisms and Processes Four **42**
Introduction 42
Processes involving violence and harassment of
women and other 'outsiders' 42
Processes that reinforce the inclusion and
privileging of the 'insiders' 47
Summary 50

How are Universities Responding
to the Big Challenge? Five **51**
Introduction 51
Institutionalised resistance 51
There is no problem: The nature and importance of
legitimating discourses 52
Other manifestations of institutionalised resistance 54
Initiatives to tackle inequality 55
Athena SWAN (AS) 57
Gender Equality Plans (GEPs) 60
Summary and conclusions 62

Leadership, Whiteness and Masculinism Six **63**
Introduction 63
The attractiveness of the concept of leadership 63
Leadership and power 64
Who accesses leadership positions in higher education? 66
Typology of leadership in higher education 71
Summary 74

You and 'Your' University **Part Two** **75**
Stephen Whitehead

The Politics of Belonging **Seven** **77**
Identity 78
Belonging 83
Intersectionality 84
'Others' 87
Conclusion 90
Notes 91

An International Learning Community? **Eight** **92**
Internationalised HE 93
What type of internationalisation? 97
Female internationalisation of HE 98
Tortoises on steroids 99
Contented communities of HE learning? 103
Identity politics 104
Collaboration? 106
Free higher education 107

Privilege **Nine** **111**
Ivory towers? 113
Unearned privilege 114
A story of privilege – Earned and unearned 118
What to do about it? 119
Unconscious bias 121
How to respond? 123
Conclusion 124
Notes 125

'Free' Speech? **Ten** **126**
Introduction 126
Positions 126
Your standpoint? 128
A febrile Climate 128

Can speech ever be free? 130

Totally inclusive speech 131

Trans women are women? 134

Academic freedom? 136

Lamenting a 'simpler age'? 139

Notes 142

A Crisis of Love **Eleven** 143

Wellbeing and safety indicators 144

The invisible student 156

Notes 158

What Next for Universities? **Part Three** 159
Stephen Whitehead

The Totally Inclusive University Audit **Twelve** 161

Introduction 161

Continuum on becoming a totally inclusive university 163

Summarising the actively discriminating, failing university 164

Summarising the tokenistic, rhetorically correct university 166

Summarising the reflectively unsettled,contradictory university 169

Summarising the tentative – working to become a learning university 172

Summarising the Rebuilding, transformative and advancing university 174

Summarising the totally inclusivity university 176

Where is your university on the totally inclusive continuum? 177

What Next for You? **Thirteen** 182

Male dominance 182

Intersectional leadership 184

No 'love song' to leadership 184

What can you do as an TI advocate to advance intersectional leadership? 186

Examples of total inclusivity-approaches in action 187

Strategy and empathy need each other 192

Notes 194

Bibliography 196

Acknowledgements

Our thanks to Dr Alexander Gardner-McTaggart and Dr Sadie Hollins for their contribution to the initial design and structure of the book. Also, our appreciation to Katie Peace and Kendrick Loo, the Routledge duo who supported us throughout the writing and production stages. We also acknowledge the many individuals who have been part of our respective journeys as writers, lecturers and researchers into issues pertaining to diversity, equity, inclusion and justice in and outside of higher education and over many years. We thank all of them for their invaluable contributions.

Acknowledgements

This is the second in a series of books on Total Inclusivity published by Routledge in 2022. The other two are:

Total Inclusivity at Work (S. Whitehead)

Becoming a Totally Inclusive School: A Guide for Teachers and School Leaders (A. Aow, S. Hollins, S. Whitehead)

While each book has its own style and content, their focus and aims are identical; to define, identify, examine, and promote the philosophy and practice of Total Inclusivity in organisations, institutions, society – in this book's case locating it in the context of an analysis of global higher education.

While three books on Total Inclusivity is impressive in itself, we are not unaware of the challenge that TI poses to us all. It will take more than a few books to change the world. Because in the final analysis, that is what is required to bring in Total Inclusivity across all of humanity and in such a way that no one ever need write such a book in the future because the principles underpinning diversity, equity, inclusion and justice will not only be present across society, but they will be accepted across society.

One can take the long view and consider that society is making progress towards a place of universalism, international-mindedness, international care and empathy. And, not least, non-violence.

Or one can look at the state of the world in 2022, the year the concept of Total Inclusivity was first introduced, and despair.

It all depends on one's perspective.

The perspective we adopt for *Creating a Totally Inclusive University* could be described as cautious optimism. The fact that universities exist at all is a tribute to humanity. But the fact that they exist on a tremulous foundation, one riven with inequality, discrimination, violence, elitism and entitlement is no tribute at all.

There cannot be anyone anywhere with even the smallest stake or interest in the future of global higher education who considers universities to have reached some plateau where diversity, equity, inclusion and justice flourish. Certainly, we don't believe that. As this book confirms, there is still a mountain to climb if we are ever to get to that place where higher education is available for all, is a safe and healthy place for all, and with all equally benefiting according to their potential. But, no matter, that is the aim of this book – to head off in the direction of the Totally Inclusive University. Please join us on the journey.

Stephen, with Pat (April 2022)

One

Have we reached the most profound moment in human history? it sure feels that way to a great many of us. Yes, there have been pandemics far deadlier than Covid-19. There have been more conflicts, worse famines, and far more numerous threats to individual safety; at least, for most of us.

But never before has humanity recognised its interconnectedness.

The internet, globalisation, advanced technology, social media, 24/7 news or simply the fact that there are now over 7.7 billion of us all living in close proximity to each other, means that we are now waking up to a new reality; that we are interdependent and that what happens next will impact every one of us – personally.

Covid-19 is a simply the canary in the coalmine; remorselessly delineating how interconnected we really are and how reliant on each other for our individual wellbeing and safety.

Climate change will bring further disruption if not devastation on a scale far beyond that experienced with Covid-19. Indeed, far beyond anything humanity has experienced in its 300,000 years on earth. For climate change is itself connecting to every other aspect of human existence; starting from our basic needs for shelter, food, water to our desire for self-actualisation and higher-level understanding and learning. No one is going to get a pass on this.

And then there is the continuing threat of nuclear war, rendered horrifically stark for all of us by Vladimir Putin's invasion of the Ukraine on the 24th February 2022.

That is why this moment is the most important one in the human story so far – because we are all exposed, all vulnerable, all at risk, not just to pandemics, climate change, and disruption to our comfortable lifestyles, but also exposed to the consequences of the worst aspects of human behaviour. Because how our neighbours react, how our friends and family react, how our work colleagues react, how our

DOI: 10.4324/9781003277651-1

community reacts, how people living on the other side of the world react, and how you react, will determine whether what happens next is a continuation of human advancement or the endgame.

DEFINING TOTAL INCLUSIVITY

What is that opening section saying to you and why have we written it that way?

It is written to appeal to your self-interest. We are respectfully, but unapologetically, warning you of where humanity is right now, and asking you to reflect on the threats to you personally and to consider how you will respond.

That is one dimension of Total Inclusivity; the realisation that it protects everyone so long as everyone, or the vast majority of us, embrace it.

In other words, Total Inclusivity is in your best interests.

There is, of course, another dimension to Total Inclusivity: the moral and ethical one. Maybe you don't need to be prodded into Total Inclusivity through pragmatic self-interest, not least because you've already recognised that diversity, equity, inclusion and social justice are essential for the wellbeing of all of us and therefore there is a compelling humanist reason for embracing these values.[1]

So, what is Total Inclusivity?

> **Total Inclusivity means recognising, valuing, protecting and nurturing diverse identities, including those of race, gender, sexual orientation, class, disability, age, religion and language.**

If you recognise the inherent worthiness of that intention, if it speaks to both your heart and your head, then you are on your way to being an Advocate for Total Inclusivity.

You may ask why we do not include every other possible aspect of human identity within this definition. The answer is simple: it would be impossible to create such a definition without losing its impact; the list would, in theory at least, have no end. Why? Because every single one of us, each of the 7.7 billion people alive today, is unique, occupying and experiencing a different mix of identities across different cultures and communities. And there is a second, equally valid reason;

anyone who can accept to 'value, protect and nurture' race, gender, sexual and class differences, together with those of age, religion, language and disability and do so across the human spectrum, will be for inclusivity in total.

So, does anyone get excluded from Total Inclusivity?

No.

Those for Total Inclusivity exclude no one.

Those against Total Inclusivity exclude themselves.

TOTAL INCLUSIVE PHILOSOPHY

We cannot know how you feel about Total Inclusivity (TI) before you've started reading our book, but we certainly hope you'll have embraced TI by the end of it.

Because without you, there is no Total Inclusivity. And without Total Inclusivity, the future looks grim indeed – for all of us.

Which is why our definition of Total Inclusivity comes with an underpinning philosophy, one now increasingly referred to as the 'new humanism' and neatly summarised in 2010 by Irina Bokava, Director-General of UNESCO.[2]

Being a humanist today means adapting the strength of an age-old message to the contours of the modern world...It means building bridges between North, South, East and West and strengthening the human community to take up our challenges together...This work of 'self-fashioning' is a collective requirement, and here lies the importance of another critical aspect of the [new] humanist message, which emphasises the necessarily collective dimension of all accomplished living. Individuals become whole in society, as members of a community...Now more than ever before, our task is to work towards building this ideal community. Humanists posit the existence of a community of humanity that binds every individual to all others. Conflicts may arise from misunderstandings or superficial disagreements, but that which unites us is stronger than that which separates us.

(Bokova, 2010)

That statement was made a decade before Covid-19 rudely awoke us to the fact that globalisation isn't simply about flying around the world on Boeing jets. Globalisation is defined by physical, emotional and economic connectedness and means taking mutual responsibility for the welfare not only of ourselves, but all of us.

Covid-19 is a warning of what humanity faces as this century unfolds. It is a test of people's willingness to work together to resolve such crises. Climate change will most definitely bring even greater challenges, it already is doing. What will be your role in addressing these problems? Do you believe only in yourself, your own potential, and demonstrate that, for example, by refusing to vaccinate, wear a face mask, make no effort to reduce your use of plastic or carbon footprint? Or do you recognise yourself as a member of the global community, with the need to play your part in trying to ensure its future?

If the latter, then you are already demonstrating new humanist values and therefore it is a small step towards Total Inclusivity.

In short, you cannot be a new humanist and also be racist, sexist, misogynistic, LGBT+-phobic, a hater and a discriminator. You cannot always put your individuality above the common good. To be a new humanist you must recognise the need, indeed the urgency, to contribute to the human community – for all our sakes. Always remembering that:

Total Inclusivity won't happen unless you make it happen. Total Inclusivity is no one person's responsibility – it is every person's responsibility.

TOTAL INCLUSIVITY AND UNIVERSITIES

You may have reflected on what might be seen as an inherent contradiction within the title: Creating Totally Inclusive Universities. For, isn't that an oxymoron? Aren't universities by definition designed and intended to be exclusive?

Yes and no.

They certainly must be centres of knowledge both in terms of teaching and research. In which case they must be exceptional, but that doesn't mean they should be exclusive.

As we argue in Chapter 9, why cannot university provision be made available to every single school leaver and adult who wants it and who can benefit from it? No one can claim it cannot be afforded, certainly in developed countries. Nor can anyone justify exclusiveness on the basis of ability to benefit.

In the 1950s, the idea that over 50% of school leavers, the majority of them females, could or should go on to higher education (HE) at university would have been laughed at by most pro vice chancellors and Ministers for Education.

No one is laughing at that prospect today. Indeed, it is an expectation. What has happened in the past 70 years? Have we suddenly been producing cleverer daughters? Perhaps, but what this data shows – and it is mirrored around the world – is that no one can or should put a limit on developing human potential. TI in HE means:

- Opening the doors to anyone, regardless of their identity mix and background.
- Treating equally everyone who enters these gilded halls of learning.
- Ensuring universities are not separate from but embedded in their societies and communities.

This book is the second in a trilogy we've written on Total Inclusivity. The above philosophy, value system and definition, are common to all of them. These books are connected and self-supporting in that they retain the central premise, which is that Total Inclusivity cannot be compromised or marginalised if individuals and organisations are to meet their ethical, moral, professional, communal and safeguarding obligations to their organisational, local and global communities. This principle applies equally to a fast-food restaurant, local tax office, police department, online department store, or school.

However, we do make an exception for universities.

And that is because of all public and private organisations, universities are the most privileged spaces and therefore should be **exemplars of Total Inclusive values and practices** even while they exemplify and symbolise educational achievement.

We believe universities should be modelling Total inclusivity, setting the standards for all organisations to follow. They have a duty to do so, born of their privileged, powerful, influential and authoritative position in society. We believe this principle applies to all universities, regardless of their position in any global HE league table.

At the same time, we are very aware that this book is presented at a particularly testing and pivotal time for universities around the world. Not only is there intensifying global competition, as we recognise in this book there are intensifying funding pressures. Aligned with this, the dominance of the neo-liberal discourse (managerialist language, knowledge, practice) has been growing in higher education at least since the late 1990s. But what has also been growing in volume and quantity are the voices of those who are marginalised, discriminated against, disempowered, rendered invisible, silenced and threatened in society.

As the Chinese artist and dissident Ai WeiWe puts it:

> *You know, whenever we talk about democracy, we're never talking about a perfect state, but rather continuous questioning and argument...**We are living in a time when interpretation and judgement are changing.***
>
> (*The Guardian*, 2021, our emphasis)

Inevitably, universities are at the centre of this vortex.

Whether it be concerned with academic freedoms, free speech, student safeguarding, a racist history, LGBT+ identities, performativity, managerial powers, or 'simply' the ability of a university to survive post-covid, universities are now in a place of increasingly public critical scrutiny and uncertainty.

The aim of this book is to provide a clear vision and convincing basis for the future direction of any organisation that deems to claim the title 'university'. Therefore, we speak equally to Oxbridge, the Ivy League, and to any private HE institution.

Our message is this:

> *More than any other public or private entity, universities must represent the very best of humanity – not just intellectually but in terms of how they address issues arising from diversity and inclusivity. Universities are arguably the most influential bodies in a civilised society, consequently, they should aim to be communities of learning with the highest standards of knowledge attainment, alongside being exemplars of organisational practice. These aims can only be met in an HE climate and culture which is Totally Inclusive. This must be the standard for any university to aim for, not only in its teaching but in its fundamental principles and its everyday practices.*

So, who is this book for, who is that message aimed at?

First and foremost, this book is written for anyone who is in any way associated with higher education – anywhere.

You may be a first year undergraduate or a distinguished professor. You could be a faculty administrator or head of HR. You might be the vice chancellor. It matters not, because if universities play some part in your life, have done or could do in the future, then what we say in this book matters to you. You have a personal and very direct investment in universities becoming Totally Inclusive.

In truth, global society has an investment in universities becoming Totally Inclusive.

Universities are the advance guard of society, not governments and politicians. Social and scientific progress originates in universities, not in Silicon Valley. Universities are the treasurers, engine drivers, standard bearers for the best of what humanity has achieved and can achieve.

No country, no community, no organisation can hope to grow, prosper, adapt and thrive in the 21st century unless it has the knowledge and skills to do so. And those knowledges and skills come via education and higher-level research. Universities have, from their humble if elitist origins in the 12th century[3] become the engine of globalisation, the passport to a better life for all of us, and the symbol of individual hope and national aspiration.

Arguably the most important social change to occur is not globalisation but massification – the massification of further and higher education. Indeed, could globalisation have occurred in quite the way it has without this global explosion of higher education? Certainly, as we reveal in our respective biographies below, we would not be writing this book without the opening up of HE from 1980 onwards (see, for example, O'Connor, 2014).

We have long passed the era when, for example, 1% of British school-leavers undertook degree-level study and most of them were male and privately educated.

But while we write this book for all, we also recognise the continuing influence of the elite.

As in all three Totally Inclusivity books, this book on universities holds that power is a central element determining whether or not an organisation can become Totally Inclusive. Traditionally, power in Western universities has been held by white males, with all leaders of whatever race or gender required to operate within a masculinist, performative culture. This continues to be the case and is one important aspect of university life which must therefore change if these organisations are to embrace the demands for inclusivity fast emerging around the world.

A second aspect that we address is the way in which power engages with professional identity to generate a highly competitive silo-mentality within university life. This is reinforced not only by rankings and similar performance indicators designed for public consumption, but by a creeping corporatisation. We offer a resistance to this culture by encouraging you to recognise yourself as an Advocate for Total Inclusivity in your personal and professional lives, to take personal responsibility for progressing your institution towards the goals of Total Inclusivity.

A third aspect, one which we argue can act as a counter-narrative to corporatisation and unreflective elitism, is the growing discourse within university student bodies now demanding inclusivity, safeguarding, accountability, and that universities recognise their history, their present and their privileged place in society. These Generation Z and young Millennial voices offer hope while also asking critical questions of universities, and our book aligns with them.

SOLVING PROBLEMS?

Let us assume you are a university lecturer and have just experienced, and perhaps are continuing to experience, the most stressful, chaotic, and isolated few years of your working life – due to Covid-19. Your only small comfort is knowing you are not alone in feeling emotionally wrung-out. Around the world, there are thousands of HE staff, and millions of educationalists, feeling exactly the same.

Unfortunately, this book doesn't offer you any answers to that dilemma. After reading it, you will still be faced with the demands of your students, bosses, government – and maybe also a continuing global pandemic. But what we do offer you is the sense and actuality of unity and the possibility of belonging. And as we explain in this book (see Chapter 7), we all need to belong. Unfortunately, as we also explain, whether or not you'll be accepted, permitted to belong, depends a lot on who you are – your identity mix.

Here is one example of 'not-belonging' in a university:

A major university with three campuses in Shanghai is making a list of all 'non-heterosexual' students, according to a leaked document. Shanghai

University is ordering its schools and colleges to report students who iden-
tify as LGBT+ or sexual minorities. The school is targeting 'non-heterosex-
ual' and 'LGBT rainbow' groups.

(Feng, 2021)

Sure, the first thing you spot is that this is a Chinese university, and the chances are that you don't work in one. But don't dismiss this as just another bizarre example of the Chinese government's propensity for social control. Is it any different where you work? Just how inclusive is your institution, your department?

Okay, we doubt your university managers are drawing up lists of 'undesirables', nevertheless, so-called developed countries still have a long way to go to tackle inequality in higher education, not least the UK and US as these quotes below confirm.

There has been absolute resistance to facing the scale of racism in British
universities. If you're in a climate where you think that people don't under-
stand the problem, don't take it seriously, don't have procedures and poli-
cies that seem to be effective, why and how would you make a complaint?

(Suki Ali, quoted in The Guardian, July, 2019)

In recent years, many studies have uncovered overwhelming evidence that
Ivy League Universities and other selective schools have been engaging in
systematic and continuous discrimination against Asian-Americans in the
[US] college admissions process.

(AACE, 2015)

I am determined that nobody experiences a worse outcome solely on the
grounds of their ethnicity. Which is why the Government is making a clear
and concerted effort, alongside higher education partners, to tackle these
injustices.

(Lidington, 2019. Chancellor of the Duchy of Lancaster.
UK Dept. of Education)

We all know such reports are just the tip of the iceberg because if you've worked in a university then you will have experienced discrimination first hand and/or witnessed it. Scratch the surface of most institutions, and something not very pleasant will appear. To expect universities to be different is unrealistic.

Or is it?

We believe it is not only totally realistic to expect universities to be better than the rest, but is well within their power to be so. At the same time, we recognise they have a long trek to undertake before they get to that particular nirvana.

It would be wonderful, indeed quite remarkable, to write a book which could resolve all the diversity, equity, inclusion and social justice issues now surfacing in global HE and exacerbated by several decades of neo-liberalism; together with entrenched masculinism, colonialist values, and white privilege.

This book is not it.

What the book will do is highlight and critically examine these issues, situate them in the context of Total Inclusivity, and offer practical suggestions for taking the first steps towards addressing them.

To this end, we place Total Inclusivity as a rallying call for the HE global community, asking all stakeholders in this field to address the question as to what TI means for them? Do they personally and professionally align with TI? If not, why not? And if they do align with it, what actions will they take to help ensure TI becomes embedded in their institution and individual practice?

It would be entirely possible to write substantial monographs on topics such as trans identities; free speech; disability; woke culture and cancel culture; each in the context of global HE. We do not therefore claim to be addressing all these issues in detail, though what the book will do is align them with the TI concept and its inherent and unchangeable values. The book will certainly have a position on these issues, and this will be underpinned by theory; notably feminist institutionalism, intersectionality, critical race theory, poststructuralism, hegemonic power. Drawing on these theories and their concepts, the book aims to undermine all binary thinking including that which generally informs notions of gender, sex, sexuality, race, and disability.

To summarise our position, we envisage this book as the flagpole to which any HE institution can hoist its DEIJ flag. How individual universities address TI is up to their stakeholders, leaders, staff and students. We do offer practical guidance, but we are not offering prescriptive solutions on all issues or questions; that would be impossible and inappropriate. Our aim is to establish, define, and clearly articulate a Totally Inclusive value system, rooted in contemporary theory and philosophy and which we believe any HE institution heading into the 21st century with any degree of DEIJ awareness should at the very least consider and ideally, implement.

SO, WHO ARE WE?

At first glance we might appear an unlikely duo to be presenting advice on how to deliver DEIJ in global universities; none of us has ever gotten close to heading a university. But we have each been leaders in education, and we've taught in state schools, international schools, further education colleges, redbrick universities, regional universities, technological universities and elite global universities. Also, we know Total Inclusivity; we've tested it in our teaching, leadership and as researchers. Both personally and professionally, Total Inclusivity defines us.

We each have a unique, personal/professional relationship to higher education and these combined experiences directly inform our writing and our position on Total Inclusivity. We believe it is therefore important to present our individual reasons as to why we write this book. For many readers, our brief positioning statements will likely have resonance.

PAT: 'A MERE WOMAN...'

My career has spanned 46 years in five academic organisations in Ireland and the UK. During that time, I never had a woman boss. One of two daughters, with a mother who did not fit the procrustean bed of Irish female domesticity and a father who thought I was wonderful, I never absorbed the idea that women were inferior to men.

I went to University College Dublin at 16 and graduated with a first-class honours' degree in Social Science at 19. My first job was as a contract research assistant in Dublin. When I told the new Director there that I wanted to do a Masters, his response was: 'Why would you do that? You will marry,' (the Marriage Bar did not end in Ireland until 1973). It was a chilling moment.

My next job was in a research unit in the University of London. There, I finished my 524 page M.Soc Sc. thesis in my spare time. I started a PhD on a new topic, supervised by my boss there. I noticed (eventually...) that most of his PhD students did not finish... We were destined to sit at the feet of the Master for ever, it seemed.

I needed the immediacy of teaching, and got a permanent lecturing position in Ireland in 1982. After six years in that job, with my PhD and publications, I saw an opportunity for the development of a new degree. However, the Director backed a degree led by a male footballer. My assumptions about merit were challenged. It was time to move on.

But I was a woman, over 40. Eventually, in 1992, I got a job in the University of Limerick as a lecturer, and was given responsibility for women's studies. It was back to the 1970s in terms of misogyny.

The position of women in universities emerged as an issue there in 1995. I took it on. In 1997 with a bionic leap, I became an overnight success after 27 years, being appointed to a Chair in Sociology and Social Policy, the first woman at full professorial level in that university, and the first female professor of sociology in Ireland. My appointment reinforced my commitment to gender equality. I had seen discrimination and cronyism. I wanted change. I was appointed Faculty Dean in 2000 and re-appointed by three Presidents over a period of 10 years.

In the 1990s, I started what has become an almost thirty-year period of research and activism around gender equality in academia at local, national and international level. Between 1997 and 2012, the proportion of women at full professorial level in my university increased from zero to 34% (much higher than the Irish and EU average of 19%). In 2015 I was invited to be a member of a five-person national expert group which recommended a professorial gender quota of 40% and led to the creation of 45 senior leadership posts for women.

My 120 publications include eight books, over 80 refereed journal articles and 30 chapters. Dogged by self-doubt, in my late 40s I was still a lecturer on the first step of the academic hierarchy. Many people have helped and supported me in what has been an always interesting, if sometimes frustrating, career.

Mere women should know their place, I was told – but like many other women, I have refused to accept the place assigned to me – and have tried with relentless energy to widen the space for us women in the academy. This book is part of that attempt.

STEPHEN: A LATE STARTER

The year I was born, British men were still marking their class by what they wore on their heads: workers, cloth caps; upper classes, trilbies. My family were neither – we were members of the lower middle-class bubble shortly to explode across the UK. We were shop-keepers. So we wore brown overalls. And that is what I wore for several years after I left school in July 1964, just two weeks before my 15th birthday, to start work in my family's florist business in a seaside town in northern England. An 11+ failure, but fortunate to get a place at the age of 12 in a technical school, which at least taught me typing. That came in handy. Now aged 72, with a PhD behind me, this will be my 15th book. How is that possible? Answer: Luck, determination, higher education – and feminists.

Florist; Pub/Restaurant Manager; Athletics Coach; Assistant Secondary School Teacher; Further Education Lecturer/Manager; University Lecture/Professor; Writer/Researcher; Director of International School Consultancy based in South East Asia.

Yes, an interesting journey, and one neither predicted nor conventional.

There have been countless 'pivotal moments' during those 70+ years, though one particularly relevant to TI and this book is when I was accepted as a mature student on a part-time MA in Human Potential at Leeds Metropolitan University, in January 1990. Despite the rather pretentious title, this was essentially a Masters in Sociology, and that is what I became after graduation – a sociologist. Though continuing my job as HoD of Leisure, Tourism and Sport, in a Leeds city FE College. The pivotal moment was not so much getting the first serious qualification of my life (I still have no first degree), but meeting Professor Sheila Scraton and her team of brilliant lecturers. In the second year of the MA I shut my eyes and nervously opted for the module on Feminist Theory. I never looked back. I got my MA, and then three years later graduated from LMU with a PhD titled 'Public and Private Men: Masculinities at Work in Education Management'. Sheila and Prof Jeff Hearn (Manchester Univ.) were my joint supervisors. Within a year I was lecturer in Education at Keele University. Conference papers, academic journal articles, and books flowed quickly after that. They've kept flowing, at least the books have.

How does one go from 11+ failure to, 50 years later, Professor in Gender Studies (Shih Shin University, Taipei) and International Programme Coordinator (Asia) for Keele University? Only with help. And that help came especially from people in higher education.

Universities turned my life around. They opened my eyes, opened my mind, and caused me to reflect on who I was as a male, a man, a heterosexual, a white middle-class Brit, and on my masculinities. Without feminists, I doubt that would have happened. There have been others, too; key individuals who helped me understand and recognise (not least in myself) white privilege, the toxicity of institutionalised racism, and how to gauge the mental state of societies/organisations/communities/individuals by their level of inclusiveness, not least regarding LGBT+ identities.

Yes, I was the archetypal 'late starter', but since then I've had the opportunity and privilege to help a great many other late starters pursue their HE potential and aspirations. I am still doing that. This book is merely my way of saying 'thank you' to all those in HE who had patience with my first stumbling steps into academia, into better understanding DEIJ. You are the reason I can write this.

THE STRUCTURE

Following this Introduction, the book is structured into three parts.

Part One: How inclusive are universities?

In this first part, Pat critically examines the challenge of creating an inclusive university in what is largely a neo-liberal world, obsessed with the institutional prestige and global rankings of universities is identified. Pat asks how inclusive do universities look from the viewpoint of academic staff, who are not only involved in the creation and transmission of knowledge but are also potentially role models to their students? This question highlights issues related to the centralisation of power; increasing precarity of front-line staff and the structures, criteria, procedures and career timelines which favour the reproduction of a predominantly male elite. The focus then turns to the practices and attitudes which reflect and reinforce the position of 'insiders' by looking both at those which denigrate and marginalise the 'outsiders' as well as those which privilege the 'insiders' and foster a sense of entitlement. Rape and sexual assault are at the extreme end of this continuum, but they are aspects of a power-based continuum which plays a very real part in actively excluding, encouraging self-exclusion and fostering a sense of self entitlement and the normality and legitimacy of such practices. The last chapter in Part One examines universities responses to these troubling questions about power and inclusion. It highlights the types of institutionalised resistance that frequently occur, including challenging the data; focusing on 'fixing the women'; engaging in rhetorical, marginal or 'compensatory' activities which effectively leave power structures and culture unchallenged. The role of leaders at the very top in challenging such collusive activities is highlighted as is whiteness and masculinism.

Part Two: You and 'your' university

Organisations are not only essential to societal cohesion and progress, but they also provide an existential space within which the individual can be, become, and belong. In Part Two, Stephen critically examines this relationship as it gets enacted in universities. Central to this focus is the concept of identity – as functional group membership, the inclusive collective, and as the striving individual. Each of these three elements of identity work are vivid in universities underpinned by legitimising discourses of excellence, exclusivity, rarity, and (intellectual) isolation. In examining the relationship between the self and the (HE) institution, this section explores; the politics of belonging within higher education and the conditions which configure this existential place for staff and students; the notion of the international learning community and how close universities are to this ideal; the concept of privilege and its relationship to different power formations with higher education; the contentious issues now surrounding the concept of 'free speech' and how this apparently compelling phrase actually hides serious challenges for universities in aspiring to Total inclusivity; and in Chapter 11, the relationship between staff and student wellbeing, safety, employment conditions and violences.

Part Three: What next for universities?

In Part Three, guidelines towards becoming a Totally Inclusive university are presented, using as a model the university Total Inclusivity audit. This device is taken from the other two books in the Total Inclusivity trilogy but slightly redesigned to meet the particular needs of universities and their members. The concluding Chapter 13, will return to the central aims and objectives of the book and in doing so will ask two questions of the reader – what next for you and what next for your university? In reality, these two questions are the same because one of the key positions within Total Inclusivity is that while an organisation (university) has no existential identity, the identities of organisational members are directly affected by the power regimes that exist in such spaces. In other words, the actions of the individual within the organisation become actions of the organisation. Which is why the key aim of this book is to spur individuals to become Advocates for Total Inclusivity in their own institution, thereby opening doors for others while eliminating the concept of 'the other', at least in higher education.

NOTES

1 For an excellent definition of Diversity, Equity, Inclusion and Justice, see www. lancasterfriends.org/deij
2 We are using the term 'new humanism' not as a theory of literary criticism, but to describe a humanist agenda for the 21st century and beyond.
3 There is much debate on when the first university was established, but general agreement that they became fully part of societal advancement during the 12th and 13th centuries.

How Inclusive are Universities?

Part One

Pat O'Connor

Two

INTRODUCTION

This chapter asks the question: who really cares about total inclusivity in higher education? Underlying this is a question about the purpose of universities. Are they simply concerned with the education of students? Or embedding democracy through creating an educated and responsible citizenry? Or is their purpose the perpetuation of elite knowledge through peer-reviewed journal articles? Generating international revenue through the attraction of international students? Facilitating the development of patents for industry? Or is their purpose the consolidation of white, male hierarchies of power and its legitimation? Is there any difference between the purpose of public versus private universities? Who are the key stakeholders – students, elites in society, industry, the state? This chapter asks whether higher educational institutions are increasingly diverse, so that there is no need for TI. Finally, it identifies possible levers or stakeholders for promoting a TI agenda.

WHAT ARE INSTITUTIONS OF HIGHER EDUCATION FOR?

At first glance, this can appear to be a facetious question. Universities have existed for centuries and at one level their purpose is simple: the creation, application and transmission of knowledge. However, in different countries and at different times, their purpose has varied. Thus, universities have been established to transmit professional skills; to progress nationalism; to promote democratisation; to create a professional elite; to legitimate access to power; to train young people for employment; to enhance economic growth; to promote internationalisation; to enhance individual or collective social and cultural life, etc.

The ambiguities about their purpose has enabled them to become part of wider social projects, which have legitimated their activities and provided funding for those involved in them. These wider social

DOI: 10.4324/9781003277651-3

projects have influenced who has access to higher education in particular societal contexts as well as access to positions of power within them. Thus, for example, traditionally, universities were concerned with the education of a (male) elite and the reproduction of gender and class privilege (Morley, 2005). Thus, middle-class men got access to higher education, and this was also the typical profile of those who occupied positions of academic power and leadership in them.

The 21st century can be seen as: 'an existential moment for universities ... universities have to decide how they are to be in the world' (Barnett, 2011: 16). Are they to be concerned with meeting the needs of students, industry, or with serving the wider public good? The whole purpose of universities, their appropriate relationship with the state and with private for-profit organisations is very much in a state of flux, nationally and globally. The difficulty for embedding TI lies in identifying the powerful stakeholders who will support that vision, with consequences for access to and leadership of higher education.

WHAT DO STAKEHOLDERS SEE AS THE PURPOSE OF HIGHER EDUCATION?

Typically, higher education is depicted is concerned with teaching, research and service. This kind of definition obscures the issue of power and purpose, although it can be seen as capturing much of what universities actually do in practice. However, at different times and places these activities have been differentially valued. Thus, the classic Newman vision of a university saw teaching students as the defining characteristic of a university, albeit that the curriculum was very much narrower than would be normal today. His perception of teaching as a core activity is still a taken-for-granted assumption by students and their parents in most societies, and is frequently presented as such by the state.

On the other hand, the Humboltian dream of a university in nineteenth century Germany was concerned with the production of original scholarship. In that context the focus was on appointing the best researchers in arts and science; providing them with academic freedom, and building curricula around their area of expertise. This concept is still very powerful. However, the dominant position frequently accorded to (limited areas of) science and technology today has implications. It marginalises subjects (such as the humanities and the social sciences) which are seen as of little relevance to industry although they evoke high levels of student demand.

Although institutional autonomy is frequently seen as central to the definition of a university, the Napoleonic university was not self-governing, and was effectively part of the state and potentially politically controlled (Graham, 2008) and this is still reflected in the status of academics in France as effectively civil servants. Thus the state is another potential powerful stakeholder in higher education. Its interest in higher education can be multifaceted. In burgeoning nation states, higher education can be used in nation building at an imaginative and cultural level. The state can also be concerned with the revenue generated by the attraction of international students (as in the case of Australia or the UK). More broadly, the perceived contribution made by higher education to economic growth is a key concern of many states. Educational attainment accounted for 50% of the increase in economic growth in 30 OECD countries (1960–2008). However, the idea that higher education always creates economic growth is contested (Meyer et al., 2007). As levels of education increase in the society as a whole, the economic and social advantages conferred on an individual by higher education decreases within that particular society (although it does provide individuals with a global competitive advantage, increasing their likelihood of getting a well-paid job in societies with lower levels of education).

One of the indicators of state power is its ability to define what policies are in the national interest. For Franzway et al. (1989: 18), state control operates 'as much through the production of dominant "discourses"…as it does through naked force'. In some countries higher educational institutions have overtly become part of a state knowledge production system. Less overtly, higher educational institutions worldwide, directly and indirectly valorise particular kinds of knowledge and expertise and legitimise the underlying discourses which explain and justify existing patterns of access to university as a whole or to senior positions within those structures. Such legitimating discourses include those of choice and excellence – with the implicit suggestion that those who do not access senior positions in these organisations have either chosen not to do so or are not excellent enough (O'Connor and White, 2021a).

The importance of the state as a stakeholder has also been reflected in a focus on the role of higher education in creating a viable democracy and an active citizenry (Giroux, 2002, 2011). This was a particular focus in the 19th century United States, although it continues to exist in part of that higher educational system; e.g., in community colleges there. It reflects the assumption that the more educated individuals and societies are, the greater the possibility of social justice and equality (Meyer et al., 2007). This perspective includes assumptions about the value of science and arts as fields of study. Underpinning it is also the idea that the university is a place for public intellectuals (O'Connor, 2012) who bridge the gap between the academy and the wider society. However, there has been an increasing tendency not to value the opportunities for everyone that are created by public education (Marginson, 2007). There is currently no global policy space to discuss education in these terms; i.e., as a public good. The main global forum for higher education is the World Trade Organisation/GATS negotiating framework, which commodifies education and sees it as simply increasing individual cultural, social or economic capital.

Students are also key stakeholders in higher education since higher education has been seen as one of the few public spaces where they can learn to question authority and develop a capacity for critical thinking. For Lynch (2006: 11 and 2), the ultimate purpose of public universities is 'to promote independence of intellectual thought, to enable scholars to work outside the control of powerful vested interests'. From this concept of a university comes the idea of individual academic freedom with the opportunity to pursue a search for truth (Carvalho and Machado, 2011: 91). However, this raises the question of the extent to which a critique of power holders is likely to be seen as useful or appropriate by those same power holders. It ignores the ability of power structures (external and internal) to subtly dictate agendas within higher education, reflected in the concept of stealth power (O'Connor et al., 2019b) – power that operates covertly, including invisible forms that are reflected in people's desires, and not interpreted as power. It also ignores academics' career ambitions and the possibility of self-censorship by them.

In summary, the purpose of higher education varies within societies and over time. It is linked with the interests of key stakeholders in those contexts.

THE IMPACT OF NEO-LIBERALISM: THE MARKET AS A KEY STAKEHOLDER

Until recently, the stages in the development of higher education identified in one society did not map easily on to other societies. However, global convergence appeared to be emerging from 1995 onwards (see Peterson, 2007). This era is seen as involving very rapid societal and cultural change; high expectations as regards the contribution of higher education to national economic performance; increases in student diversity; changes in the mode of academic delivery; increased pressures as regards quality and accountability; increased competition for students; decreased willingness by the state to fund higher education and expectations around accessing wider sources of funding. It also implicitly reflects a preoccupation with science and technology in the context of an alliance between the state and the market.

Many of these trends have been seen as reflecting neo-liberalism. Implicit in neo-liberalism is a valorisation of the market; a hostility to state intervention, and an endorsement of light regulation in a context where private interests maximise their profits. A number of processes have been identified as having an impact on higher education internationally, many of them reflecting its influence including corporatisation, marketisation, commercialisation and commodification (Gallagher, 2012; Lynch et al., 2012).

Neo-liberalism is indifferent to social justice, equality and the rights of citizens. Although claiming ideological neutrality, neo-liberalism 'depoliticises debates about education by hiding its ideological underpinnings in the language of economic efficiency' (Lynch, 2006: 7). Managerialism as an internal mode of governance, reflects the adoption by public sector organisations of policies and practices from the private sector. It is 'the organisational arm of neo-liberalism' (Lynch, 2014: 968). The purpose of higher education is redefined as serving the needs of the market, with a stress on the transmission of employment related skills and the undertaking of commercially useful research. In some cases, the focus is on meeting the needs of local industry or where there is a more global perspective, it is reflected in a focus on international research and global university rankings and the creation of international patents to support scientific and technological developments (for example, in the pharma and information communication areas). Those disciplines that are seen as having the greatest use value in both contexts (for example, particular areas of science and technology: O'Connor, 2014) are prioritised. Areas such as humanities, and those parts of the social sciences that are seen as having little relationship to the market, are devalued, except in so far as they provide transferrable skills.

The state's tacit support for these neo-liberal processes has played an important part in affecting the current shape of higher education. Corporatisation involves universities being seen as very similar to other large businesses, and as such being expected to earn a greater proportion of their revenue from the market. This process is frequently seen as interrelated with commercialisation, marketisation and the commodification of knowledge (Slaughter and Rhoades, 2010). These processes have been seen as weakening the student–teacher relationship; reducing the involvement of academic staff and students in governance; distorting research activity; increasing the levels of casualisation among teaching staff; depicting students as customers and fostering a narrow instrumental approach to education.

Neo-liberalism has been associated in many countries (such as the US and the UK) with a shift from 'government, where the state takes responsibility for the daily administration and universal provision of services; to that of governance, where the state steers indirectly from a distance' (Blackmore and Sachs, 2007: 31). There is a 'hollowing out' of the state, which was expected to hold 'the ring between many different actors as the ultimate guardian of the public interest' (Ferlie et al., 2008: 328). In practice in a neo-liberal context, the state is effectively subordinate to the market, which directly and indirectly dictates the shape and purpose of higher education.

Global league tables reflect the global marketisation and commercialisation of higher education (Marginson, 2007). They have been presented as useful in informing international students, governments, private investors, academic and industrial partners and employers. Two of the most widely used ranking schemas (THE and QS) both include a narrow measure of impact, which focuses only on citations in peer-reviewed journals on the web of science. These global league tables are linked to commercial interests who favour journal research output (such as those of the journal publishers, Thomson Reuters), and hence underestimate wider societal impacts (Hazelkorn, 2015,

2018). All of these ranking systems, to varying degrees, operate with a bias towards science, and because they focus on the citation of journal articles in the web of science, they exclude all books, and a very substantial proportion of other publications in arts and literature, education and most social sciences. They also privilege articles published in English, relative to other languages. They implicitly validate a particular concept of higher education and a very narrow definition of knowledge, with peer scientists rather than the general public as stakeholders. They reflect and reinforce the transformation of higher education into a marketable commodity.

The commercialisation of higher education is not new, what is new is its 'pace, intensity and moral legitimacy' (Blackmore, 2002: 423). In the twenty-first century, universities are no longer the sole repositories of knowledge. International and national structures which privatise and commercialise knowledge could threaten the very survival of public universities, particularly public support for them (Lynch et al., 2012). A neo-liberal state may effectively erode public universities' monopoly over credentials as a way of reducing public expenditure on higher education, through its support of private institutions (Carvalho, 2011). In this situation the unique contribution of public universities is hard to identify.

In advanced capitalist countries, the relationship between the state, the market and class position is close and typically has been depicted as gender neutral. Yet the higher echelons of the ideological apparatuses of the state, the media and the institutional churches are likely to be under male control. Either through their presence in the state or the market, (male) upper-middle-class professionals can promote their own interests and legitimate those as in the national interest (for example, restricting entry to university courses in medicine and pharmacy and so increasing the remuneration of such graduates).

In summary, neo-liberalism and the market seems particularly unpromising as a possible stakeholder for advancing TI.

IS HIGHER EDUCATION NOT DIVERSE TODAY?

At its simplest diversity can be defined in terms of variety in the characteristics of those gaining access to higher education and/or to positions of power in it (in terms of gender, class, race/ethnicity etc).

Increasing the size of the student cohort can be seen as increasing inclusivity. Increased access to higher education is a virtually global phenomenon, with roughly 20% of the global cohort in higher education. However, the 'outsiders' may end up on shorter courses and/or in less prestigious institutions leading to less well-paid or precarious jobs where there is little opportunity to challenge power structures. Internationalisation has increased student diversity in terms of nationality, but not in terms of class, since overwhelmingly only those from well-off families are able to afford to send their offspring to higher education institutions abroad.

Within western society, increased access can be seen as reflecting a number of phenomena, such as the development of binary structures of higher education; fewer restrictions on the numbers admitted, and increased access by women. These processes, and their implications have been little discussed. In many countries, universities remain elite institutions, explicitly concerned with the reproduction of privilege. This is their attraction for their students and a badge of honour among their staff, whose own elite position is legitimated by ideas about excellence. Are these universities willing to reject a concern with global rankings? Will they then be seen as second-class institutions for students and staff who in turn, are seen as second class? Is inclusivity to be the preserve of non-elite institutions? What does this say about its importance?

Diversity policies may exist in all these institutions, but may lack embeddedness in the power and resource structures and so become largely symbolic – a kind of virtue signalling. In these contexts, although much is made of initiatives to improve access to under-represented students, management and leadership positions remain overwhelmingly non-diverse in these elite institutions.

POSSIBLE LEVERS TO PROMOTE A TI AGENDA?

It is possible to identify four very different kinds of stakeholders who might support or promote a TI agenda: students; minority, precarious and disaffected staff; non-elite HEIs and international organisations. The motivations of each of these is somewhat different as are their vulnerabilities in advancing that agenda.

In higher educational institutions, students, who in many cases are identified publicly as the key stakeholders in higher education are also at the lowest level of the internal organisational hierarchy, and so have least investment in the existing structure and culture. At least a minority of them are idealists with global views, as reflected in the global #MeToo, #BlackLivesMatter, and climate change movements. They are also typically digital natives and so can mobilise globally. Thus, they are at least potentially an important stakeholder for TI within and between organisations. They are however a transient group, as the leaders are likely to graduate and move on to challenge TI in other sites within a number of years.

The second possible stakeholders are staff who benefit least from the existing system. This includes those who are outside the hegemony – whether this is defined in terms of gender, class, age, race/ethnicity etc (Lipton, 2020). In western society, frequently those in these positions gain access to the margins of higher education – but they do not for the most part access positions of power or leadership. Potential staff stakeholders also include those who are in precarious positions on temporary contracts (including post-doctoral positions) as well as those who are on solely teaching contracts or on various types of 'mommy tracks' or career cul-de-sacs. For them the disjunction between the policies that legitimate their access to higher education and their difficulties in moving up is apparent. They are potential stakeholders in promoting TI in institutions. Transience is an issue for some of those in these positions – as is the structural vulnerability of many of them and the fear that generates. Thus, they may simply be afraid to be seen to dissent since that may endanger their already precarious position.

The third potential group of stakeholders are non-elite institutions who want to find an alternative way of framing their status and contribution. They may include regional universities, institutes of technology, new universities, teacher training institutions etc. For various reasons, including the weighting of reputation in traditional global ranking schemas, and the typically heavy teaching loads and professional service obligations of their staff, they tend to score poorly in global ranking schemas. They frequently have a much more overt commitment to goals that are compatible with TI, whether these are reflected in a focus on students' all-round development or an inclusive professional ethos and so are already positioned so as to be receptive to TI. As institutions, they are potentially in a much stronger structural position than the individuals in the second category. Hall and Tandon (2021) suggest that such higher educational institutions need to engage the local/regional/global communities as stakeholders, establishing partnerships with them so as to foster inclusion – drawing not only on experiences from South Africa, but also, they suggest, Kyrgyzstan, Malaysia and the Ukraine. The focus on what are, in Western terms, marginal geographical areas is interesting, indicating as it does the importance of working with those who are outside the spatial hegemony.

However, non-elite institutions may be unable to resist pressure from the state which funds them. Furthermore, by embracing a TI agenda, they may also copper – fasten their position as lower status institutions. This does little to promote the valorisation and legitimacy of TI. Elite institutions may remain effectively untouched by TI – although they may give rhetorical commitment to it by having policies, providing limited scholarships to minority students and even promoting minority staff. But power and the ideologies which legitimate elite access may remain untouched.

The final possible source of stakeholders in the TI project are international organisations. The European Union has been concerned with gender equality in academia since the 1990s. It has endeavoured to move the focus in higher educational institutions from fixing the women to fixing organisations and knowledge, by funding research and action projects in such institutions. Thus, for example, Horizon 2020, with a total budget of €11 billion, included a focus on gender balance in research teams, panels and advisory groups and on integrating the gender dimension into the context of the research. Additional programmes such as the Science with and for Society have funded specific gender equality initiatives. Horizon Europe (2021–2027), the most recent research funding schema promoting gender balance has a budget of 95.5 billion euro (see Chapter 5). Thus, the EU has endeavoured to create oases of best practice both in individual organisations and in constellations of them. The publication She Figures has over the past 20 years facilitated monitoring progress at the national level; albeit, that the indicators are crude. Overall, there has been some progress in the promotion of gender equality in academia, but it has been slow and uneven with and between countries – with a general move away from the more overt forms of discrimination to more subtle forms of gender-based violence and inequality. Bencivenga and Drew (2021: 3) highlighted the lack of harmonisation among EU projects and concluded that despite the EU's efforts: 'There is no common or shared vision on what constitutes the best strategies'.

The most important of the global stakeholders is the United Nations. In its 2030 agenda (UN, 2021), it identifies 17 Sustainable Development Goals – including inclusive and equitable education (Goal 4) and gender equality and the empowerment of all women and girls (Goal 5). Goal 4.3 specifically refers to ensuring equal access for all women and men to affordable and quality tertiary education including universities (UN, 2021). There is also a specific reference in Goal 4.5 to eliminating gender disparities in education; while Goal 4.7 refers to including human rights, gender equality, a culture of peace and non-violence, global citizenship and sustainable development in the content of education(UN, 2021). Goal 5.1 refers to ending all forms of discrimination against all women and girls, and Goal 5.5 to facilitating women's leadership at all levels of decision-making in political, economic and public life. Thus, quite clearly in its identification of these goals, the United Nations agenda is compatible with that of TI in higher education. THE Impact Ranking (THE, 2021) measures university performances against these 17 UN Sustainable Development Goals. The ranking of HEIs in these terms, in which both the state and the HEIs have an interest, may be a useful way of moving a TI agenda forward.

Further support for one element of this agenda – viz the elimination of gender inequality-comes from another international body – the OECD (2012). It found that over half of the economic growth attributed to higher education was in fact due to increases in female educational attainment; with additional positive effects arising from greater gender equality in educational attainment. Thus, although higher education has increased economic growth (Fitzgerald, 2012), it is not clear to what extent it will continue to do so other than through its impact on women's participation in paid employment. Hence the OECD's focus on the importance of women's paid employment and on ways of increasing and facilitating this – a nuancing which is ignored by many states.

However, the underlying problem is that the promotion of TI effectively demands a challenge to the existing power holders and their definition of the nature and purpose of higher education. Human

Resources (HR) are a potentially logical site for the advancement of TI. However, particularly in neo-liberal contexts, HR have become corporate apologists – concerned with the image and public presentation of the institution. In that context they are unlikely to support an agenda which is effectively challenging the powerful. COVID 19, which has posed substantial societal and educational challenges, provides yet another excuse for failing to tackle TI, although it may yet undermine existing power structures in the long term.

The most important sites for the advancement of TI are in the area of access, recruitment and promotion. As outlined in the next chapter, these are also the most difficult to change. However, since the focus is on higher educational institutions, TI must also become embedded in the core curricula and in the research priorities of the institution. It is obvious that it is not acceptable that the literature that is recommended to students at undergraduate and post graduate level valorise the achievements of a homogenous elite. Changes in these areas are important in shifting the culture. Equally at a symbolic level, whether in terms of the composition of conferring platforms; the types of valued art and objects displayed in the organisation or its media presence, the continued dominance of white, male, middle class men is unacceptable. Such symbolic changes are relatively easy to bring about. They cannot, of course, substitute for more fundamental structural and cultural change, but they can be useful indicators that such change is necessary.

SUMMARY

In this chapter we have posed fundamental questions about the purpose of higher education, highlighting the close relationship between the characteristics of key stakeholders and those who have access to and occupy positions of power within these institutions. We have suggested that the neo-liberal market driven ethos, endorsed by the state and the market and in collusion with many higher educational institutions, is particularly unhelpful in promoting TI. Finally, we have identified possible individual, sectoral and global levers that might promote a TI agenda: students; minority, precarious and disaffected staff; non-elite HEIs and international organisations.

Three

INTRODUCTION

The characteristics of academic staff potentially affect students' aspirations since the symbolic absence of people like themselves may affect their perceptions of their own future in academia. Thus, insofar as those at the top are overwhelmingly white, middle-class men there is a clear message about the characteristics of the people who have a place there.

In this chapter we look first at concepts that have been used to understand the extent to which higher educational institutions are not inclusive at academic staff level, including the evidence as regards vertical and horizontal gender segregation. We suggest that these concepts tend to obscure the experiences of those who are differentially included in such higher educational organisations. We put forward the classification from Sumer et al. of four ideal types of citizenship (full, limited, transitional and non-citizenship) so as to open up the issue of what inclusivity actually means in such contexts.

HIGHER EDUCATION: GENDERED ORGANISATIONS

The theoretical perspective of feminist institutionalism (Mackay et al., 2010; Mackay, 2011) builds on the work of Acker (1990, 2006) on gendered organisations and Connell (2002) on gender regimes. Acker (1990) suggests that organisational processes are gendered and create/sustain gender segregation in paid work and between paid and unpaid work; gender pay gaps; the differential valuation of predominantly female/male areas; stereotypically male/female cultural images as well as individual gender identity. Organisations are also typically 'care-less' (Lynch et al., 2012) insofar as they are premised on the existence of paid workers without caring responsibilities.

31   Academic Staff

DOI: 10.4324/9781003277651-4

In these organisations gender operates at the structural and cultural level. Mackay et al. (2010: 580) sees gender as a 'constitutive element of social relations based upon perceived (socially constructed and culturally variable) differences between women and men, and as a primary way of signifying (and naturalising) relations of power and hierarchy'. Thus, they suggest that a devaluation of women is implicit in the very construction of gender. Gendered structures, procedures and practices legitimate that devaluation, with both men and women potentially colluding with it.

Each institution has a particular gender order or 'gender regime' (Connell, 2002: 53) that operates not only formally but also on a 'hidden' day-to-day basis – defining what is expected, allowed and encouraged for women and men in different contexts. For Connell (2005), that gender order involves a patriarchal dividend i.e., financial resources, autonomy, status, support and other benefits are given to men because they are men, particularly if they uphold that unequal gender order. Thus, gender inequality is embedded in these organisations, and shapes and is shaped by the individuals in them. There is no agreement on whether organisations are inevitably gendered (Ferguson, 1984; MacKinnon, 1989) or historically gendered (Connell, 1994) – and if the latter, what are the conditions which affect that.

In academia, women appear to have equal rights and privileges in what purports to be a gender-neutral world. The reality is however much more complex. Higher educational institutions have historically been hierarchically male dominated. In such institutions globally, despite the illusion of gender neutrality, male privileging and masculinity is seen as normal, as is women's subordinate position. 'Gender is thus practiced within a power context that amplifies its toxic aspects for women' with the 'concerted – or joint, practicing of masculinities by men at work' being particularly harmful to women (Martin, 2006: 268).

There is increasing recognition that the purportedly gender-neutral concept of excellence (which has been widely used to legitimate the under-representation of women in senior positions: see Chapter 5) is a problematic concept, without a clear definition, and that it ignores context (Campbell, 2018; Ferretti et al., 2018; O'Connor and Barnard, 2021). Despite the rhetoric around excellence, recruitment involving just one candidate (which is more likely to favour men) has been identified in a number of countries (Van den Brink and Benschop, 2012a; Nielsen, 2016). Even where competitions are open, the criteria are more likely to favour men than women (e.g., the privileging of research over teaching).

Criteria may also be defined so narrowly that effectively they are set up to suit an individual candidate, despite a veneer of transparency (e.g., posts are advertised, but the preferred candidate is already known and will ultimately be appointed). Even where detailed evaluative criteria are available, gendered practices may persist (O'Connor and O'Hagan, 2016). The interpretation of criteria in decision-making fora may also be gendered in the sense that similar material is differentially interpreted if it is on a man's rather than a woman's CV (Moss-Racusin et al., 2012). Procedures may advantage men, not least because of informal processes such as homosociability (see Chapter 4). Indeed, Lamont (2009) argued that since evaluation is a social process, and since gender is a social construction, it is inevitable that gendered practices will exist.

The purportedly gender-neutral, but, in fact, masculinised stereotype of the 'ideal' scientist or leader is also in tension with the 'ideal' mother stereotype (White, 2014; Van den Brink and Benschop, 2012b: see Chapter 7). Although frequently stereotypes are depicted as immutable, there is evidence that their strength varies between countries (O'Connor and Goransson, 2015) and under particular conditions they can change in organisations. Management can play a key role in fostering a culture where stereotypes can be challenged by empirical data (e.g., about salaries or appointment processes). Stereotypes can also be challenged by the identification of targets and quotas and through the making of non-stereotypical appointments. Since higher educational institutions are ultimately about the creation and transmission of knowledge, the content of the curriculum and of core and supplementary texts can also challenge stereotypical thinking.

One of the most common concepts used to understand the position of women in higher education is the 'glass ceiling'. The glass ceiling has been described as a metaphor for the invisible structural and cultural obstacles that prevent women and other non-hegemonic minorities from accessing senior positions. It potentially recognises that the under-representation of women in these positions cannot be seen as a purely individual phenomenon and that its existence necessitates attention to career paths; workload models; the ratio of senior to junior posts; recruitment and promotion practices and processes; organisational culture, stereotyping etc. However, it has been critiqued for its focus on women rather than men; for the suggestion that what is going on above the ceiling is clear (as implied by glass); for the failure to identify the specific organisational processes and procedures that privilege men and for its implicit focus on effects rather than causes (Benschop and Brouns, 2009). Although this concept has long been part of the public discourse, academic organisations typically still focus on 'fixing' individual women rather than the organisation (O'Connor, 2014, 2020; Burkinshaw and White, 2017).

The pipeline metaphor (Allen and Castleman, 2001) is also popular, with its implicit suggestion that gender inequalities will disappear as more women become available (the assumption being that it is the absence of suitable women that is the problem). This metaphor provides a convenient rationale for those who have a vested interest in maintaining the status quo and has been widely critiqued (Heijstra et al., 2013). Metaphors such as the maze or the labyrinth (Eagly and Carli, 2007) highlight the lack of transparency around career paths and around the mechanisms through which male privilege is maintained; while the metaphor of the medieval court (O'Connor, 2014) evokes the image of centralised power and the importance of informal relationships in facilitating advancement in such male dominated contexts.

As will be discussed in Chapter 4, with a small number of notable exceptions (such as O'Connor et al., 2021; Phipps, 2020) relatively little attention has been paid to those organisational characteristics which create/maintain the structure and culture facilitating/undermining TI in universities.

THE EVIDENCE: GENDERED SEGREGATION IN HIGHER EDUCATION

The systemic pattern globally in higher education is one of gendered segregation. This includes vertical segregation, with men typically occupying the majority of the senior positions; and horizontal segregation reflected in predominantly male/female disciplines.

Across the OECD countries (which include Canada, the United States, Australia, Japan, Israel, Chile, Columbia, Mexico, as well as many European countries), a higher proportion of women than men aged 20–24 years are enrolled in tertiary education (OECD, 2021: 151). Women are also more likely to graduate from tertiary education than men. However, they earn less than men who have that same level of educational attainment and less than those men who have graduated in the same discipline (OECD, 2021: 11). Thus, although women are included in the higher educational system, their rewards in terms of earnings are less than men's.

The EU has been a long-standing supporter of gender equality in higher education (EC, 2021a). Across the EU women now make up more than half of the students and graduates on bachelor's and master's programmes and just under half of those on PhD programmes. Thus, it can be argued that women are being included. However the proportion of women who are in academic positions in higher education in the EU is inversely related to level. Thus, women constitute 47% of academic staff in starter positions (Grade C); 40% in mid-level ones (Grade B) and 26% of those in the equivalent of full professor (Grade A: EC, 2021b). These patterns are not peculiar to the EU. Women make up 34% of full professors in the United States; 30% in Australia; 24% in India and 28% in South Africa (see O'Connor and White, 2021b). Thus, although women are admitted to higher education, they are subordinate within it. This pattern has been described in academic circles as reflecting vertical segregation – a concept that detoxifies the implicit subordination of women.

The same gendered pattern appears when we look at the profile of heads of higher educational institutions (Rectors/Presidents/VCs) both in the EU and outside it. It has been recognised that 'progress has been particularly slow and insufficient in the area of gender equality in leadership positions' (EC, 2021b: 176). Thus, higher educational organisations in the EU remain mostly male dominated: with women making up 14% of the heads of universities and just under 24% of the heads of all higher educational institutions (EC, 2021b). Similarly higher educational institutions outside the EU remain mostly led by men at Rector/President/VC level – with women constituting 34% of those in these positions in the United States; 24% in Australia; 17% in India and 15% in South Africa (see O'Connor and White, 2021b); with similar patterns being identified elsewhere in Africa (Sidelil,

2020; Igiebor, 2021). Sweden and New Zealand are exceptions (see below).

Thus, the most common pattern globally in higher education is one of male dominance of both academic and managerial leadership positions in higher education. The most popular explanation for these patterns is that they reflect women's deficiencies (e.g., lack of confidence, lack of political 'nous') or their priorities (e.g., childbearing, rearing and other caring activities). Such explanations are difficult to sustain in view of the variation existing between and within countries. Thus, for example, in the EU, the proportion of women at full professorial level varies from 51% in Romania to 13% in Cyprus (EC, 2021b: 184). It also varies within countries. In Ireland, 27% of full professors are women, but the proportion of women at this level varies from 17% in NUIGalway to 32% in Trinity College Dublin and 34 per in Maynooth (HESA, 2021). Similar variation exists in the proportion of women heading up universities (i.e., as Rector/President/VC). Women make up roughly half of those in these positions in Sweden and New Zealand. On the other hand, only 7% of these positions are held by women in the Czech Republic, and 9% in Turkey (O'Connor and White, 2021b). In Ireland, for 429 years, up to 2021, no woman ever headed a public university. This pattern changed dramatically that year with seven of the now 13 universities being headed by women – including Trinity College Dublin (the oldest and most prestigious university). Such variation between and within countries undermines explanations that focus on women and their physical, social or psychological characteristics in a context where the dominant global pattern is one of male dominance and female subordination.

Horizontal segregation has also been identified i.e., the tendency for men and women to predominate in particular disciplines/areas. Thus, in Science, Technology, Engineering and Mathematics (STEM), only one-third of the students and graduates at bachelor's and master's levels are women, with just under 40% of PhD graduates being women in several STEM areas (EC, 2021b). There are also somewhat lower proportions of women in academic staff positions in STEM i.e., 35% in Grade C (starter grade); 28% in Grade B (mid-level ones) and 19% in Grade A (the equivalent of full professor). However, the concept of horizontal segregation obscures the fact that it is not only that men and women are concentrated in different disciplines, but that those disciplines are differentially valued.

Thus in western society, STEM is seen as a particularly important area, crucial to the national interest. It is not clear whether this valuation reflects its predominantly male profile or the priorities of a capitalist neoliberal society. Compared to predominantly female academic staff areas (for example, nursing and midwifery) this importance is questionable. This has become very clear during the Covid-19 pandemic when the ability of the health services to cope determined whether the economy could function. Nevertheless, in academia, resources are higher and working conditions better in STEM (Steinporsdottir et al., 2018). In universities in Ireland, there is also a tendency for senior positions to be more available there (these being initially created by industry or by state-funded organisations, with the expectation that they will be subsequently funded by the university: O'Connor, 2014), thus affecting the ratio of senior to junior posts in those disciplines – with implications as regards individual's access to senior positions in those organisations.

To summarise, issues surrounding the inclusion of women or other non-hegemonic others are obscured by the apparent gender neutrality of the concepts of horizontal and vertical segregation.

AN ALTERNATIVE CONCEPTUALISATION...

In order to highlight the position of women and non-hegemonic others in higher educational institutions, Sümer et al.'s., (2020) classification of types of academic citizenship is useful. It identifies three key components in such academic citizenship: membership (yielding certain rights and duties); recognition (yielding power, voice and respect) and belonging (yielding a sense of identity, entitlement and 'fitting in'). This framework enables us 'to analyse the subtle processes and complex practices of inclusion and exclusion, privilege and discrimination, reward, recognition and denigration, and the ideologies that legitimate those processes and practices in the academic context' (Sümer et al., 2020: 20). Unlike the concept of gender segregation, it makes clear that there are structural, cultural and experiential consequences reflected in these types of citizenship. Sümer et al. (2020) identify four ideal types of academic citizenship: full citizenship, limited citizenship, transitional citizenship and non-citizenship-differentiating between them on the basis of membership, recognition and belonging. These are described below. The gender and intersectional profile of those in each of these types may vary somewhat in specific contexts, but it is possible to identify some trends.

1) **Full academic citizenship** is granted to tenured academics who are usually employed on a permanent and full-time basis and paid relatively well compared to other members of the academic community. These academics are able to participate in decision-making fora and to define what constitutes valued knowledge. However, there is a potential for hierarchy, marginalisation and inequality within this group. Thus, for example, female or intersectional academics in this type, may have less status and experience less belonging than their male counterparts. Gendered departmental micropolitics (see Chapter 4) may result in their marginalisation and reduce their impact on decisions and on the identification of valued knowledge.

Those who have full academic citizenship globally tend overwhelmingly to be men. The assumption that access to such positions reflect women's meritocratic inadequacies has been challenged (Van den Brink and Benschop, 2012a, 2012b; Nielsen, 2016; O'Connor and Barnard, 2021). Across the EU men are twice as likely as women to have a full professorial position: roughly 16% for men and roughly 8% for women: EC, 2021b: 185). This is not peculiar to the EU. Drawing on a unique data set, Brower and James (2020) found that in New Zealand, a man's odds of being professor or associate professor were more than double a woman's odds, with a similar research score, age, field and university.

2) **Limited academic citizenship** is associated with institutional positions that are generally less prestigious and rewarding than those of the full academic citizenship, with lower salaries, poorer promotion prospects and less voice in institutional decision-making. Compared to full citizenship, limited academic citizenship implies reduced recognition and sense of belonging – akin to second-class citizenship. The power inequalities associated with this status are reflected in limited influence on the professional ethos of the academic community. Their presence is critical to the self-definition and functioning of full citizens.

Again, this is not an undifferentiated category, as it is fraught with its' own internal hierarchies. Many jobs in organisations are career cul-de-sacs; i.e., positions that are essential for the functioning of the organisation, but which do not provide opportunities to demonstrate that one is a 'next level' person. Some of those in this type are in career cul-de-sacs or 'mommy tracks', with teaching and pastoral care being overwhelmingly allocated to them. Thus, for example, increasingly in West European societies, undergraduate teaching and pastoral care of students is seen as 'housekeeping' (Heijstra et al., 2017: see also El-Alayli et al., 2018). Such low profile and low-status activities are frequently stereotyped as particularly suitable for women in general and mothers in particular. This has consequences for feelings of belonging, as well as for recognition and voice and for opportunities to attain full citizenship. Activities that are seen as high profile and high status (for example, postgraduate teaching and opportunities for research) which are likely to position the person as a 'next level' person, are most likely to be allocated to men. The net effect is that women are less likely to appear to be the 'obvious' next level person when opportunities for recruitment/promotion to full citizenship come up.

3) **Transitional (or probationary) academic citizenship** occurs at a specific point in the career trajectory and is experienced by early-career academics who are currently located on the periphery of academic institutions in terms of membership, recognition and belonging. These early-career academics run the risk of becoming trapped in this position or of being relegated to non-citizenship. Transitional academic citizenship involves particular forms of subordination, to individual senior academics and/or to university departments. The duration of this period and the chances of accessing limited academic citizenship are coloured by the structural and organisational characteristics of particular higher education institutions as well as by the broader societal context.

The creation of a pool of precarious early-stage academics who have little possibility of a permanent academic job is a global phenomenon (see also Chapter 11). Precarious employment is variously defined internationally, with the proportion of the academic labour force on precarious contracts varying from 70% in the US (Zheng, 2018) to

40–50% in Australian universities (Blackmore, 2011) to roughly a quarter in France (Bataille et al., 2017). Many of these are post-doctoral researchers (post docs). Two-thirds of post docs in a global study, and 80% of those currently working in North America or Europe saw academia as their preferred career destination (Woolston, 2020). In that global study, the proportion who were satisfied was highest among those holding that position for less than two years – although roughly half had in fact been post docs for more than three years. Although these positions were depicted as developmental, more than half got less than an hour of one-to-one time each week from their academic supervisor/principal investigator. The situation of women in such positions is further complicated by the fact that this stage is likely to coincide with the most intense childbearing and child rearing period.

Although one would expect that those with less valued characteristics (in terms of gender, race etc.) would be most likely to be on precarious contacts, this may not always be the case. Thus, for example, in Ireland although women are more likely to be on precarious *academic* contracts, they are less likely to be on precarious *research* contacts where the processes of recruitment are less transparent.

4) **Non-citizenship** is the fourth and final form of academic citizenship. Those in this category lack even basic entitlements. Non-citizens score low on all of the three dimensions of membership, recognition and belonging. They are allowed to work in the organisation but are effectively treated as disposable 'hands and minds'. Increases in the numbers of PhD students (which potentially looks inclusive) creates a pool of such non-academic citizens who have little possibility of a permanent academic job – not least because in many countries, the number of such permanent positions has fallen. These are the *gastarbeiter* (guest workers) of the academic community, whose contribution to undervalued work such as teaching is critical, but who are individually considered as marginal, transient and disposable. This form of academic citizenship involves casual hourly paid work with relatively low wages (Murgia and Poggio, 2019).

Again, this is not an undifferentiated category, as it is fraught with its' own internal hierarchies. For the most part it is women and others with less valued characteristics who are most likely to be non-citizens. Many continue in such positions for many years in the hope of moving to transitional citizenship.

SUMMARY AND CONCLUSIONS

In this chapter we have looked at higher education institutions as gendered organisations where vertical and horizontal segregation exists. Various concepts including that of the glass ceiling were described and critiqued. Exclusionary processes operate in terms of other indicators (such as race/ethnicity) as well as gender, although there is less systematic information available on them.

Reflecting vertical segregation, women are for the most part not included in professorial or senior leadership management positions although they make up roughly half of those at PhD level and are the high academic achievers. Horizontal segregation focuses on the identification of predominantly female and male areas – without recognising that these areas are differentially valued and that this has consequences. These gendered segregation patterns are typically explained with reference to women's individual characteristics or priorities (an individual deficit perspective). However, the variation that exists between and within countries suggests that the societal and organisational context is important.

The concept of segregation under-estimates the impact of the absence of Total Inclusivity. Hence a typology of academic citizenship was put forward involving full, limited, transitional and non-citizenship. It is necessary to empirically research the gender and intersectional profile of those in each of these types in specific organisations and countries. However, it was possible to identify some trends, including the dominant position of men as full citizens. It is difficult to avoid the conclusion that higher academic institutions are overwhelmingly organisations created by and for men.

Four

INTRODUCTION

The focus in this chapter is on the organisational context and specifically on the organisational processes – both formal and informal – that reflect and reinforce non-inclusion/inclusion. Particularly in organisations where senior positions are held by men, there can be a resistance to the inclusion of women or those who are 'different' in some way at senior level. This can be reflected not only in the formal procedures and processes but also in day-to-day interaction which perpetuates this differential evaluation of insiders/outsiders. Here we focus on two different kinds of mechanisms and processes: those involving violence and harassment that denigrate and marginalise 'outsiders' whether these are defined in terms of gender, race/ethnicity, disability etc. and those that ereinforce the inclusion and privileging of the 'insiders' and they include homosociability (a preference for interacting with people of the same sex), the sponsorship of those who are seen as social mini-me's and inbreeding.

PROCESSES INVOLVING VIOLENCE AND HARASSMENT OF WOMEN AND OTHER 'OUTSIDERS'

At the most extreme these processes can include rape and sexual assault. These are part of a wider continuum of power related behaviours which exclude, demean, belittle, ignore, ridicule, blame, devalue etc. The purpose of these processes is to perpetuate privilege by actively excluding the 'outsiders' or by wearing them down so that they exclude themselves. Such behaviours have often been referred to as gender-based violence and harassment – behaviour 'that is not necessarily sexual in nature but is targeted at individuals or a group of individuals *because* of their sex or gender' (Foley et al., 2020: 1). They can also be extended to other 'outsiders'. Implicit in this perspective is a focus on power and the abuse of power by those in powerful positions. Such abuses are

DOI: 10.4324/9781003277651-5

more likely to occur in situations where power inequalities are substantial and normalised. This situation characterises higher educational institutions, and is particularly likely to be experienced at the early career stage, when dependence by post graduate students, post-doctoral researchers and junior staff on senior academics for references, research funding and sponsorship is at its highest, particularly but not exclusively in STEM (O'Connor et al., 2021).

Most of these behaviours can occur face-to-face or online. Most of them are not peculiar to higher education. They can extend beyond gender. In each case their purpose is to consolidate power and to use it to diminish/devalue/exclude those who are outside the acceptable hegemony. Many of these behaviours reflect the exercise of informal power and have been referred to as micropolitical practices (Morley, 1999; O'Connor et al., 2020) or micro-aggressions. These are essentially power related and can include devaluation (Tepe, 2019; O'Connor et al., 2020); condescension, disparagement, threats (Miner et al., 2019, Naezer et al., 2019); invisibility, ridiculing, withholding information (As, 2004); scientific sabotage, including taking unearned credit for others work (Naezer et al., 2019). 'Doubt raisers' such as questioning women's intellectual independence and devaluing women's achievements have been identified by observers on Swedish funding boards (Ahlqvist et al., 2013). Typically, we do not think of many of these as violence.

Frequently, much of this behaviour is underpinned by stereotypes; i.e., the repertoire of actions and behaviours that society makes available (Martin, 2003). These stereotypes are reflected, for example, in biases against women or other 'outsiders' in assessments of applications for research funding (Wenneras and Wold, 1997); in the criteria and the procedures used in the assessment of senior staff for appointment/promotion (Van den Brink and Benschop, 2012a; Nielsen, 2016; O'Connor and O'Hagan, 2016) and in the evaluation of early career researcher's potential (Herschberg et al., 2019; Benschop, 2021). Such biases have also been reflected in reference letters; in success in funding applications and in student teaching evaluations (see Vettese, 2019). They emerged in experimental studies of job applications where men and women in research intensive universities in the US were asked to assess identical CVs with male and female names, with both men and women favouring the identical cv with a male name, and recommending a higher starting salary for him (Moss-Racusin et al., 2012). These biases are of course not peculiar to higher education. They also emerged in the evaluation of players for top orchestras, and they were only reduced in that context by holding auditions behind a screen and in bare feet so as to conceal the gender of the performers (Goldin and Rouse, 1997).

Bias is frequently not seen as such – but is legitimated by assumptions that the evaluations on which it is based are 'natural', 'traditional', 'inevitable'. Frequently, too, the underlying power relationships are legitimated by ideas about entitlement based on characteristics related to gender, race/ethnicity etc, which are embedded in wider cultural evaluations. Thus, women or those from non-white races/ethnic backgrounds may be depicted as unsuitable for leadership positions, or seen as needing to be 'protected' 'for their own good' from the pressures assumed to exist in such positions These patterns have been shown to exist in higher education institutions in various countries including the United Arab Emirates, India and Ireland (O'Connor, 2015; Galant and Agarwala, 2021; respectively).

Overlapping power bases frequently exist in higher educational institutions (e.g., power based on organisational position, on expert knowledge, and the ability to reward those who are subservient). This increases the likelihood of abuses of power and makes it more difficult to identify them. It also heightens the negative consequences of calling out abuses of power, and increases the likelihood of power being used to protect perpetrators. These processes are exacerbated by the hierarchical male dominated character of higher educational institutions (O'Connor et al., 2021): workplaces which are less hierarchical enable women and non-hegemonic minorities to speak up, with higher numbers of women in leadership positions also being helpful (Zippel, 2021).

Power can be exercised more subtly by persuading women and other non-hegemonic groups that they do not want these positions/ that they conflict with their gender or other identities or by making it so difficult for them that they withdraw/give up (Linkova et al., 2021). Thus, for example, tenure tracks which coincide with women's peak time for bearing and rearing children maximise difficulties for women who want to have children; as do grant arrangements which make no allowance for maternity leave; while a failure to provide state funded childcare also make it very difficult for women to continue in academia. Dropping out or not progressing can be presented as a 'choice' – one which fails to recognise that in less masculinist structures, the 'choice' might be very different indeed. It can be difficult to see these as violence, unless we broaden out the concept of violence beyond the use of physical force by A over B (O'Connor et al., 2020). Workloads, for example, where women disproportionately carry pastoral care, course administration or other service activities may be legitimated as stereotypically appropriate – reflecting and reinforcing women's subordinate status (O'Meara et al., 2017).

A neoliberal managerialist ethos in higher education with its focus on markets and on individual responsibility (Lynch, 2014; Cooper et al., 2020); its concentration of power at Vice Chancellor/Rector level (O'Connor et al., 2019a); its highly individualised, hyper-competitive, performance-driven focus, and its valorisation of research, global rankings, 'research stars' and long hours culture (Naezer et al., 2019; O'Hagan et al., 2019; Bondestam and Lundqvist, 2020) reinforces the power dynamics in higher education. It encourages a perception of contract workers as essentially disposable. It strengthens the power gap, and increases the likelihood that abuses of power will occur and that they will not be reported. In neoliberal universities the perpetrator may be a major source of research funding and be depicted as a 'star' whose reputation is valuable to the organisation. In this context, there is an incentive to ignore the actions of the perpetrator (Phipps, 2020).

The relationship between neoliberalism and precarious work contracts is contested. Such work contracts are a way of freeing up research 'stars' by delegating routine tasks such as laboratory work or undergraduate teaching to contract workers who provide low-cost research assistance to senior academics. Traditionally, the post-doctoral researchers (post docs) were 'groomed' in career terms by permanent senior academics. It was accepted that the relationship would be exploitative and personally advantageous to the senior academic for a limited period of time, after which that academic would facilitate the post doc getting an academic position. This arrangement reflected an implicit patriarchal bargain (O'Connor, 2022). The likelihood of this 'payback' to the post doc has substantially declined in most western higher educational systems as the number of PhD students and post docs has increased. Senior academics are under increasing pressure to deliver research outputs in such managerialist neoliberal contexts.

Thus, there is pressure to maintain and legitimate the exploitative arrangements well beyond the traditional three to five years after the submission of the PhD, particularly in STEM where temporary exploitative relationships have long been depicted as legitimate and normal.

A recent Irish initiative (called Speak Out, 2021), by the Minister for Further and Higher Education, Research, Innovation and Science involves an online and anonymous system for reporting gender and other based violence and harassment. It is an attempt to deal with the fact that overwhelmingly these experiences are not reported. It may provide some insight into the extent to which they occur and the situations, positions and categorical identities of those involved. However, since the system is anonymous, there is no possibility of identifying or penalising perpetrators. Furthermore, in a societal context where there has been little discussion of forms of violence other than sexual harassment it is not clear to what extent negative micropolitical practices and episodes of what has been called 'everyday' sexism/racism will be reported.

The aspect of such behaviour which has been formally recognised to date is bullying. However, it has been overwhelmingly treated by higher educational institutions as an individual problem, best handled by individual mediation, thus ignoring the power dimension (Hodgins et al., 2020). Indeed, gender-based violence in higher education has overwhelmingly been seen as an individual problem which can be solved by discouraging complainants or allowing perpetrators to leave quietly (Phipps, 2020). This ignores the fact that those experiencing it may have difficulty identifying it as such, and may be unable or unwilling to report it.

The function of Human Resources (HR) has become more concerned with 'image over substance' (Lynch, 2013: 9) moving from a concern with the wellbeing of personnel to presenting the organisation in the best possible light (Smyth, 2017), with implications for recognising and dealing with violence and harassment (Ferber, 2018). Frequently HR favours informal mediation, which ignores the power dimension (Bondestam and Lundqvist, 2020; O'Connor et al., 2021). This approach assumes that once an alleged perpetrator is informed about the impact of their negative behaviour, he/she will change: a problematic assumption (Bennett, 2009; Hodgins et al., 2020). Frequently, too, their focus is on individuals rather than seeing that behaviour as reflecting the organisational structure and culture: with the onus of proof being placed on the individual victim/survivor and at most informal mediation being encouraged.

Thus, power related processes involving violence and sexual harassment of women and other 'outsiders' are one way of marginalising and devaluing them. They are not the only ones.

PROCESSES THAT REINFORCE THE INCLUSION AND PRIVILEGING OF THE 'INSIDERS'

It is important to also recognise those processes and practices that reflect and reinforce bonds between the 'insiders'. These processes play an important in fostering a sense of entitlement among insiders and in the acceptance of the normality and legitimacy of such attitudes and practices. At a fundamental level, powerful men's relationships with other men in male dominated organisations are a key element in the perpetuation of patriarchy, which Hartmann (1981: 14) defines as 'a set of social relationships between men, which have a material base, and which, though hierarchical, establish or create interdependence among men that enable them to dominate women.' Such relationships with other men play an important part in opening opportunities for some and closing them for others in higher education. They are reflected in the presence of affinity bias or homosociability (i.e., the tendency to favour those who are similar to oneself: Grummell et al., 2009) – a social rather than a sexual preference. They are also reflected in sponsorship and inbreeding.

In a context where constructions of masculinity are fragile, and where men are defined as superior to women, homosociability can be seen as important in providing both a sense of identity and security to men and supporting their construction of themselves as entitled 'insiders'. The culture of higher educational institutions has frequently been depicted as homosocial with a 'mate-ocracy' existing: one in which men are 'looked after' (Cooper et al., 2020: 16). In this context the strategy of 'paying forward' (O'Connor, 2020) so as to create indebtedness in those involved in evaluative activities, reflects an important element in sponsorship relationships.

Sponsorship includes not only a preference by those in senior positions for interaction with men, but a higher evaluation of them, facilitating their greater access to information, creating greater opportunities to know and trust them and greater identification with and sponsorship of them. It encourages the reproduction of 'sameness' in terms of gender, race/ethnicity/class etc rather than diversity. Valian (2005: 35) has highlighted the impact of these multiple small acts-arguing that each individual event in which a woman does not get her due is a mole hill and: 'Mountains are molehills, piled one on top of the other'.

Nepotism – the practice of favouring friends or relatives by giving them jobs – is widely deplored as unethical. However other processes, such as sponsorship, which are based on the prioritisation of relationships, and hence similar to nepotism, are frequently not defined as such. This 'patriarchal' support system (Bagilhole and Goode, 2001) has been obscured by not differentiating between sponsorship and mentoring, and not recognising the differential relationship of the two processes with male dominated power structures.

Sponsorship involves senior managers with influence leveraging off their own power, reputation and influence to advance the careers of their protégés whether by advocating for or recommending them for assignments, opportunities or promotions and generally using their power and reputation to advance their protégé's career. It is an investment that must be earned because sponsors are invested in their protégés/ées' (Hewett, 2013). The benefits to sponsors include an enhancement of their reputation, the effective creation of a dependency in the sponsee which can be called on in the future, as well as the ability of sponsors to delegate parts of their own workload to the protégé.

Ibarra et al. (2010) found that men are more likely than women to be sponsored, and by a senior member of the management team. In higher education, men are also more likely than women to be sponsored by their PhD supervisor and by other senior male academics, with most women indicating a lack of access to such senior academics (O'Connor et al., 2019a). Sponsorship can be seen as one of the mechanisms involved in perpetuating the position and privileges of those at the top (who in higher education, are overwhelmingly men), through reflecting and reinforcing ties between men. It can be seen as a kind of nurturing relationship between men: one which reproduces the absence of diversity in the occupancy of positions of power. Sponsorship frequently reflects an unconscious affinity or homosocial bias. Equalising access to such sponsorship relationships perpetuates a clientelistic culture. Thus, while it can increase an individual woman's chances, it is essentially a form of nepotism since it involves a focus on relationships rather than objectively defined merits.

Mentoring involves the relationship between a relatively more experienced academic staff member and a younger, less experienced individual, which provides a place to discuss anxieties and uncertainties. Its key elements have been seen as providing emotional support, feedback, increasing mentees' sense of competence, enhancing their personal and professional development, guiding, advising, sharing experience and knowledge (Ibarra et al., 2010; De Vries and Binns, 2018). It is seen as enabling young academics to deal with the often-conflicting demands of teaching, research and service and learning the tacit as well as the explicit organisational rules. Mentors can be at any level of the hierarchy, although Ibarra et al. (2010) found that women's mentors had less organisational power with mentors and mentees being matched on the likelihood of frequent contact and what was referred to as 'chemistry'. Mentors typically expect little in return and the relationship involves little reputational risk.

Where those occupying formal positions of power are providing mentoring, where they are open to detecting common patterns across mentees and have at least some structural awareness of gender inequality, mentoring can promote organisational change (De Vries and van den Brink, 2016). Such a context occurs rarely. Typically, the main focus of the mentoring relationship is on the mentee changing themselves. Ibarra et al. (2010) concluded that women are over-mentored but under-sponsored, with consequences for their likelihood of moving upwards. The focus on mentoring also distracts attention from the fact that the 'normal' process for the reproduction of 'sameness' and the male dominated character of the organisation itself is through the process of sponsorship.

'Inbreeding', or the favouring of in-house candidates, also frequently involves sponsorship. It has been identified as important in the Spanish university system (Sanz-Menéndez et al., 2013; Montes López and O'Connor, 2019). It reflects unofficial and unwritten rules that each new member of a department should be selected from the members of the internal dominant group. A focus on local fit is a less extreme variant of it (Lynch et al., 2012). Like inbreeding, it is rooted in a discourse which favours familiarity, loyalty and affection. In male dominated organisations when combined with homosociability, it seems probable that it will favour men rather than women.

One of the less recognised difficulties for women who do gain access to positions of power in higher education is that their relationship with these male dominated structures is potentially more complex than their male counterparts. This is particularly so if they want to create further change by increasing diversity. Then, they are seen as disrupting the usual patterns of 'paying forward'. These difficulties are reduced if women share some similar characteristics with those in power, and if their main focus is on the reproduction of privilege/sameness in terms of these characteristics. Thus, for example, Carvalho and de Lourdes Machado-Taylor (2017) showed that a limited increase in the presence of women in senior positions in higher education was tolerated in Portugal, provided that these women were from the same class backgrounds as the male power holders and were chosen by them.

If women or non-hegemonic minorities attempt to sponsor 'people like themselves', these attempts are likely to be challenged, and attempts made to discredit them. In addition, in so far as women or others' embody diversity, they are less likely to be attractive targets for sponsees who are uncertain if 'paying forward' to them will yield the 'normal' results. Thus, sponsors are less likely to be able to delegate the routine aspects of their job and to count on the self-interested co-operation of actual or potential sponsees. Their attempts at increasing diversity are also particularly likely to be viewed with suspicion by those who are marginal to the formal power structures and who are interested in institutional transformation. In addition, they may face difficulties arising from the construction of leadership – a topic that we return to in Chapter 6.

Thus, relationships between 'insiders' are an important element in the processes involving inclusion/exclusion. It has been suggested that these are rooted in an appreciation of the importance of power in facilitating advancement-refracted through a homosocial lens.

SUMMARY

In this chapter, the focus has been on two kinds of processes: those that denigrate and marginalise the 'outsiders', and those that reinforce the inclusion and privileging of the 'insiders'. It also identifies some of the characteristics of higher education institutions that are associated with these processes, such as their male dominated hierarchical structure, heightened by neoliberalism and its impact on increasing the power gap between those at the top and bottom of the hierarchy.

Five

INTRODUCTION

There are many types of responses globally by universities to the promotion of gender and other kinds of equality in higher education. A common one can be described as institutional or organisational resistance. It is reflected in the endorsement of legitimating discourses such as excellence, choice, gender neutrality and a revitalised biological essentialised discourse. All of these implicitly deny that there is an organisational problem. Other strategies include challenging the data or focusing on 'fixing' those experiencing inequality. In so far as gender or other bases of inequality are recognised, the institutional focus can be on undertaking time consuming activities which deliver organisational awards (such as Athena SWAN (AS)) or Gender Equality Plans (GEPs). Such activities can increase awareness of gender and diversity, can create rhetorical or marginal change while not actually producing change in the gender profile of academic staff, in the organisational culture or in bringing about organisational transformation.

INSTITUTIONALISED RESISTANCE

We have become accustomed to thinking about resistance as something that feminists or other activists do to tackle inequality in organisations. Here, we suggest that it is necessary to recognise the reality of institutionalised (i.e., organisational) resistance to tackling inequality. Agócs (1997: 918) defines gendered institutionalised resistance as "patterns of organizational behaviour that decision makers or people in power positions employ to actively or passively deny, reject and refuse to implement, repress or even dismantle gender equality change proposals and initiatives". Such institutionalised resistance may be reflected in the endorsement of ideologies that legitimate the current situation by suggesting, for example, that those who are excluded are not 'excellent' enough; that they have 'chosen' other

DOI: 10.4324/9781003277651-6

routes or priorities, or that the current situation reflects 'natural' patterns. Institutionalised resistance can be reflected in an unwillingness to problematise the existing organisational structures, culture, procedures, allocation of resources and informal practices and to see them as implicated in the failure to promote inclusion. It may be combined with a recognition of the need to be seen to 'do something' about gender/racist or other bases of inequality. In that context issues surrounding two of the most popular attempts to promote equality i.e., Athena SWAN (AS) and Gender Equality Plans (GEPs: which are a European phenomenon: EC, 2021c) are explored later in this chapter.

THERE IS NO PROBLEM: THE NATURE AND IMPORTANCE OF LEGITIMATING DISCOURSES

Legitimating discourses are social constructions which implicitly legitimate the status quo and present it as 'natural' and 'inevitable'. They 'provide normative justifications for existing policies and practices through which they are seen as appropriate, reasonable, and fair' (Tyler, 2005: 211). In Western higher education settings, as well as in many others, excellence and choice are two of the most common such discourses in explaining why power remains centralised in (white) male hands. The argument is that women and non-hegemonic groups are not excellent enough to access such positions or that those who are excellent do not choose to access them. These discourses may be underpinned by those suggesting that higher education is gender neutral and/or that men and women's relative positions are 'natural'. These legitimating discourses serve to justify the existence of inequality on the basis of characteristics such as gender, race etc.

At first glance, such explanations appear to have a great deal of validity. Common sense suggests that people should be qualified for positions of power and that they should be free to choose whether or not they want such positions. However, on closer examination it is clear that the situation is a good deal more complex than this. O'Connor and Barnard (2021: 55–56) concluded, based on a policy analysis of documents related to recruitment and promotion as well as national policy documents related to the Research Evaluation and Teaching Evaluation Exercises in the UK that 'excellence' is used rhetorically as an empty signifier and contextual interpretation is key…. excellence can be mobilised, distorted or constructed as stakeholders see fit'. Definitions of excellence are typically vague and circular, with candidates being required to have a record of excellent research and teaching but with little indication as to how vague excellence criteria such as originality or significance are to be operationalised for those at different levels of the academic hierarchy. Nobel prize winning is obviously one definition of excellence – but there are far fewer of these than there are academic positions in higher education.

Since senior positions in higher education are dominated by men, most of those defining excellence are men who have been recruited and promoted within masculinised structures and cultures and their positioning and priorities influence who is defined as excellent. Yet this hegemonic subjectivity is presented as objective reality and its impact on the reproduction of sameness is obscured.

A similar problem arises from the assertion that the crucial factor is individual choice with women's under-representation in senior positions being explained in these terms. Again, this appears at first glance to have a degree of face validity. However, it ignores the fact that the structures, criteria and procedures are for the most part designed by men for men. Women themselves often collude with the internalisation of these individualised choice discourses, and blame themselves rather than challenging the conflicting greedy institutions of paid work and family (Linkova et al., 2021).

Underpinning these discourses is the idea that higher educational institutions are disembodied bureaucracies, staffed by automatons, so that resource allocations, recruitments, promotions and informal interactions are all uninfluenced by the positioning and relationships of those, such as white, middle-class men, who are in positions of power. This was the classical Weberian definition of a bureaucracy, which ignored the impact of informal ties, personal and categorical agendas in defining excellence. It also ignores institutionalised resistance to change in a context where it can be seen as threatening the existing power holders' entitlements and revealing their vested interests.

In Eastern Europe, in India and in other parts of Asian and African countries, a revitalised biological essentialism persists. In this perspective women and other non-hegemonic groups are seen as naturally suited to subordinate, low paid positions, while men are depicted as naturally suited to well-paid powerful positions. These beliefs are seen as unproblematic – 'natural' and inevitable. Under pressure from external forces, a small minority of women or non-hegemonic others may be admitted to senior positions, not least to legitimise the system, but these will tend to be those who are of 'good behaviour' in the sense that they do not challenge the existing structures of power and privilege (Tiernan and O'Connor, 2020).

These discourses conspire to make 'the problem' of inequality disappear as an organisational issue. Insofar as they are not totally successful and individuals or groups continue to raise issues, other strategies become necessary.

OTHER MANIFESTATIONS OF INSTITUTIONALISED RESISTANCE

If organisations want to deny the existence of inequality, the failure to collect and present data on it is a useful strategy. Typically, the collection of this data is done by an individual academic or groups of academics, often funded by the EU and involving case studies and action research on individual higher educational institutions or groups of them. A common response to the presentation of such data within academia involves a challenge to the methodology used; a suggestion that the results are not applicable to their particular organisation, or that if these trends existed in the past, they no longer do so. Van den Brink (2015) noted that two out of every three of the responses to her presentation of data on gender inequality to university leaders in academic settings were defensive, with these leaders criticising the approach adopted or the study's findings. Such responses are aimed at discrediting the study and/or the author, and hence invalidating the findings.

Whistle-blowers' accounts are also usually discredited, with an attempt made by the power holders in an organisation to 'circle the wagons', and to deny the accusations and undermine the credibility of the whistle-blower. Frequently, the insights provided by whistle-blowers do not come into the public arena, since an attempt is made to forestall the resultant publicity through the existence of non-disclosure agreements.

Occasionally, the outcome of an individual case becomes public, and this creates challenges. This happened in the case of Micheline Sheehy Skeffington, who took a gender inequality promotion case in 2009 against the National University of Ireland Galway (NUIG), her employer for 34 years. The Equality Tribunal (2014) found that in the promotion competition to senior lecturer, the university had discriminated against her because of her gender (describing the promotion process as 'ramshackle'). It ordered the university to promote her to senior lecturer from 2009, and to pay her the salary difference as well as a tax-free lump sum of €70,000. The case garnered further publicity since she gave that money to the other five women who had been shortlisted but not promoted in that competition to help them to fight their cases. The dispute involving four of these five women went to the High Court but was eventually settled by NUIG in 2018 with their promotion and an undisclosed financial settlement. The fifth woman had earlier received promotion and compensation through the Labour Court.

This process dragged on for ten years and made it very difficult to claim that gender inequality did not exist in NUI Galway. The best that the then President of that university could do was to argue that it was not unique. This, amongst other pressures, culminated in the setting up of *National Review of Gender Equality in Irish Higher Education* by the Higher Educational Authority (HEA, 2016). As part of that review, it undertook an online survey involving roughly 5,000 people working in Irish higher education. The report showed that men were less likely than women to think that gender inequality existed in Irish higher education institutions or to see it as extremely important. Men constitute the majority of those in senior academic and managerial positions in Ireland as elsewhere (see Chapter 3). Their disinclination to take action makes sense in a context where most of them do not see gender inequality as existing and/or as extremely important.

INITIATIVES TO TACKLE INEQUALITY

Effective initiatives to tackle inequality are more apparent in the research funding sector than in mainstream higher education institutions (Benschop, 2021; Husu, 2021). This may be because a permanent cohort whose career prospects and privileges would be affected by such initiatives are less prevalent in funding organisations than in such higher educational institutions.

The EU has been active in the attempt to reduce gender inequality, including most recently in Horizon 2021–2027, a research funding schema with gender – balance in research teams being a ranking criterion in equally ranked projects (Husu, 2021). A number of research funding bodies have also implemented innovatory practices. The Irish Research Council found that anonymising STEM postdoctoral applications increased the percentage of women achieving an award from 35% in 2013 to 57% in 2017 (IRC, 2018). Yen (2019) found that accepting individual postdoctoral applications (rather than HEIs institutional nominations); including a meeting facilitator who could interrupt the evaluation process if bias arose and giving an unranked list of candidates to the funders, increased the offers made to women fivefold in a context where the female pool of applicants increased only marginally. The European Research Council extended female applicants window by 18 months per child and in 2014, the success rate for women in its Consolidator Grant was higher than that of men. The Swedish Research Council, having documented gender inequality in the allocation of research funding for a number of years, put observers on to these boards. They identified gendered processes, including, for example, 'doubt raisers' i.e., the questioning of women's intellectual independence if their applications came from prestigious research centres, while the evaluation of male applications increased in similar circumstances (Ahlqvist et al., 2013).

It cannot be assumed that increasing the success of women in acquiring research funding will inevitably translate into their success in moving upwards in higher educational institutions. Brower and James (2020) showed that in New Zealand, although women improved their research scores by more than their male counterparts, they still moved up the academic hierarchy much more slowly, with men having more than twice their female counterparts' chance of accessing a professorship or associate professorship.

Even where attempts are made to put in place workload models or to link performance and even pay to what purport to be objective metrics, the gendered nature of the performance indicators may still perpetuate male privilege. Steinporsdottir et al. (2018) found that early career researchers in STEM (who are predominantly men) compared with those in Social Science and Humanities (who are predominantly women) enjoy greater access to research funding, lower student–staff ratios, higher evaluations of their research output and hence are more likely to get additional payments, access to sabbaticals and hence increased chances of career advancement.

Much of the focus has been on what has been called the 'best practice' model on the assumption that 'decontextualised tools' can be imported without regard to the local specificities. Ni Laoire et al. (2021) argue that both the national context as well as the organisational context matters. Processes and criteria related to promotion and recruitment may be centralised at national level or located at the local level- and this has implications for the identification of sites of institutionalised resistance. Ni Laoire et al. (2021: 578) are critical of 'models that view organisational change as an *outcome* [sic] resulting from the importation of policy, rather than as an ongoing *process*, [sic] involving complex interactions between policy and practice'. Thus, they stress the importance of the organisational structure and culture, the history of gender equality initiatives and infrastructure, the positioning of those attempting to initiate change as well as the power relations, agendas and vested interests of those operating there. This raises fundamental issues about co-design or co-creation methodologies since internal middle management stakeholders may fail to support transformative initiatives if they see them as undermining their own position, privileges and future career possibilities.

In Western higher educational institutions, insofar as it is accepted that gender inequality exists, the two most common responses are application for an Athena SWAN (AS) quality mark and the formulation of a Gender Equality Plan (GEP). These are discussed below.

Athena SWAN (AS)

Athena SWAN (AS) is a United Kingdom quality mark awarded at bronze, silver and gold to institutions or departments (Barnard, 2017). Versions of it have now been adopted in Ireland, Australia, Canada and the United States (see also Chapter 11). It was initially focused on advancing the careers of women in science, technology, engineering, mathematics and medicine (STEMM) and now includes all professional, support and technical staff, all disciplines, all genders and all intersectional inequalities (O'Mullane, 2021).

The popularity of AS in the UK dramatically increased with the linking of eligibility for funding from the National Institute of Health Research to the attainment of an AS Silver award (Tzanakou and Pearce, 2019). In the UK, it is delivered through Advance, a limited company with charitable status. It is thus in a structurally weak position since it has no leverage for incentivising the promotion of gender equality in higher educational organisations other than in terms of the linkage to medical research funding, or through competition between higher educational institutions for an AS quality mark. In contrast, in Ireland, AS is ultimately under the aegis of the Higher Educational Authority, which allocates state funding to higher education, and so is in a structurally much stronger position.

The application for an AS award involves quantitative data collection, self-assessment under a chair (sometimes called an 'AS champion'), potentially at senior management level. It involves the design and implementation of an action plan to tackle gender and other inequalities. Potentially, that plan can include a range of areas including 'leadership, organisational culture, recruitment, promotion and retention policies, gender in research' (Bencivenga and Drew, 2020: 181).

Although the ultimate aim of AS was to bring about structural and cultural change, little research has been done on its impact. Graves et al. (2019) in one of the very few extensive evaluations found no relationship between the organisational length of engagement with AS and increases in the proportion of female staff or students. There was also no clear trend over time in the UK in the proportion of professorial promotions that went to women in organisations with an AS award. Indeed, the respondents in the 13 case studies, undertaken as part of the evaluation, noted that 'the greatest challenge remains in addressing gender balance in the most senior positions (e.g., professorial, senior management),' (Graves et al., 2019: 54).

The percentage of female professors in science, engineering and technology (SET) nationally increased very little between 2010 and 2014 in the UK, despite this being the then focus of AS, while the proportion outside those disciplines increased substantially (SET: 15% to 18%; non-SET: 25% to 44%; Barnard, 2017). Amery et al. (2019) found that there was no evidence that the AS award or its level (that is, bronze, silver or gold) had any impact on the gender pay gap. The study by Ovseiko et al. (2019) also recognised that AS had limited ability to address power and pay imbalances, persisting work–life balance issues and wider structural and cultural changes in the organisation and in the wider society. They noted that under certain circumstances it could become a rhetorical box-ticking exercise.

Case studies of the tiny minority of individual Gold departments in the UK did show increased female representation at senior academic levels (Graves et al., 2019). Thus, for example, in the Department of Chemistry in Edinburgh the proportion of female professors increased from 15% in 2007 to 27% in 2014, well above the sector average. It is not clear whether this reflects the impact of AS or the leadership of such departments. In any case, given the tiny minority of such departments, it seems inappropriate to use their success (as O'Mullane 2021 does) to suggest that AS is a generator of institutional change. Indeed, even in the UK gold-winning AS departments, there tends to be little emphasis on mid-career, senior academic or management level (Barnard, 2017). Even there, the main focus is on 'fixing' the women (training them to manage time better, to become more confident or more politically aware etc.); the assumption being that it is women who need to change.

There was a tendency for promotions to senior lecturer/reader/associate professor to become more gender-balanced in the period up to the submission of an Athena SWAN application (Graves et al., 2019). The proportion of departments with gender-balanced (40/60) shortlists also increased (from 27% to 37%) over a three-year application period. However, the fact that women remained a minority on most shortlists clearly indicates the ongoing difficulties, since when there is only one woman on a shortlist, her chances of appointment are mathematically low (O'Connor, 2020).

Graves et al. (2019) surveyed almost 3,000 staff and students in institutions with an AS award, and showed that male academics were generally more positive about AS than their female counterparts. Even in these AS award-winning institutions, women were less likely than their male counterparts to be familiar with the criteria and processes for promotion; less likely to see such processes as evidence-based, unbiased and fair; less likely to have been encouraged to apply for promotion; less likely to be satisfied with their most recent performance review; and less likely to be optimistic about their career prospects. In addition, women were less likely than men to have been encouraged to take up such training opportunities as were available, although they were more likely to be mentored. This suggests that even in those organisations that had won an AS award, there was a focus on 'fixing the women' through mentoring, while at the same time ignoring routine organisational processes and practices that perpetuated inequality (Peterson and Jordansson, 2017).

Athena SWAN does create a context which makes it easier to raise gender equality issues, and it elicits positive responses from participants, particularly champions (Graves et al., 2019). However, in both the medical and social science departments in Oxford which had won an AS award, more women than men felt less confident in their ability to move forward in their career, were less convinced that the university treated women equitably and less convinced that their department supported the advancement of black and minority ethnic faculty equitably (Ovseiko et al., 2019).

Most of the work done by Self-Assessment Teams on AS applications, even in those departments with silver awards, is done by women (Tzanakou and Pearce, 2019), with varying effects on their careers (Graves et al., 2019). This combined with the failure of AS to produce clear increases in the proportion of women at professorial level or to impact on micropolitical practices (such as encouragement to apply for promotion), raises fundamental questions about its ability to seriously challenge male dominance in higher education.

Higher educational institutions are increasingly sensitive to global ranking systems which, up to very recently ignored issues related to gender equality in general and male privilege in particular. However, the impact of gender equality practices on United Nations Goal 5 (Gender Equality) is assessed on the THE (2021) ranking system. However, only a small proportion (15%) of the 100 marks are allocated to measures related to the advancement of female staff. There is no attempt to look at structural mechanisms such as the implementation of the cascade model i.e., where the proportion of women to be promoted is based on the proportion of each gender at the grade immediately below (HEA, 2016). Nevertheless (see Chapter 2) it still constitutes a potential lever for T1.

Gender Equality Plans (GEPs)

The EU increasingly favours the development of Gender Equality Plans (GEPs). It defines them as 'a set of commitments and actions that aim to promote gender equality in an organisation through institutional and cultural change' (EC, 2021c: 5). Research funding applications under

Horizon 2021–2027 must include them; they must be public documents; with dedicated resources and expertise to implement them; they must include data collection and monitoring as well as awareness raising and training elements. Five thematic areas are also recommended for inclusion in these GEPs: work–life balance and organisational culture; gender balance in leadership and decision-making; gender equality in recruitment and career progression; the integration of the gender dimension into research and teaching content and the inclusion of measures to tackle gender-based violence, including sexual harassment. However, reference to the 'sustainable transformation of organisational culture' (EC, 2021c: 6) is a recommended, rather than a mandatory element of such GEPs.

GEPs vary widely in their focus and ambition. They often assume that best practices can be transferred easily between different contexts (assumptions that have been challenged: Ni Laoire et al., 2021). Frequently, they are developed by junior staff who are remote from power and dependent for their implementation on key stakeholders who may have other priorities and interests. Such plans may fail to take into account the particular characteristics of the organisation; their track record on tackling inequality and the absence/presence of infrastructural support as well as the compatibility of an equality agenda with the strategic priorities of the organisational and national power holders.

In these contexts, Ni Laoire et al. (2021: 585) suggest that their key focus becomes 'building relationships and legitimacy.' This can however be at the expense of attempts at organisational transformation. Thus, for example, stakeholders may encourage the drafting of GEPs which are then largely ignored. Support from key stakeholders may be withdrawn if the focus is on the implementation of procedures surrounding recruitment or promotion if they are seen as undermining what are depicted as valued patterns of sponsorship and entitlement. GEPs may also depict success as an individual phenomenon. Finally, difficult issues may be deferred until EU funding has been exhausted and then quietly abandoned.

In a case study evaluation of an Irish university, it was noted that there was a good deal of reliance on an uncritical 'fix the women' approach (O'Connor, 2014) in the GEP There were 20 references to leadership in it, all reflecting the idea that women were deficient in such skills (Hodgins and O'Connor, 2021). A focus on busy-ness involving de-politicised actions was also identified. Thus, although the GEP contained 89 actions, neither power nor inequality were mentioned, and 'discrimination' was only mentioned once. There appeared to be a strong a preference for 'safe' actions that did not challenge the power structures (reflected in for example, a video showcasing senior women in leadership roles and the creation of parental support networks). Gender quotas based on a flexible cascade mode were in the Gender Equality Plan 2019, but they were not explicitly referred to in the promotional documentation, implicitly raising the question as to whether there was an institutional acceptance that they were not necessary and whether they would be implemented (Hodgins and O'Connor, 2021).

Although a huge amount of effort is being expended on the development of GEPs, there has been little systematic evaluation of them, and it is not clear to what extent they promote organisational transformation.

SUMMARY AND CONCLUSIONS

In this chapter we have suggested that higher educational institutions have tended to resist the identification of inequality by legitimating it through discourses such as excellence, choice, gender neutrality or a revitalised biological essentialist discourse. Where data documenting such inequality has been produced, power has been deployed more overtly to challenge the data and to undermine the credibility of those presenting it. The innovative response of funding organisations contrasts with the institutionalised resistance in higher education organisations. The chapter also explored two of the most popular types of organisational interventions: Athena SWAN (AS) and Gender Equality Plans (GEPs). Although both are useful in facilitating discussion of inequality, it is by no means clear that either of them can promote the kind of institutional transformation that is necessary for the elimination of inequality and the promotion of a Totally Inclusive agenda.

Six

INTRODUCTION

All organisations have a 'climate' or culture. This may not be visible but it is certainly felt. It becomes concretised over time through values and deeper cultural roots that are reflected in and reinforced by leadership within the organisation. Typically, and historically, for higher educational institutions these dominant (albeit often unrecognised) values have been associated with whiteness and maleness.

The majority of those in leadership positions in higher education globally are men whether this is defined as holding the rector/president/vice chancellor position or that of a full professor (see Chapter 3). Critical leadership studies problematise the concept of leadership as well as asking whether changing the gender profile of those in leadership positions is sufficient to create inclusive organisations. In this chapter we challenge the attractiveness of the concept of leadership and suggest an explicit focus on power; we ask who accesses leadership positions in higher education and the implications of this and present a typology.

THE ATTRACTIVENESS OF THE CONCEPT OF LEADERSHIP

Leadership tends to be seen as the key to all kinds of organisational success. This has been seen as 'leaderism' which 'suggests that certain subjectivities, values, behaviours, dispositions and characteristics can strategically overcome institutional inertia, outflank resistance and recalcitrance and provide direction for new university futures' (Morley, 2013: 116). Critical leadership studies challenges 'excessively positive constructions of heroic leadership' that are 'often reluctant to address issues of power and privilege' (Collinson, 2019: 266).

Leadership has been defined as a process of influence (Gunter, 2010). Alvesson and Spicer (2014: 40) noted that; 'The term *leadership*

DOI: 10.4324/9781003277651-7

(sic) is seductive, has a strong rhetorical appeal, and is therefore heavily overused'. Frequently it is presented in unambiguously positive terms that fit 'nicely into a culture of grandiosity' (Alvesson, 2019: 27). It tends to create and sustain an overly positive view of organisational relations and glosses over issues related to consent and subordination and the different interests of leaders and followers (Learmonth and Morrell, 2017).

Considerable attention has been paid to the characteristics or personal attributes of leaders. Frequently these tend to be stereotypically male: 'irredeemably masculine, heroic, individualist' (Grint, 2011: 8). Morley (2013: 188) suggested that masculinism 'denotes the ideology that naturalises and justifies men's domination over women'. The criteria, rules and routine practices used in gendered organisations evaluate men's potential differently to women's; see men as more entitled to hold powerful positions and evaluate women's performances and achievements through a lens that devalues them relative to men. When leadership is seen as 'naturally' male, male dominance and female subordination is legitimated. This explains and justifies privileging, not only of male leaders, but of all men since as men they are all potential leaders.

Despite the popularity of the concept of leadership, heroic ideas about leadership behaviour, styles and characteristics break down when those in leadership positions in higher education are asked to describe what they actually do. Behaviour such as listening, which might be seen as quite unremarkable (or even typically female) if it was done by non-leaders, becomes transformed when it was enacted by those in leadership positions. Critical leadership studies suggests that the crucial element is neither the characteristics, styles or behaviour of the leader, but their power. With a small number of exceptions (Sinclair, 2014; Lumby, 2019; O'Connor et al., 2019b), the relationship between leadership and power has attracted little attention.

LEADERSHIP AND POWER

Universities have been intimately linked with interest groups at particular times and places (see Chapter 2). If leadership is seen as understanding and shaping these external factors (Power, 2021) the recruitment of leaders who accept the existing power structures reduces any pressure to create change. It enables leaders to avoid challenging the political projects of those who fund higher education. Given the overwhelming acceptance of neoliberalism by nation states in western society, it is highly unlikely that men or women who gain access to leadership positions will be opposed to it: thereby positioning them from the start as supporters of this aspect of the status quo.

Power (2021: 144) suggested that the leaders of academic institutions 'continue to see their role as implementers rather than leaders... focused less on change and more on doing the same tasks more efficiently, effectively or accountably'. Hence the concepts of leadership and management are used interchangeably in this chapter. Other than in crisis situations the leaders' role may be largely symbolic; with the assumption that the existing structure, culture and allocation of resources will continue. Thus, power and its mechanisms are obscured. In many organisations, this is the normal face of leadership.

Lumby (2019) identified power as key to leadership and an important element in affecting the ability of power holders to make something happen in line with their wishes. However, many of those in senior management positions in higher education attempt to obscure power (O'Connor, 2014). The critical leadership approach has rarely been applied to leadership in higher education – perhaps because power tends to be obscured or denied there. Lumby (2019) identified what she called 'subtle forms of power' reflected in shaping discussions and decisions; acquiring support and weakening opposition. The concept of stealth power (Webb, 2008; O'Connor et al., 2019b) is useful in identifying a continuum of such covert power. It includes opaque decision-making fora where deals are struck behind the scenes and where invisible forms of power exist, reflected in people's desires. Power may also be reflected in attempts 'to frame others' reality (Smircich and Morgan, 1982: 258), by defining situations in ways that suit the purpose of the power holders for example, through discourses that portray their sectional interests as universal, and that depict inequalities as 'natural', 'inevitable' (O'Connor and White, 2021a). Leaders are able to exert stealth power because they have at their disposal power and resources, and these 'encourage' others' co-operation, including those who hope to share that power in the present or future.

Connell (2005: 82) argues that:

A gender order where men dominate women cannot avoid constituting men as an interest group concerned with defence and women as an interest group concerned with change. This is a structural fact, independent of whether men as individuals love or hate women or believe in equality or abjection.

The power dynamics involved in leadership play a crucial role in reproducing the system involving male power and privileging through what has been called patriarchal bargains (see Chapter 4). These bargains involve informal relationships between seniors and juniors, often including sponsorship, and frequently based on identification between them so as to maintain the status quo. In this context little effort is needed by those in positions of power to do that: but a great deal of effort is needed to change the taken-for-granted structures, cultures, criteria and informal practices maintaining it.

The weave of patriarchal support (Bagilhole and Goode, 2001) also extends to relationships between senior men, where, other than in extreme circumstances, the norm is one of mutual support and their avoidance of public conflict, on the understanding that this support will be repaid in kind. In this transactional environment the unspoken ethos is: 'You scratch my back, I will scratch yours'. In this masculinised context, the expectation is that men will benefit from perpetuating a context where male privilege is embedded. Women may think that they will be included in this system if they behave as honorary males. But this status may be withdrawn at any time:

'You may find a place as long as you simulate the norm and hide your difference. We will know you are different, and continue ultimately to treat you as different, but if you yourself specify your difference, your claim to equality will be nil'.

(Cockburn, 1991: 219)

Evidence from a number of studies show that many women in senior positions do not fully recognise that 'academia remains predominantly a site of men's power, privilege and mutual support' (Hearn,

2021: 101) characterised by the perpetuation of male-dominated, masculinist structures that maintain that male privilege. Thus, they are surprised by the failure to discuss issues openly at senior level; by the failure of most men to publicly back a woman (even when they agree with her) and by the low level of public dissent between men (O'Connor, 2014, 2015).

WHO ACCESSES LEADERSHIP POSITIONS IN HIGHER EDUCATION?

Organisational processes and practices reflect and reproduce wider social inequalities. Crenshaw's (1991) concept of intersectionality contributes to an understanding of who is included in/excluded from leadership positions (see also Chapter 13). The main focus here is on leadership and gender since this data is most widely available. However, intersectionality 'makes a discussion about power dynamics and the actual 'doing' and processes of inequality unavoidable' (Woods et al., 2021: 11).

The culture of the organisation has been used to refer to a complicated fabric of management myths, values and practices that legitimise the differential evaluation of activities/areas/people. In male-dominated masculinist organisations, it is frequently underpinned by stereotypes which legitimise the allocation of devalued activities to particular categories of people (such as those based on gender, race/ethnicity etc.).

The most obvious leadership position is the rector/president/vice chancellor one and in neoliberal managerial contexts power is centralised in it (O'Connor et al., 2019b). Some power also exists at vice rector/vice president/deputy/pro-vice chancellor level. However, typically, academics in these positions are assigned by the rector/president/VC to these positions on a temporary basis, thus limiting the extent to which they can effectively challenge his/her power – or indeed the extent to which they may wish to do so. The position of full professor is also important in leadership terms, not only because it plays an important role in shaping the relevant discipline, but also because it is frequently a route to these senior management/leadership positions.

There is considerable variation between countries in the proportion of women at rector/president/VC level (see Chapter 3). Thus, for example, women make up roughly half of those in these positions in Sweden and New Zealand, as compared with one-third in the United States; roughly a quarter in Australia; 7–9% in the United Arab Emirates, Turkey and the Czech Republic (O'Connor and White, 2021a). Given such variation, it is difficult to sustain the argument that the bearing and rearing of children by women is the determining factor in affecting the proportion of women in such positions. In some countries (for example, Sweden), the state's endorsement of gender equality and its role in signing off on these appointments plays an important role in affecting gender parity at this level.

The disciplinary backgrounds of those in such leadership positions tend to vary over time and between countries depending on the main stakeholders' project (e.g., national identity or research). The current tendency in much of western academia is to favour those with a science, technology, engineering or mathematics (STEM) background. Those recruited from STEM are more likely to be men and reflect the stereotype of the ideal academic:

> Western Science and technology are culturally masculinised. This is not just a question of personnel.... The guiding metaphors of scientific research, the impersonality of its discourse, the structures of power and communication in science, the reproduction of its internal culture, all stem from the social position of dominant men in a gendered world.
>
> (Connell, 2005: 6)

Women are frequently in female-dominated areas (e.g., nursing or midwifery): areas that are perceived as low status and not ones for the identification of future leaders.

Countries vary in the number and power those in senior positions who have had experience outside academia. Blackmore and Sawers (2015) found that in their study of Australian academia, over half of the senior managers (including those in non-academic positions) had spent time in industry or government. Those in such non-academic positions are typically permanent employees, and hence constitute potential bases from which challenges to the power of the rector/president/VC could potentially be launched.

Blackmore and Sawers (2015) also noted that in Australia academic senior management positions that were internally oriented (such as teaching and learning) were less prestigious. They were also more likely to be held by women, with greater variation in the disciplinary backgrounds of those in these positions. Senior management positions that were more externally oriented (such as research) were more likely to be held by men with a background in STEM, and were more likely to lead to the position of rector/president/VC.

The position of full professor is another position of leadership in higher education. The proportion of women in such positions also varies between countries (see Chapter 3). Thus, for example, it is just under 34% in United States; 30% in Australia; 24% in the EU but only 12–15% in the Czech Republic and the United Arab Emirates The two countries – Sweden and New Zealand – with the highest proportion of women at rector/president/VC level perform modestly on this indicator (29 and 27% respectively: O'Connor and White, 2021a). What little evidence there is on those with intersectional characteristics (such as gender and race/ethnicity) suggests that they fare particularly badly – with the proportion of black women among tenured female academics in the US falling since 1993 and with only a handful of black female professors in the UK (see Vettese, 2019).

In higher educational institutions, it appears that women as leaders do not fit. Stereotypes create considerable challenges for them (Fitzgerald, 2018). The masculinist definition of the characteristics and behaviour of a leader mean that women are wrong-footed: if they behave like women, they are not seen as leaders; if they behave as leaders, they are criticised as women (Schein et al., 1996). They are exposed to interactional pressures that reflect and reinforce a perception of them as being out of place (O'Connor, 2015). Women who are seen as powerful leaders 'will attract particularly vicious and brutal efforts to drive women into silence or submission,' (Sinclair, 2013: 17). A study of 9,000 staff at the prestigious Max Planck Society in Germany (Abbott, 2019) found that women in leadership positions reported experiencing negative gendered behaviour at a higher rate than other women. Women's performance in leadership roles is also more likely than their male counterparts to be negatively evaluated (Morley, 2013; Vettese, 2019) and there is considerable pressure on them to 'pass' as honorary males. Finally, their materiality, whether this is their physically embodied appearance, or their requirements around maternity leave are also seen as problematic (Sinclair, 2013; Fitzgerald, 2018).

The convenient explanation for women's under-representation in leadership positions in higher education is 'the notion of women's missing agency' (Shepherd, 2017: 82) i.e., the idea that women lack confidence, ambition or an ability to deal with rejection. In contrast to suggestions (Morley, 2014) that women have little interest in senior leadership positions, Shepherd (2017) found that there was little difference between men and women in terms of their aspirations for the positions of deputy and pro-vice chancellors in (pre-1992) UK universities or in terms of their applications for such jobs. They also differed little in their ambivalence about assuming these positions. Thus, she suggests that efforts to 'fix' the women through women only development programmes (such as Aurora) are unlikely to be successful.

Moratti (2021) also found, in her study of access to professorships in Norway, that there was no support for a deficit hypothesis involving women's reluctance to apply or to relocate. However, she identified an external candidate penalty for women, in the sense that they were less likely to be appointed outside their own university. Shepherd (2017) also found that men were more than twice as likely as their female counterparts to apply for a job in another university. External men are more likely to be seen as exceptional ('Sheep with five legs': Van den Brink and Benschop, 2012a). This tendency for men to perceive themselves and other men more favourably than they perceive women (called vanity by Vettese, 2019) was documented in the US even at undergraduate level and is conducive to their selection for leadership positions. The UK Leadership Foundation found that female alumni of its Top Management Programme who subsequently applied for a more senior management role were more than twice as likely as their male counterparts to have been unsuccessful (Manfredi et al., 2014). However, Moratti (2021) found that there was an internal candidate bonus for women; i.e., they were more likely to be appointed in their home institution. Internal women are arguably seen as useful for the bread-and butter-low status work. The implicit suggestion is that internal women (regardless of their ability) who are not willing to do that low status work will not get leadership positions.

Female leaders may be appointed in 'glass cliff' situations (Ryan and Haslam, 2007) when the chance of failure is high: ultimately affecting women's perceived suitability for such positions. Targets or quotas implicitly challenge the inevitability of equating senior positions with maleness, and the reproduction of male-dominated structures. Of course, the presence of women does not necessarily transform the system since not all women are feminists (Carvalho and de Lourdes Machado-Taylor, 2017). However, having more women as editors in chief of important journals increased the rate of first authorship by women, sometimes to more than double the rates of comparable journals headed by men (Filardo et al., 2016). It is not clear if this reflected editorial decisions or role modelling.

Male-dominated higher educational institutions are particularly vulnerable to pressures to normalise a culture of male entitlement, one that tolerates or even valorises toxic masculinities (Whitehead, 2021a); a culture that legitimates 'Othering', where bullying and micro-aggressions are normalised and remain hidden (McKay and Fratzl, 2011; O'Connor et al., 2021). Where leaders lack knowledge about gender as a social construct and are unwilling to tackle gendered power structures, leadership can be seen as gender incompetent (Lipinsky and Wroblewski, 2021).

Implicitly and explicitly, the culture created by those in positions of power in higher education has tolerated gender-based violence and harassment, failing to take complaints seriously, failing to sanction perpetrators and failing to protect complainants from retaliation (Bondestam and Lundqvist, 2020). Conversely, a UK wide review highlighted the importance of 'the visible, vocal commitment from senior leaders' in changing the culture (Smail and Waye, 2019). Efforts by organisations to recruit, retain and promote women, which themselves reflect an organisational appreciation of diversity have been shown to prevent sexual harassment, as does leadership which shows that sexual harassment will not be tolerated (Lee, 2018). Higher numbers of women in leadership positions are also helpful in changing that culture (Zippel, 2021).

The dominant pattern, however, in higher education globally is one of male dominance.

TYPOLOGY OF LEADERSHIP IN HIGHER EDUCATION

There has been a reluctance by leaders in higher education to reflect on their position of privilege as (white) men so as 'to fully comprehend how they are perceived and how they represent particular forms of leadership that may 'other' some forms of masculinity, most forms of femininity and indigenous ways of being and leading' (Blackmore, 2013: 147; see also Hearn, 2021). Connell (2005: 77) defined hegemonic masculinities as embodying 'the currently accepted answer to the problem of the legitimacy of patriarchy, which guarantees (or is taken to guarantee) the dominant position of men and the subordination of women'. Women in leadership positions in male-dominated organisations are part of a predominantly male group, where the ultimate authority is male and the organisational culture is masculinist. In that context they are often given the message that they should develop a 'male' style.

Hegemonic masculinity refers to the most culturally valued form of masculinity in a particular society. Its content will vary between societies. Thus, for example, aggression reflects a particular construction of hegemonic masculinity (Connell, 1995). However aggressive behaviour was rarely mentioned, much less endorsed by university senior managers in Sweden (O'Connor and Goransson, 2015), underlining the contextual content of hegemonic masculinities. However, they all involve the subordination of women and other nonhegemonic masculinities. Difference is evaluated against a male norm so that women and these others, by definition, are seen as 'not good enough'.

Although only a minority of men in higher education may actively subordinate women (hegemonic masculinity) the majority benefit from the patriarchal dividend 'in terms of honour, prestige or the right to command. [They] men also gain a material dividend' (Connell, 1995: 82). This dividend is facilitated by the fact that hegemonic masculinity is used to organise such structures, so that men and women are not treated the same within such male-dominated structures. It is possible to identify four ideal types amongst those in leadership positions in higher education:

1. Overtly masculinist in ideology and practice

Those in this ideal type overtly endorse male superiority and prioritise areas where male faculty predominate. They see attempts to change such priorities as reflecting unacceptable social engineering. Policies involving any kind of gender equality measures are openly challenged. They show minimal conformity to gender balance policies (e.g., one woman and ten men on an interview board being seen as balanced). They see little problem with all male interview boards, and when challenged, suggest that asking female interviewees if they have any objection to this is adequate. They see any attempt to raise gender issues as undermining meritocracy and are active in discrediting and stereotyping those raising these issues. Firm believers in men's superiority, they can on occasion be verbally abusive to women in decision-making fora. For the most part however, they do not see the need to do this in a context where male hegemony is taken for granted, one where women are routinely devalued, marginalised and patronised.

2. Apparently gender neutral but complicit in masculinism

Those in this type present themselves as indifferent or neutral on gender issues. They value the existence of patriarchal privileges but are less confident about their legitimacy. Hence although they do not typically play an active role in proposing masculinist policies, they equally do not oppose them. They see higher entry level positions for academics in overwhelmingly male areas as 'natural' and inevitable' and the allocation to women of low status 'housekeeping' activities in the same light. They favour vague criteria and loose marking schemas at critical access points-both of which have been shown to be unhelpful to women. They quietly subvert attempts to ensure real gender balance on important boards and revise models of promotion or appointment that seem to benefit women. They use a variety of strategies to ensure that a culture of sameness' persists. Some of them try to be different kinds of men and are empathic and sensitive in their responsiveness to requests for aid but only from younger men. They typically evaluate men's potential and performance more positively and are extremely reluctant to recommend women for leadership positions.

3. Supportive of challenges to masculinism but not a priority

Those in this category are supportive of challenges to masculinist ideology and practice, although it is not a priority for them. In some situations, they deliver on gender balance and discourage practices that are hostile to women. In other cases, where such decisions affect their own work or comfort zone, their decisions reflect homosociability – with their successors being similar in key attributes (such as gender, management style and even physique). Under pressure from other priorities, they over-use compliant women who do not endorse a feminist agenda and under-use women who are reputed to be difficult as a way of meeting organisational gender obligations. Unwilling to 'think outside the box' they are not interested in the gender implications of state or organisational policies. Although nominally supportive of gender equality at the organisational level, it is not a priority, and it is typically given only rhetorical assent.

4. Feminist or pro-feminist in ideology and practices

Pro-feminist men are advocates for feminist concerns and opposed to the marginalisation and devaluation of women (Whitehead, 2021a). Those in this type do not endorse ideologies of male superiority and see gender issues as power related. Uncomfortable with hegemonies of any sort, they overtly support policies and practices that limit male dominance; support gender auditing and seek to ensure that the appropriate gender and nonhegemonic balance exists in decision-making fora, with women being appropriately represented in leadership positions.

SUMMARY

This chapter has outlined the attractiveness of the concept of leadership and has explored the importance of its relationship with power, using a critical leadership studies perspective. In higher education that power is exercised in male-dominated organisations and reproduces both these structures and the constructions of masculinity embedded in them. It is difficult for women to access such positions and to fit comfortably in them, since hegemonic masculinity is based on the subordination of women and nonhegemonic masculinities. The presence of women in such positions does not inevitably transform higher education, although it can facilitate some change by providing role models and reducing gender-based violence and harassment. Finally, the chapter identifies four ideal types of leadership based on their relationship with the ideology and practices of hegemonic masculinity.

You and 'Your' University
Part Two
Stephen Whitehead

Seven

The first time Lucy set eyes on the manicured, historic university campus she panicked. Feeling massively intimidated, she turned anxiously to her girlfriend, who was accompanying her to the undergraduate open day, and, almost in tears, told her "No way can I study here. This is not for me." The only thing that stopped her turning around and catching the next bus home was her friend insisting that she at least "just check it out". Lucy's reaction was hardly surprising. The campus may only have been 30 miles from her home (situated in one of the most depressed housing estates in northern England – a drug-infested, violent environment, cursed by dysfunctionality and hopelessness) – but in terms of class and identity, it might as well have been on another planet.

A decade later, and Lucy is still at the very same university department which subsequently accepted her for a BA. Only now she is Dr Lucy; a full-time lecturer.[1]

If you work in higher education anywhere in the world, then this vignette will likely be familiar to you. You'll have witnessed the same progressive identity work which occurs when young (and not so young) people embark on higher level learning. You may have been a guide to them on that journey, both as academic tutor/supervisor, and a friend/mentor. Perhaps you were their sponsor?[2] You may even be a 'Lucy' yourself.

Have you reflected on what is happening here with regards to identity?

Have you reflected on the amazing capacity of higher education to transform people from insecure beings, lacking confidence and belief in themselves and their potential, to highly agentic individuals?

Have you reflected on the power of it all?

We have, which is why we write this book.

DOI: 10.4324/9781003277651-9

Any level of education has the potential to change people, to move them from a state of ignorance to a state of understanding. Indeed, is that not the very point of education – to bring about intellectual development in the individual? It is certainly the point as far as we are concerned though for a great many politicians and others, education is simply about getting a better job, or worse, socialisation to a dominant ideology or creed.

We totally reject any such limitations imposed on education and consequently imposed on the individual (and society). We do so not only from a personal/political standpoint but from an intellectual one. And a key foundation of that position concerns theories of identity.

IDENTITY

It is not only hairstyles and clothes which go in and out of fashion – so too do sociological and psychological theories.

It is not that long ago when, if you'd enrolled in almost any UK (or European) university department which drew on sociological theories, then you'd be writing and learning about Marxism, neo-Marxism, or any of their associate (structuralist) theories.

Two examples are business and management, and organisational Studies. What was the 'big theory' informing much of the research pouring out of such departments by sociologists during the 1990s?: Labour Process Theory.[3] And which theories were its 'arch-enemy'? Postmodernism and Poststructuralism.[4]

One theory that wasn't getting much traction within global academia back then was feminism. Partly because most male academics didn't understand or value it, and partly because feminists themselves were having the same theoretical battles as the organisational/business studies researchers. During the 1980s, and through to the early part of this century, feminist theory was dominated by Marxist-feminism; socialist feminism, radical feminism and liberal feminism.[5] And which theories were their 'arch-enemy'; yes, you guessed correctly – postmodernism and poststructuralism.

To those outside the intellectually intense world of heavy theoretical analysis, this might all have looked irrelevant if not nonsensical. Actually, it wasn't. What these sociologists were projecting, even if they didn't realise it at the time, was the emergence of global identity politics.

Nowadays, it is impossible to move anywhere, read anything, without bumping into 'identity'. The word, and concept, has assumed a dominance in thought, culture, language and politics which surpasses even Marxism at its height – this ideological tiger of the 20th century has now migrated to remote outposts inhabited only by the most devout. Today, university students are enveloped with identity issues, from trans = woman debates to whether or not to pull down the Oxford University Cecil Rhodes statue because it symbolises a racist, colonialist past.

But while 'identity' is now ubiquitous across pretty much every aspect of human discourse, informing analysis of everything from Brexit to terrorism, Trumpism to racism, few commentators delve deep into its complex constitution.

And the reasons for this are not hard to fathom. After all, how easy is it to analyse one's self? Not easy at all, but that is where one must start if one is to unpick this catch-all word.

Importantly, it is not possible to explore, never mind implement, Total Inclusivity, unless one first understands a number of key aspects concerning identity, and at the same time is prepared to hold on to those understandings and allow them to coalesce into the foundations of diversity, equity, inclusion and justice as practice.

And this is the single most important aspect to grasp with relation to identity and Total Inclusivity – that the identities which TI seeks to protect, nurture and value are for the most part social constructs not biological ones. Even that identity which is biological and not socially constructed, sexuality, is lived and expressed socially.

In other words, identity is work in progress not a predicted, fixed or settled state.

In poststructuralist terms, there is no sovereign self, no fixed authentic 'I' behind the deed, behind the thought, behind the mask, behind the social performance. Indeed, the very notion of 'I' is problematic:

A thought comes when 'it' wants, not when 'I' want…'It' thinks but that this 'it' is identical with the good old 'I' is at best only an assumption.
(Nietzsche, 1973: 16–17)

The individual is an illusion, reified and reifiable only in social immersion and representation…the individual's very presence in the social is both a condition and consequence of the social, a point that problematises any idea that the individual and the social are separate entities.

(Whitehead, 2002: 214)

I can never be totally defined, nor can I escape all definition. I am the quest for myself.

(Sarup, 1993: 13)

There is no gender identity behind the expressions of gender...identity is performatively constituted by the very 'expressions' that are said to be its results.

(Butler, 1990: 25)

You don't need to be a sociologist to instantly recognise what is being stated above – that biology is not destiny, because identity, and therefore one's potential, is not determined by biology.

So, what is identity determined by?

Actually, the answer to that question depends on where you situate yourself on the agency-structure continuum or indeed whether you recognise that such a continuum exists in the first place.

We cannot answer for you, and this book is not the place to try and convince you either way. But for us, there is indeed a continuum operating in society; in fact, countless numbers of them, approximately 7.7 billion to be precise: one for each of us.

In other words, it all depends on the many variables which have informed your being since the time you were first exposed to the social world – certainly at birth, very likely before. The structure-agency battle goes on around us, in our environment, and in our heads. Some structural constraints we absorb by osmosis (e.g., religious belief, language, culture, social rules) and very quickly these discourses become us; they define who we think we are. We become bound by their soft and comforting, but very firm and inflexible, embrace.

Other discursive constraints we might reject and subsequently reinvent. An example is someone being raised in a homophobic environment but eventually coming to reject this discourse and become LGTBT+ positive. Or the violent criminal who in time rejects the path of violence and adopts an alternative discourse/path, which leads him to become a mentor of young juvenile offenders.

Who is to declare any individual incapable of this self-fashioning, what Foucault terms the 'artistry of self' (Foucault, 1991)? Certainly not us. Indeed, we see self-fashioning as central to TI, new humanism and to diversity, equity, inclusion and justice, because it can offer a way of both rejecting those discourses which speak to our anger, fears, insecurity and ignorance, while providing us with deep and satisfying existential and ontological connections across humanity.

That said, rejecting discourses (or ideologies) which speak to our more toxic emotions is not easy, especially if our identity, sense of self, is being validated by them. In order to reject them we first have to have the courage to reinvent ourselves and that can only begin once we decide we no longer want to be the person we were before. Not easy to do:

> *Individuals act in certain ways because it would violate their sense of being to do otherwise.*
>
> (McNay, 2000: 80)

A stark example are incels and white supremacists. How many incels and white supremacists (often the same thing) do you imagine will read this book? Let us be realistic and say 'none'. Everything written in these pages is not only an affront to their world view, but it also undermines what they have become and who they think they are.

We are not psychologists, but that level of intervention is invariably required to help someone who is deep in the 'cave of male fundamentalism' (Whitehead, 2021a) to emerge into a safer, healthier, more inclusive and less violent place.

Incels and feminists are at opposite ends of the political (identity) spectrum, but there is one thing they have in common: they are both caught up in discursive fields of knowledge, practice and power; as are we all. In poststructuralist terms, no human becomes an individual, exercises power, assumes an identity other than through discourse:

> *...discourses are historically variable ways of specifying knowledge and truth – what is possible to speak of at a given moment. They function...as sets of rules...Discourses are, therefore, powerful.*
>
> (Ramazanoglu, 1993: 19)

We must not imagine a world of discourse divided between accepted dis-
course and excluded discourse, or between dominant discourse and the
dominated one; but as a multiplicity of discursive elements that can come
into play in various strategies...Discourse transmits and produces power;
it reinforces it, but also undermines and exposes it, renders it fragile and
makes it possible to thwart it.

(Foucault, 1984: 100; quote in Ramazanoglu, 1993: 19)

This book is an example of discursive creation, or at least discursive adaption. We offer the concept of Total Inclusivity and frame it within a set of previously defined and established theories, all reinforced by a relevant evidential base and analysis. Total Inclusivity is a 'new' concept in one respect but ancient in another. Its origins go back to the first person who spoke out against injustice, spoke (their) truth to power, and challenged discriminatory practices.

In creating a discursive strategy for the subsequent implementation of TI, the writing must first connect to your subjectivity, ideally by resonating with who you are or want to be – sociological theories such as poststructuralism won't achieve that on their own, there have to be other more potent hooks and we employ them in this book.

This is discursive power at work and all writings which aim to convince people to change, to action, use it. Though few writers will openly admit it or acknowledge the process at work here. However, we recognise your capacity to refashion yourself into an Advocate for Total Inclusivity. We know you have that potential. Which is why we have adopted this approach with all three books. The aim in each is to connect with the individual reader rather than with an amorphous organisation or institution.

And the reason is quite simple; the organisation or institution (e.g., university) has no identity – so it cannot create TI; only you can do that.

One of the most common mistakes we all make when imagining, thinking
about, or working in organisations is to render them real. Organisations
have no ontological identity. They are not existentially functioning beings
with all the characteristics of humans. Organisations may have a website,
an HQ, a thousand employees, a worldwide image and huge profits, but
they do not have a mind and nor do they have emotions.

(Whitehead, 2022)

BELONGING

Of course, it is one thing to expose the fallacy of organisational identity and entirely another to expect individuals within organisations to remain ontologically separate from them.

Knowing something as an intellectual argument is not the same as being able to live it out in our daily lives, our everyday practice.

And this is especially true of our relationship with an institution such as a university.

The existential vacuum at the heart of human identity has to be filled somehow, and this need for being and becoming can be temporarily satisfied in any number of ways and in any number of arenas, but most effectively with institutions and organisations which offer community, association, progression, and, consequently, an identity.

Universities do that very well indeed. They are big, powerful, impressive, authoritative, desirable, and effortlessly middle/upper class. Many are ancient, almost mythical, making them appear more enchanting, while even the newest offer hope of personal and professional advancement. No surprise that many students, and staff, become seduced by the institutional image and wrap it around them, not just physically with a scarf or jumper, but with all the signifiers confirming that "yes, I went to Oxbridge", 'yes, I'm a Harvard/Yale graduate', and so on.

If you wish to see this evidence of the desirability of universities beyond educational achievement, just visit Oxford any summer's day and witness the crowds of people (pre/post-covid), from all around the world, none of them students at the university, but all eager to have a selfie taken outside the famous college gates. Instant association and instant belonging, albeit for an hour or two.

In respect of TI it would be far healthier if all this disappeared and going to university became nothing more than an inevitable next step on the ladder of maturity and development for all individuals regardless of where they lived, originated from, or any other aspect of their identity.

But we are still some way off that as a global reality. As our 'Lucy' vignette demonstrates, universities are not yet for everyone even though they could be.

What Lucy and every other young (and not so young) person wants and needs is the feeling of being existentially and ontologically connected: a sense of belonging ideally to something which can protect them and be aspirational. Of course, the university is not the only space which can provide this, but for a great many of us, especially young folk, 'going to university' is more than an educational achievement, more than a rite of passage: it is a declaration that one has been accepted by the powers that operate in society. Yes, we know that many young people who do not go to university go on to become 'successful adults'. But these relatively few prove the point – that university experience can change people for the better. It advances their intellect, their confidence, their very sense of who they are.

The university graduate emerges with a greater sense of social belonging because society has embraced them and provided the means, the 'starter pack', for their life thereafter.

This is identity at work and the university is a powerful space for its enabling, experimentation, and achievement.

But for this to happen for every university student and staff member, every university must embrace every student and staff member regardless of their 'identity mix'.

So, what is meant by and how do we theorise the concept of 'identity mix'?

INTERSECTIONALITY

Poststructuralist theory not only exposes the absence of any core to identity, the lack of a 'sovereign self', it reveals the contingency, multiplicity and variability of identity. And this was one of the key areas of contestation between various feminist camps during the 1980s and 1990s especially. That is, if there is no fixed identity core then can there be, for example, a feminine epistemological reality which is held by women and not by men? And what about power? If all is contingent and power is diffused then where, for example, does gender power, and especially patriarchy, originate from and how is it sustained?

These are big questions, not least because a key aim of feminism is to critique and destabilise patriarchy, hegemonic masculinity, the whole gamut of masculinism and its accompanying assumptions and beliefs. The goal of all feminists, and of Total Inclusivity, is to change those practices (of men especially) that hinder or confront the possibility of gender equity. Because without gender equity then there is no chance of Total Inclusivity.

> ...a number of tensions then arise for critical gender theorists, one of which occurs in the attempt to reconcile or straddle the nature-nurture dualism. The dilemma is how far to go in seeing women and men as biologically inspired gender categories, albeit with material and epistemological differences, or in deconstructing the terms 'men' and 'women' from any biological or essential basis – in so doing possibly losing the sense of men as a political grouping with particular power effects.
>
> (Whitehead, 2002: 8)

That was written by one of us over 20 years ago. Intellectually, the complex questions raised above have never been fully answered – partly because they cannot be. But what has happened over the past two decades is rejection of gender as a biological state, acceptance that sex identity too is contaminated by social 'performativity' (Butler, 1990) – and the recognition that each of us is unique. Enveloping this subjective, discursive uniqueness are different power effects, call them hegemonic, patriarchal, racial or whatever, they do exist, and they are potent. We see them all around us, we experience them in our lives.

So, what name do with give to this condition?
Answer: intersectionality.

Poststructuralism and to a lesser extent postmodernism may have assumed a persuasive theoretical authority in sociology and related disciplines over the past two decades but that has only been achieved because they have given birth to a much more attractive child: intersectionality. And the reason intersectionality is so attractive is because most critical gender theorists can see their own particular theoretical position mirrored within it – somewhere.

> Intersectionality...recognises that each life and each individual identity exists in the intersections of many aspects of self and social powers; encourages the recognition that gender intersects with, for example, race, sex, sexuality, ability, ethnicity, age, culture and class to "produce" the individual.
>
> (quoted in Whitehead, 2022)

Intersectionality investigates how intersecting power relations influence social relations across diverse societies as well as individual experiences in everyday life. As an analytical tool, intersectionality views categories of race, class, gender, sexuality, nation, ability, ethnicity and age – among others – as interrelated and mutually shaping one another. Intersectionality is a way of understanding and explaining complexity in the world, in people, and in human experiences...Rather than seeing people as an homogenous, undifferentiated mass of individuals, intersectionality provides a framework for explaining how categories of race, class, gender, age, and citizenship status, among others, position people differently in the world.

(Hill Collins and Bilge, 2020: 4/19)

To fully appreciate intersectionality, it is important to recognise its feminist poststructuralist roots; indeed, it also has a lot in common with feminist postmodernism.

Intersectionality tells us nothing new in terms of advancing theories of identity – we are still firmly located within the concept of the Foucauldian discursive subject. But it has become the most popular and public face of feminist theory and for good reason, and not only because laypeople can easily understand it.

You want to discuss ideology and structure?

You want to examine agency and power?

You want to highlight the multiplicity and contingency of identity?

You want to theorise how gender, sexuality and class connect?

You want to examine the relationship between being Black and being a woman?

Intersectionality offers us a way into to all these complex debates. It is not a sophisticated theory of identity or of power, but it is a useful tool to show how the two connect.

Not surprisingly, intersectionality has become the 'go-to theory' for gender theories/theorists and we are pleased to align with it in our discussion of Total Inclusivity.

It bridges the apparent unbridgeable gaps between structure and agency; between juridico-discursive power and structural power; and between the individual and society. It does this quite simply, by recognising that none of us is a fixed composite being, but...

...an ever-evolving kaleidoscope of social elements, mixed in with hor-
mones and chromosomes to produce an individual; a person who is always
in the process of some degree of metamorphosis.

(Whitehead, 2022)

This is still a discursively bound individual always in a state of being and becoming (Deleuze and Guattari, 1988), and that individual/ subject remains caught up in the power effects arising from numerous discourses. But intersectionality offers us a simple lens through which to view these otherwise messy, murky and evolving dynamics of the self.

To gauge just how far intersectionality has come in influencing feminists and gender activists of all persuasions over the past few years, one only has to look at how the concept is being enlisted to fight for 'trans rights':

Holding a "feminism is for everyone" placard, Kate West, a bar manager
and student, said: Feminism is intersectional, and you don't get to cher-
ry-pick whose rights you support...Women's rights are not threatened by
trans rights.

(Brooks, 2021)

So, does intersectionality have any weaknesses?

Not unless you consider being all things to all feminists/critical gender theorists as a weakness. Though we do suggest that in order to fully understand how intersectionality works it is necessary to go back to its original feminist roots – feminist poststructuralism.

'OTHERS'

It is not possible to know how far back in the human story we need to go in order to see the first example of the politics of identity, to first witness political dynamics shaping one's sense of belonging or not belonging. Perhaps this has always been a central factor in the human condition. Indeed, is identity itself not partly to blame for the politics of belonging? After all, we invest our sense of self, our ontological connections, in both association and disassociation. Belonging, whether it be to a biker gang, a political party, a family, a football team, the

Army, the Girl Guides or a university alumnus is compelling precisely because these discursive regimes offer the subject (individual) a clearly demarked space to be and become. The rules, codes, dress, cultures and language which signify all discursive regimes welcome us in and provide us with validation so long as we stay 'loyal' to them by replicating those discourses, ways of being.

The problem is, of course, what about those who are on the outside? What about those who are not welcome in? What about the 'others'?

'Othering' has become a key aspect of diversity, equity, inclusion and social justice, at least in terms of it needing to be challenged. Which is why we write about othering in both our other two books on Total Inclusivity. Othering can occur through any number of devices, but almost inevitably it involves language as a key signifier as to whether a person is 'not one of us'; an 'outsider'; unwelcome; lesser; and different. We discuss language and free speech in Chapter 10, so we won't go into detail here, but what is important to recognise is how this othering works and what its basis in power is.

For this, we must again turn to feminist theoreticians for insight into that which too often gets ignored, is unseen, or unrecognised for what it is. But not a contemporary feminist – rather someone who bequeathed us the concept of the 'other' in her writings over 70 years ago; Simone de Beauvoir.

But before we look at de Beauvoir, we must first acknowledge her lover, Jean Paul Sartre. These two giants of 20th century philosophy were not just lovers they were intellectual soulmates and together wove existentialism into one of the great philosophies – even while they held opposing views as to the possibilities.

Sartre struggled with the subjectivity v collective contradictions inherent in existentialism. In this quote he falls on the side of the collective, having accepted that there is no self without others:

I think that an individual in the group, even if he is somewhat terrorized, is all the same better than an individual alone, even if he is somewhat terrorized...It isn't true that you are being asked to abdicate your self; it would still be too much if you had a self to abdicate...I say this without irony: it is certainly sweet to discover yourself in the fraternal eyes of others.

(quoted in Levy, 2003: 401)

Sweet indeed, which is precisely an aim of Total Inclusivity – to provide a fraternal embrace for all not least because without association the self is, as Sartre acknowledges, adrift in an existential nothingness; without essence or definition.

De Beauvoir took a slightly different stance on existential belonging, raising the point that this fraternal embrace came with a price tag attached together with a load of gendered assumptions.

> *A man's body has meaning by itself, disregarding the body of the woman, whereas the woman's body seems devoid of meaning without reference to the male. Man thinks himself without woman. Women does not think herself without man. And she is nothing other than what man decides; she is thus called 'the sex', meaning that the male sees her essentially as a sexed being; for him she is sex, so she is it in the absolute. She determines and differentiates herself in relation to man, and he does not in relation to her; she is the inessential in front of the essential. He is the subject; he is the Absolute. She is the Other.*
>
> (de Beauvoir, 1949/2009: 23)

The Sartrean male can frolic between the contours of fraternity and individuality unburdened by the existential question of the 'Other', precisely because he has already defined himself, or is defined, as the centre, the Absolute in relation to women. In short, the price for man's existential 'freedom' is paid by women.

Not surprisingly, for the past 70 years feminists of all theoretical persuasions have read those words and decided enough is enough.

> *Woman can create her own self because there is no essence of eternal femininity that prescribes a ready-made identity for her. All that is holding woman back from self-creation is society – a patriarchy this is, in de Beauvoir's estimation, reaching its end.*
>
> (Tong, 1994: 210)

> *Throughout history, men have differentiated and defined women in reference to themselves, rather than as beings in their own right. The result, as de Beauvoir says, is that woman is 'the incidental, the inessential as opposed to the essential'.*
>
> (Butler-Bowden, 2017: 45)

Of the many valuable and lasting gifts de Beauvoir gave to humanity, and to feminists in particular, the concept of the 'other' was one of the most important.

It has transcended its Sartrean existentialist origins and taken root in every place and every language where discussions of diversity, equity, inclusion and social justice are joined. It has become almost impossible to explore DEIJ without reference to the 'others' which exist not by choice, not through agency, but through imposition by those with the hegemonic capacity to maintain their dominant place in society.

De Beauvoir powerfully exposed the binary of Absolute – Other at the heart of gender and sex identities. But it is equally valid to expose this binary at the heart of the heterosexual – LGBT+ divide and the white – Black divide. Othering is not exclusive to men's existential relationship to women, it is vivid also in white supremacism, homophobia, indeed in all hatreds. As Sarte pointed out, when we hate a particular Other in reality, we hate all Others.

It is this hatred, this anger, this fear of the Other, which Total Inclusivity seeks to overcome. And in the overcoming so are we all made free – and hopefully a little wiser as to who we are and why we are.

CONCLUSION

There cannot be a university in the world which does not like to see itself as a 'citadel of learning'. Indeed, was that not their very *raison d'etre* all those centuries ago when the first 'university' was conceptualised? But that was then, this is now. Today exclusivity and elitism won't cut it, and for the many the reasons this book explains. In which case stakeholders and leaders in every university must today ask themselves these questions:

Who is this institution designed for?
What identity mix must you have in order to be accepted, welcome, successful here?
Who are we deliberately excluding and why?
Who are we unintentionally excluding and how?

There are many variables entwined in these questions but ultimately, they come down to two – identity and power.

This chapter has explored identity from the theoretical perspective of the non-essential self – the discursive subject of poststructuralism; the power-enveloped multiple identities of intersectionality, and the 'Other' of existential feminism. In so doing, we've exposed through theoretical discussion the politics of belonging.

You may have alternative theories to deploy which you believe make the point stronger and more convincingly than the ones we present above. That is fine. This is not a competition between theories or even between political standpoints. Total Inclusivity rises above all that – it has to.

TI does not privilege any identity over another and nor should any institution which embraces this value system, embeds it in practice and systems, and works to ensure it permeates every corridor, office and lecture theatre.

We, the authors, may be accused of some naïvety and idealism in arguing for TI in HE. But our response is that between us, we have over 80 years' experience of working in education, mostly higher education, and we cannot declare to you which identities should be excluded from the opportunity to undertake higher level learning. Our conclusion is, therefore, that none should.

NOTES

1 This an anonymised vignette and can be verified by one of the authors.
2 Sponsors are defined as people who metaphorically open doors/create opportunities for others to take advantage of (see for discussion, O'Connor et al., 2019a).
3 See Knights and Willmott (1990) for discussion of Labour Process Theory.
4 'Postmodernism' is defined as the 'culture, including theories, of postmodernity – the historical period that is believed by some to mark the end of modernity; in includes any culture or theory that studies, practices or celebrates, or otherwise takes seriously the breaking apart of modernity' (Lemert, 1997: 67). 'Poststructuralism' embraces a number of theoretical perspectives but all question the notion of a unified consciousness; a foundational, singular identity; complete and absolute meanings in language; and the Cartesian conception of the unitary subject – the originating authority for all meaning and truth. (see Sarup, 1993).
5 See Whitehead et al. (2014) for overview of feminist theories and timeline.

An International Learning Community?

Eight

This chapter explores the concept of international learning communities and how such communities relate to global diversity, equity, inclusion and justice.

If Total Inclusivity is the objective, then one of its most powerful tools is internationalisation. However, internationalisation has no innate agenda. It does not come with a particular script, nor does it need to carry a particular message. Therefore, Total Inclusivity will not be automatically promoted by internationalisation unless the dynamics, values and signifiers of internationalisation are purposefully designed to promote Total Inclusivity, which is why universities and their members are so central to Total Inclusivity: because without them embracing it, leading it, modelling it, then global Total Inclusivity will struggle against those forces which draw energy and sustenance from division, elitism and discrimination.

In a world that appears increasingly chaotic, polarised and unequal, universities are potentially powerful global influencers on young minds. The knowledge and learning generated by universities not only advances human society scientifically and intellectually, but it also has the potential to stabilise it.

All of which raises the concept of an 'international learning community' within and of universities to one of crucial importance; of concern to anyone seeking to promote global diversity, equity, inclusion and justice. So how close are we to meeting that goal?

DOI: 10.4324/9781003277651-10

INTERNATIONALISED HE

The internationalisation of higher education has, since the 1990s, been rapid and profound. It embraces study abroad programmes and transnational education, overseas branch campuses and global research collaborations, student and staff exchanges and international student enrolments. However, to imagine all these otherwise worthwhile activities are driven by intellectual enquiry would be at best naïve.

At some point in the second half of the 20th century universities ceased being solely devoted to advanced learning with some becoming multimillion-dollar business ventures. A few have flown high, generating billions of dollars of annual revenue (Neate, 2021) while most have struggled in an intensely competitive, higher education neo-liberal market economy that like true capitalism tends to weaken the weak and enrich the rich (see, for example, Harvard Finance, 2021; Statista, Cambridge, 2019; MIT Facts, 2021). Little wonder, then, that every university worthy of the title is busily chasing its share of the £300 billion which international students contribute to the global economy each year (Perez-Encinas and Rodriguez-Pomeda, 2018).

Yet despite the veritable avalanche of money arising from the internationalisation of HE, students have become (indebted) consumers; academic jobs have become less secure, more casual and temporary; and administrators and managerialism have multiplied (HESA, 2021).

The whole face and body of higher education has been transformed in just a few short decades into one where Pro Vice Chancellors have to think and act like CEOs while academics must, like mice on an ever-turning treadmill, devote their time and energy to 'delivering measurables'; invariably defined as articles in 'highly ranked' journals. Though in truth, such academics are the fortunate ones; increasing numbers are on teaching-only, fixed-term, hourly paid contracts not dissimilar to those enjoyed by Uber staff (Hall, 2021a).

When managerialism rules, performativity defines ability and value, and students are weighed down by insecurities and facing a life of indebtedness, what chance of an advanced international learning community emerging?

According to students and tutors around the world, not much.
USA:

Graduate workers in America's higher education system are organizing a response to high tuition fees, cuts to staff and faculty positions, reduced budgets and suppressed graduate workers' rights to organize unions...Job losses have been substantial at US universities and colleges.

(Sainato, 2021)

Netherlands:

After a month of occupation of university buildings University of Amsterdam students are increasingly winning support for their protest against pressure on universities to focus on 'effectivity' – producing measurable products as efficiently as possible.

(Myklebust, 2015)

Norway:

We question the way our [Norwegian] universities are increasingly run as businesses and how policy choices are more and more based on financial returns and efficacy rather than guided by scientific and societal needs [this] commodification of higher education [is occurring] at a time when corporate agendas are dominating universities and intellectual integrity around the world.

(Myklebust, 2017)

UK:

Senior academics are refusing to act as external examiners in protest at pay and working conditions...29 professors said they were resigning as external examiners and refusing to take on new contracts because of pension cuts and insecure contracts throughout the sector, as well as gender and ethnicity pay gaps, heavy workloads and stress.

(Adams, 2020)

Another way of looking at what has happened is to enlist popularist imagery:

> 'Mickey Mouse' degrees offered by McDonaldised HE institutions, leading to a situation where the *'contemporary McUniversity'* becomes a *'generally hostile environment for both professional self-governance and intellectual autonomy. More specifically, [under these constraints] what kind of intellectual [emerges] within a contemporary McUniversity?'*
>
> (Parker, 2002: 139/151)

That was written by a prominent young UK professor over 20 years ago. Since when, not much has changed that might spur him, or anyone else, to ask different questions. Indeed, all that has changed is that the rise of the McUniversity has become global and normalised.

If you have witnessed first-hand the shift from academic and intellectual autonomy to the performative treadmill, whipped along by zero-hour contracts – or the threat of them – then you can only conclude as we do that universities today are a sad and pinched reflection of what they once were, or what they might have been.

Sure, a few have more money, most will have more students and more staff, and all will be controlled by more managers, but has this improved them as international learning communities?

With so much money and so many jobs at stake, you'd have thought every university with any degree of global ambition would be well versed in exactly what their overseas clients are looking for when they arrive on campus, and what support they expect thereafter.

Well according to research this is far from being the case:

> The trend towards internationalization and the increase in mobility drives the agenda for globalization in many higher education institutions, and in some cases without any clear strategy for identifying international students' perceptions and needs.
>
> (Perez-Encinas and Rodriguez-Pomeda, 2018: 20)

To scrutinise universities anywhere in the world one has two sources of information; the public rhetorical imagery emblazoned on flashy websites, or the words of those who work and study in them.

The gap between the rhetoric and the reality appears to grow exponentially according to higher education's increasingly precarious financial state, not improved by a global pandemic.

In the UK, the problem is particularly acute as tuition fee income plummets due to both Brexit and the pandemic:

> *The extent of the financial hit facing UK universities through losing tuition fee income from E.U. students is laid bare for the first time. Universities are forecast to lose an estimated £62.5 million per year in tuition fees as a result of Brexit. The number of E.U. students at UK universities is predicted to slump by half.*
>
> (Morrison, 2021)

> *About a dozen UK universities face going bust in the long run as a result of the Covid-19 crisis if they do not get a government bailout or help with debts. According to the analysis by the Institute of Fiscal Studies, the sector's long-run losses could reach £19 billion.*
>
> (Baker, 2020; also Baker, 2022b)

However, it would be wrong to blame the UK university predicament solely on Covid or Brexit; they are only parts of the story. The reality is that many universities have been on the financial brink for some years. In April 2020, the HE Statistical Agency reported that 119 of 194 UK universities were in deficit, double the number from 2019 (Clark, 2020).

Even before the pandemic, teaching hours and contact time with staff had been cut to the embarrassingly minimum. It doesn't take a clairvoyant to predict that online lectures will become the norm long after Covid is history, tucked away in the concept of 'hybrid learning'. All of which suggests that a very different student – university relationship will emerge over the coming decades and not just in the UK.

> *Dozens of [US] colleges and universities started 2020 already under financial stress. They'd spent the past decade grappling with declining enrolments and weakening support from state governments. Now, with the added pressures of the coronavirus pandemic, the fabric of American higher education has become even more strained.*
>
> (Butrymowicz, 2020)

The overall impact of the current crisis will be large and long-lasting, and [EU] universities must prepare for operational and financial difficulties in the coming few years.

(Esterman et al., 2020: 19)

A statistics Canada report is projecting a significant drop in admissions, both domestic and international, which could translate into a $1.7 billion shortfall for Ontario's post-secondary institutions in the 2020–21 year – the largest loss in Canada. Nationwide, the damage could total $2.5 billion.

(Sarrouh, 2021)

Covid-induced job losses in Australian universities have doubled since last year...with tenured rather than casual staff now in the firing line...This trend looks likely to continue as international enrolments continue to plunge.

(Ross, 2021)

Faced with such bleak scenarios, what would you do if you were a university CEO?

Answer: you would seek revenue from other sources.

And what is one major source of such money? China.

Trade tensions between Beijing and Washington have been building for years, leading the Trump administration to label the Asian nation "a threat to the world". Yet the tally of gifts and contracts from China to US universities since the start of 2013 is approaching $1 billion.

(Lorin and Kochkodin, 2020)

WHAT TYPE OF INTERNATIONALISATION?

As we can see, an internationalisation of higher education is taking place, but not in exactly the style envisaged back in 2000 by Western governments and not one which suggests universities emerging as Totally Inclusivity communities.

While Western universities are left grappling with declining international enrolments, declining Chinese student enrolments, Covid-19, Brexit, and increasing tensions between China and the West, universities across Asia and especially China expand their provision at an awesome pace.

To put what is happening in countries like the US and the UK in perspective, compare them to a relative newcomer to the global capitalist order – Vietnam.

Higher education in Vietnam, indeed all education in that country, has expanded phenomenally. And it is privatisation which has been the driver.

Take one example: the Vin Group. This real-estate company was only founded in 2013. By 2021 it had 43 school campuses across the country and a new university in Hanoi. Not only are private companies like Vin speeding to fill the almost insatiable demand for education from Vietnamese citizens, but the government is also encouraging such educational privatisation while also injecting significant resources into the state sector. According to the World Bank, Vietnam's education expenditure as a percentage of state spending shot up to 20% in 2018. That compares to a global average of around 14% (BMI Global, 2017). Between 1990 and 2016, Vietnam's GDP grew by a mind-blowing 3,033%, the second-fastest growth rate worldwide, surpassed only by China. All of which helped push the number of students in HE from around 133,000 in 1987 to 2.12 million by 2015 (Trines, 2017).

The same trends are apparent across many Asian countries, most obviously China.

While Vietnam currently has two universities placed at 400 in the Top 500 World Rankings, China now has two in the top 20 and six in the top 100. In total, East and South East Asia now have 16 universities in the Top 100 World Rankings (THE, 2021).

Higher education has become a global experience for many millions, though in the world's poorest countries less than 1% have completed tertiary education. By contrast, Canada, Japan, Israel, Korea, USA, Australia, Finland and Norway over 45% of their citizens have a college/university degree (Roser and Ortiz-Ospina, 2013; Educate Inspire, 2019).

FEMALE INTERNATIONALISATION OF HE

Which identity appears at the forefront of this global HE expansion? The female:

In the UK young women are 36% more likely to apply to university than their peers – a record high number. And it's not just the UK; countries all

over the world are seeing an increase in female applications. Panama, Sri
Lanka, Argentina, Cuba, Jamaica and Brunei to name a few have some of
the highest female to male ratios in higher education.

(Bilton, 2018)

The era when intelligent young women were routinely denied the chance to
attend university while less able men sailed into higher education is over.
In fact, the gender imbalance seen for decades has been reversed: 57% of
women in developed countries will soon enter tertiary education by the age
of 25 compared with just 45% of men.

(Baker, 2021)

Higher education in the US, UK and Europe was never designed for women. It was designed for men. However, since the early 1980s, women have become increasingly synonymous with higher education achievement, while men have remained static or languished. So, when we talk about the internationalisation of universities, we must also acknowledge the historic changes in the gender constitution of the international student body – even while the historic domination of men in university leadership, persists (see, for example, DeLaquil, 2021).

How to explain all these interconnecting if not contradictory dynamics in terms of, or possibilities for, Total Inclusivity in Higher Education?

TORTOISES ON STEROIDS

As we have described above, the impulse behind the type of HE internationalisation now apparent in most countries is neo-liberalism and it comes with its own analogous acronym – GERM. In 2012, Pasi Sahlberg devised the term Global Education Reform Movement to describe the emergence of a new 'orthodoxy in education policy'; one which operates "like an epidemic that spreads and infects education systems through a virus" (Sahlberg, quoted in Fuller and Stevenson, 2018: 1).

The neo-liberal marketisation of global education is encapsulated in GERM; notably, standardisation, performativity, (individual and institutional) competitiveness, and the use of corporate management practices within not just universities but also schools and colleges.

A central aspect of GERM is privatisation – indeed it is a logical consequence, if not objective. So, why have universities avoided the privatisation aspects of GERM that have become apparent in the state school systems of many countries, not least Chile, USA and England, reflected, for example, in the phenomenal growth of for-profit international schooling? (Machin and Whitehead, 2020). In other words, why are private corporations not rushing to buy up failing universities in the UK and elsewhere? The answer is simple; it isn't easy to make universities turn a profit. The primary customer base (undergraduate students) cannot afford it, and the deliverers (lecturers and professors) are (mostly) high salaried experts.

There are only six ways to significantly reduce costs and strengthen the bottom line in any education institution:

1. Increase student fees.
2. Reduce teaching salaries.
3. Increase student numbers.
4. Reduce class contact time.
5. Increase class sizes.
6. Increase student–teacher ratios.

Do any of these six in a university and you are immediately jeopardising the reason why you are claiming excellence. Do all six and you are no longer a leading global university.

These simple equations have long been ignored by HE policy makers in favour of GERM ideology and rhetoric. Which has led to a strange and untenable compromise. While universities remain largely reliant on state funding, albeit via student fee income, they have been co-opted into the GERM agenda, most apparently via such devices as the UK's

Research Excellence Framework; used by the UK funding bodies to assess research quality in universities and based on this assessment, allocate research funding. Under these ideological conditions so has 'academic freedom and the notion of the university as a site of independent and critical thought' been compromised if not undermined.

(O'Leary and Wood, 2018)

Consequently, and as our quotes above reveal, GERM may be a potent virus within the global education body, but it is not going unchallenged; not least by indebted students and those staff on the sharp end of Uber-style contracts. There is growing resistance, and it is taking many forms, including strikes, protests and resignations. All of which has been compounded by the Covid-19 pandemic, and this as much as any single event has exposed the flaws within the GERM model.

Today, universities are driven by money; not students. Students have become merely a key revenue source. That said, one aspect of corporatisation that universities can no longer dodge is to keep their 'customers' happy not least because this is one of the 'performance indicators' measuring their 'success' as institutions. But as Covid-19 has revealed, happy they are not:

> *The effects of the pandemic can be seen in the slump in student satisfaction at many universities. Respondents to the 2021 national student survey expressed deep dissatisfaction with their undergraduate experience, the worst results since the survey began in 2005. As Matt Hiely-Raynor, the statistician who compiled the data said, 'the whole sector's 2021 results were awful. Everything dropped on average but for some institutions it was more like 20 percentage points. There were relatively few good news stories in it all. It's a reflection on how universities coped with the pandemic.'*
>
> (Adams, 2021)

Statistics can be revealing but not so revealing as the actual words of those who are, in the final reckoning, often seen as no more than a statistic:

> *The government's neglect of students has made university unbearable. I wish I never came...The university I attend now is not the university I signed up for three years ago. The way we're treated by our senior leaders and government is vile – it's ruined my entire experience and I will never forgive them for it.*
>
> (Mooney, 2021)

Despite the most persuasive pressures of governments, all the practices and policies imposed on global universities by GERM over three decades have still not transformed them into efficient, profitable, highly entrepreneurial operations like Google, Microsoft or Apple. Instead, universities remain for the most part what they always were; slightly dusty, isolated academic worlds, only now with more layers of bureaucracy overseen by CEOs who are themselves confused as to their actual place in the overall scheme of things. Yes, there is a 'bottom line' to all this, and it is that the rhetoric/mechanisms of the market do not translate into the reality of HE. The notion that by having corporate, competitive managerialism so would be created a profitable, responsive, entrepreneurial HE environment was misguided at best and plain stupid at worse. A bit like stuffing steroids into a tortoise and expecting it to run like a greyhound.

If you have ever tried to get an entrepreneurial venture off the ground at any university then you will be able to personally attest to just how risk-averse, bureaucratic and tortoise-like they actually are.

Far better to allow them to be tortoises because that way they are at least fit for purpose. They should be free to excel at what they are designed to excel at – the creation and transmission of knowledge: but in a culture and professional climate that promotes Total Inclusivity via internationalisation.

GERM does, of course, promote internationalisation but not for the purposes of promoting global Total Inclusivity, only for the purpose of profit or at least reduced deficit.

However, it is now apparent that even creating an artificial HE marketplace through the device of student tuition fees is no longer keeping universities financially viable. Across most UK universities, for example, tuition fees from British students are not enough to meet the costs of undergraduate courses. With the threat of cuts to postgraduate fees now very real, how will universities survive?

> There is no course at UCL where the undergraduate fee covers the cost of providing the course. We've just had the maths done by an independent firm. So we're already supporting the education of British undergraduates with both international student and postgraduate student fees.
>
> (Michael Spence, UCL provost, quoted in Adams, 2021)

Yes, survival of a great many universities now lies with internationalisation. Unfortunately, this is an internationalisation driven by fear of bankruptcy, not driven by desire for creating a global inclusive HE community.

GERM, marketisation and pseudo-privatisation, through the device of creating students as paying customers, has been a terrible distraction on universities for many decades. It has failed to create the 'healthy and responsive market economy' beloved of its devotees and instead caused mayhem.

CONTENTED COMMUNITIES OF HE LEARNING?

Who is happy with this arrangement?

Not the students, who clearly recognise they no longer get 'value for money', having to incur a lifetime's indebtedness for minimum university teaching hours and support.

Not the university academics trying their best to remain loyal to their scholarly traditions while being pummelled by McDonaldised pseudo-objective measurements of professional worth: performance indicators and research output targets.

Not the university leaders often paid grotesquely inflated salaries and perks, but now on a managerialist performance treadmill which leaves them with barely a noticeable academic identity, or indeed any identity beyond 'manager'.

Not the governments and politicians who inspired this mess by believing in the rhetoric of educational advancement via educational commodification.

And not us, or indeed anyone else, who advocates for Total Inclusivity.

This is then a massive tension within global HE and one which no university is immune from. Add in the pressures from global demographics in all regions bar Africa; climate change; and reverse globalisation (Whitehead, 2021a) – with growing numbers of nation states hunkering down in their respective nationalistic trenches and using education as weapon – and the outcome may well be a broken HE system. It is certainly going to break some universities.

But dire as all this is, it is not the whole picture. There is now a further pressure on 21st century universities and their leaders, and it comes from the base of the HE power-pyramid.

IDENTITY POLITICS

Universities as institutions may well be lacking boldness but their students are not. Where the typical university Senior Management Team will retreat to a near endless cycle of meetings before making decisions of any consequence, the student body has already largely decided where it is heading and for the most part it is not where the university leaders prefer to go.

Yes, universities are now being dragged kicking, if not screaming, into the 21st century, but not by highly paid CEOs and their corporate offspring: by the very undergraduates to whom they are 'invisible' (see Chapter 11) but nevertheless answerable.

In the past decade the global socio-political tsunami labelled 'identity politics' has finally swept into the hallowed halls of the hitherto elevated and somewhat distant universities, all aided and abetted by social media.

It has not been a painless experience for anyone and there have been casualties; physical, professional and reputational.

Of course, universities have always been at the sharp (sometimes deadly) end of social and political unrest, as those who attended Kent State University on May 4th 1970 can confirm. Just two years prior, hundreds had been massacred during the Mexico Student Movement protests, while in 1976, on the other side of the world, at least 46 were killed during student protests at Thammasat University, Bangkok. To these three events we can add thousands of killings of students by government troops in a number of countries since then, including China, Nigeria, Ethiopia, South Korea, Sudan, Philippines, India and the DRC. (GCPEA, 2014).

Nowadays, however, you are much less likely to find students marching for a communist revolution as was the case in the 1960s and 1970s especially in South East and East Asia. Today, protest marches and social media attacks on university leaders and governments will instead be focused on, for example, climate change, LGBT+ rights, women's rights, MeToo Movement, Black Lives Matter, male violence, Trans = Women issues, and (physically) erasing the colonialist history of the university.

The left–right political binary may remain vivid in the minds of a great many people, but much less so in the minds of Generation Z university students.

Identity has become a political minefield within and beyond universities. Indeed, this book is evidence of that. Which should surprise no one because Total Inclusivity is inevitably political; it speaks not just to identity but to power, especially those hegemonic discourses and their power effects that seek to maintain a social order based on the identification and marginalisation of 'others'.

Sexism, classism, racism and social injustice have always been at the core of the university paradigm, and in some ways, this is to be expected. After all, they were never devised for undertaking egalitarian missions, they were devised to cream off the best and leave the rest. A few decades ago, the 'rest' constituted around 95% of young people in so-called 'advanced' countries such as the UK and USA.

Fortunately, the tide turned towards the global massification of further and higher education during the latter part of the 21st century and that tide shows no signs of ebbing.

Consequently, the masses who today enter universities come from a very different, and diverse, identity mix than those who attended them back in the 1950s, 1960s, and even the 1970s. 21st century university student bodies are truly intersectional even if university leadership cultures have for the most part, yet to become so.

What emerges, then, is an awakening within the current generation of university students, an awakening as to their privilege in being there but also a recognition that such privilege is not accorded equally across society. HE access still depends on class, culture, colour, nationality and background, but at least is no longer dominated by the male gender.

Nowadays, identity politics can be espoused by anyone, regardless of their sexuality, gender, ethnicity, class or race. Protesters are not required to be 'the other' in order to voice against the oppression of 'the others'. And that is one thing universities are especially good at – encouraging voices of protest and resistance to the powers that be.

As we are seeing, this resistance can manifest itself in any number of ways, from pulling down statues, attending senate sit-ins, to trans rights marches.

Where does this leave university leaders?

It leaves a good many of them walking a tight-rope, one stretched taut over the gaping chasm of bankruptcy. Student protests and acts of resistance by academics don't look good on the 'latest university news' to be posted on social media. Battling adverse publicity is not what their marketing departments were intended for.

Any number of ill winds could quickly sweep HE leaders into professional oblivion/premature retirement and institutions into the pit of financial default. What can save them?

Well, not further competition, for sure.

COLLABORATION?

At some point this century a major political party in the UK and USA is going to wake up to the GERM nonsense and propose a whole new paradigmatic solution, one based on collaboration between institutions, open-access enrolments for all age-groups, and no-fees for students. In other words, follow the model established by many European countries where HE provision is affordable or free and without any sacrifice on quality (Study.eu, 2020; Collier, 2021).

Yes, this will cost, but the cost of not doing it will be far greater in the long run.

We see this collaborative model as a signature of the Totally Inclusive University and it will both drive and be driven by, internationalisation.

Not an internationalisation whose outcome is the demise of 'competitor' universities, but internationalisation based on diversity, equity, inclusion and social justice. In this post-GERM world, universities would not need to compete for students because the students are welcome in all of them regardless of their identity mix. Institutions would revert to what they were designed for – the sharing and advancement of knowledge across all disciplines. And that sharing must be done internationally.

This in turn would serve to create a new type of globalisation, one not driven by capitalist 'devil-take-the hindmost' competitiveness, the silo-mentalities of insecure and pressured workers, performativity, and the sort of anti-humanist attitudes we have seen in many countries regarding the unfair and discriminatory distribution of the Covid-19 vaccines. It would be a globalisation rooted in the human desire for connectedness, sharing, advancement and mutual security.

Yes, many countries will feel threatened by this turn towards the egalitarian within universities, even those countries who espouse equality in their political manifestos. For those governments keen to control the thoughts of the masses, identity politics manifest as, for example, LGBT+ rights, feminism, and BLM movements, is deeply troubling. China, Russia, most Middle Eastern countries and indeed any country which has governments still dominated by small groups of men who consciously self-perpetuate their control via political and religious discourse, won't want the higher educational international learning community espoused by Total inclusivity.

Will that, then, stop it happening?

It might, but there is a solution.

FREE HIGHER EDUCATION

There is an impulse deep in the human psyche – personal advancement. This impulse is not equally spread across all 7.7 billion of us, but it is most apparent in parents. If you ask parents, regardless of their nationality, whether they put their children's future first or that of their country or a political party, the vast majority are likely to say 'my children come first'.

This has implications for global higher education and the possibility for the international learning community of universities.

One example of this is in China as we write. From early 2021, the Chinese government under Xi Jinping began to introduce sweeping reforms to the economy, notably the private education and technology industries. One target was the online-education business, by this time worth many billions of dollars and controlled by corporate giants such as New Oriental and TAL Education. Literally overnight, shares in these and similar companies became worthless. However, it wasn't only the online teaching industry that was targeted, so too were international and private schools across China, private tutoring agencies, school curricula, and universities themselves. Even the English language has become a target with one major city, Shanghai, banning English exams in schools amid calls for less English teaching across China. As one Western news outlet put it at the time, 'China is putting globalisation into reverse' (see Whitehead, 2021a).

Suddenly, those Chinese parents with understandable hopes and expectations that their offspring would go on to become doctors, scientists, professors, lawyers, etc, acquiring this level of professional status through access to Western universities, were left shocked and dismayed.

For them, the egalitarian levelling of education in China, driven by Xi Jinping's desire, perhaps, to ensure stability among the 1.5 billion population and avoid worsening social divisions arising from elitist private education, was a very personal disaster. For such parents, 'Xi Jinping Thought' is a very poor alternative to the benefits which accrue from studying at an overseas university (Li, 2021; Liu, 2021a).

But that is not the whole story or indeed the end of it. Because Chinese parents won't cease to seek advantage for their children just because the Chinese Communist Party removes private educational opportunities.

> *Chinese parents say they will keep pushing children to succeed despite crackdown on private education. Some people are already looking for ways around the ban, while others say they will do the extra teaching themselves.*
> (quoted in Whitehead, 2021a)

What is revealed here is the opportunity within Total Inclusivity to free Western universities from GERM and all its performative failing mechanisms. The curtailment of educational opportunity in China is not curtailing Chinese parents' desire for educational opportunity. In Asia, education matters. It is taken very seriously by both parents and students. They want, above all else, personal advancement – and they recognise higher education as the single most important vehicle for achieving this.

How much better, therefore, to simply offer higher education to everyone for free, and regardless of where they were born or where they wish to study.

If such free provision were offered in all countries and to the citizens of all countries, then the impact on global education, global politics and global society would be enormous, and it would be overwhelmingly positive. So long as quality was not compromised, it would enable universities to become truly international learning communities; to broaden minds, remove cultural myopia, and create a generation of students who understand and value, diversity, equity, inclusion and justice, not least because they are direct beneficiaries of these values.

Sure, there will be challenges contained in this model, but they are not insurmountable so long as there is the political will to overcome them. And nor are we assuming that HE is automatically personally transformative for everyone. It is for most and should be for all, although for many young people in countries such as Ireland, HE has arguably been reduced to an instrumental, functional, rite of passage, with university attendance accorded perhaps less status than thousands of 'likes' on Facebook.

This book is not the place to detail the strengths, weaknesses, opportunities and costs contained in a global project of free (or low-cost) higher education for everyone. But it is the place to flag it up as a key dimension of Total Inclusivity and thereby raise it as an aspiration, a vision, one very much acting as a counter to the current malaise which depresses universities caught up in the GERM virus.

At time of writing, globalisation, which humanity has benefited from for several decades, is stagnating; perhaps even going in reverse. Sure, much can be blamed on a pandemic but Brexit, Trump, the rise of the alt-right, and China's reassertion of communist principles framed in a China vs West standoff, are also major factors. As are economic/social/cultural inequalities between the educated 50% and the rest.

If these negatives are to be challenged if not erased, then only higher education can do it. These negatives indeed dangers to global society, won't be overcome by violence, protests, force, propaganda, more police, more aircraft carriers, or tighter visa rules for international students. They certainly won't be overcome by GERM and intensifying competition between global universities.

The world needs a new paradigm, and while we are not claiming it to be Total Inclusivity, we can see how this value system and the principles and practices it espouses, can be an ally for universities as they struggle to survive in an age when, to be frank, many (students especially) are wondering whether or not university provision is worth the cost, the indebtedness.

Far better to reverse not the globalisation gear, but the GERM gear. Swing the whole HE ship around and sail off in a different destination, one where university provision is free for all who want it and who believe they can benefit from it, regardless of their sex, gender, race, ethnicity, class and especially, passport.

The outcome will not only be the internationalisation of Total Inclusivity, but it will also be international mindedness, interculturation, enlightenment, understanding and the advancement of human society based on learning, research and global collaboration.

At some point in the future human society will cease to fight itself and begin collaborating. Indeed, that time has likely already arrived, it is right now just fogged up with GERM and nationalistic discourses. Universities alone cannot solve all the problems of humanity, but every problem of humanity can be identified, understood, analysed and offered solutions by those who work and study in these institutions of higher learning and research.

We simply need to stop treating universities as if they were a chimera; something between a Silicon Valley company and an expensive resort for school-leavers. We need to recognise their true potential at this crucial, chaotic, moment in human history and give them the resources to advance all of us, individually and as a global society.

Nine

Privilege isn't about what you've gone through; it is about what you haven't had to go through.

(Khan, 2021)

Acronyms seem to dominate our social discourse, but we have to ask, do you recognise this one: AOC?

If you are American or a follower of US politics, then you'll know that AOC denotes Alexandria Ocasio-Cortez, a US Democrat politician and, since 2019, the US Representative for New York's 14th congressional district. 43 years old, AOC was unknown just a few years ago but has rapidly emerged as an icon of American multicultural liberalism.[1] In 2011, AOC graduated from Boston University, but returned to live in the Bronx, working as a bartender and waitress to help her mother. Just eight years later, at the age of 29, she became the youngest woman ever to serve in the US Congress, gaining her seat by defeating Democratic Caucus Chair, Joe Crowley, the ten-year incumbent.

AOC may be a relative newbie politician of humble, ethnic-minority (Puerto Rican) origins, but she is not afraid to make waves with the rich and powerful. In September 2021, she attended the NY Met Gala wearing a white designer dress with the slogan 'Tax the Rich' emblazoned in red across it.

This in a country where the very word 'socialism' is perceived by many Americans to personify evil and an oppressive political tyranny.

It is interesting to consider whether AOC is an aberration or a signifier of something bigger happening not just in the USA but globally. The growing evidence suggests the latter.

Socialism is no longer a parlour game, but a political alternative taken seriously by millennials.

(Edwards, 2018)

DOI: 10.4324/9781003277651-11

Nearly 8 out of 10 young Britons blame capitalism for the housing crisis and two-thirds want to live under a socialist economic system. How did that happen?

(Jones, 2021)

Support for socialism jumps by nearly 10% among US youth amid pandemic depression...An overwhelming majority, 49% of all Americans, believe that a 'complete change of our economic system' is in order.

(Fitzgerald and Black, 2020)

What is interesting is that this rise in socialism as an alternative to neo-liberal capitalism, at least with Gen Z and young millennials, is emerging alongside identity politics while also coalescing with global fears regarding climate change. Taken together, these are powerful forces at large and not just in the West.

We are long accustomed to seeing culture wars play out in the United States, a country whose social cohesion is as frayed today as it has been in recent memory...China is in the early stages of a culture war of its own... The current battle lines have little to do with old-fashioned doctrinal ideology, and none of the parties involved have militant struggle in mind. If anything, despite this, the stakes may be even more consequential.

(French, 2021)

Across the Asia-Pacific region, girls and young women are participating in youth activism for gender equality. Such efforts have proven successful in changing long-held discriminatory attitudes and beliefs related to gender and ensuring that girls are better able to use their voice and develop leadership qualities.

(Philstar, 2021)

Young people demand change. They wonder how anyone can be claiming to be building a better future without thinking of the environmental crisis and sufferings of the excluded.

(Francis [pope], 2015: 12, quoted in O'Brien et al., 2018)

In such hothouse political conditions, privilege doesn't sit comfortably, at least with the young.

The young are hungry, and the rich are on the menu. This delicacy first appeared in the 18th century, when the philosopher Jean-Jacque Rousseau supposedly declared: 'When the people shall have no more to eat, they will eat the rich!' But today, this phrase is all over Twitter and other social media. On TikTok, viral videos feature fresh-faced youngsters menacingly raising their forks at anyone with cars that have start buttons or fridges that have water and ice dispensers.

(Jones, 2021)

Regardless of your perspective on all this, what is not in dispute is the growing sense of disenfranchisement that young people are feeling. You may dismiss it as pandemic blues or similar, but what cannot be ignored is that around the world there is growing anger towards the ruling classes, the privileged, the 1%. And very soon these young people will be in power, generating a political backlash from the USA to Brazil, Europe to China (Brownstein, 2020).

The world that follows the COVID-19 pandemic surely will be different and likely more aligned with the ideals that millennials and Gen Zs have expressed in this and previous Millennial Surveys. If anything, the pandemic has reinforced their desire to help drive positive change in their communities and around the world. And they continue to push for a world in which businesses and governments mirror that same commitment to society, putting people ahead of profits and prioritizing environmental sustainability.

(Deloitte Global Millennial Survey Gen Z Survey, 2021)

At the centre of this dissatisfaction, unrest and developing generational backlash, sit universities.

IVORY TOWERS?

University professors and leaders may not wish to see themselves at the centre of a global cultural maelstrom, not least because as we discussed in Chapter 8, they have all on just trying to stay afloat financially. But like it or not, that is where they are placed. Yet while many pro vice chancellors and their teams will fear wading into the deep and swirling waters of identity politics, other HE leaders are only too well aware of the changed atmosphere in their university and in their profession, and are busily trying to stay ahead of the curve. They recognise that achieving an inclusive campus is not simply good politics it is an imperative for university leaders.

> *The world is going to get more cultural exchange and more diversity. If we don't deal with this problem [of diversity and inclusion] we are just facing bigger problems down the line. At my institution at least the chairs if not all members of search committees have to go through implicit bias training.*
>
> (Ana Mari Cauce, President of the University of Washington)

> *We have a requirement that people must submit some information that they have done something on equity, diversity and inclusion, and a separate requirement on such information when faculty members are looking for promotion.*
>
> (Jerry Kang, VC for equity, diversity and inclusion at the University of California, quoted in Sharma, 2019)

> *For universities to act effectively on the diversity imperative requires leaders who are willing to give priority to inclusive policies within strategic plans, but also set down governance structures and implementation mechanisms which act beyond the level of strategy to change the organisational culture of higher education.*
>
> (Colin Scott, Vice President for equality, diversity and inclusion, University College Dublin, quoted in Scott, 2018)

Everything these HE actors and those like them are attempting to achieve can be summarised as an urgency to rebuild the 'Ivory Tower' image of higher education into something altogether less remote, elitist and monocultural. However, to achieve that objective they are not only up against centuries of historic and often institutionalised discrimination they are up against embedded unearned privilege.

UNEARNED PRIVILEGE

Of all the terms and concepts which configure Total Inclusivity, unearned privilege is arguably the most emotive, and yet it is the most telling. It is a potent phrase because it demands each and every one of us reflect on where we came from, how we got to where we are today, and what role privilege played in that process.

One way of looking at this is to view it from the aspect of 'the other', in this example, African higher education.

Colonial knowledge systems have controlled the information we obtain and the way we process it. These systems decide which knowledge and methodologies are considered 'modern' and which are not worthy of the academy and should thus be silenced. The invasive process of silencing expressions of indigenous knowledge can be described as a form of epistemic violence. Universities have played and still play a key role in promoting European and New World knowledge and its production as modern, rigorous and, ultimately, superior.

(Haringsma, 2021)

To be a Nigerian student, attending, for example, an elite independent school in the UK, and then going on to study at Oxford, the LSE or Cambridge, is both to experience unearned privilege by virtue of inherited social class and cultural/economic capital, and yet to also suffer one's African cultural history being erased in favour of European culture and knowledge.

If that Nigerian student is a woman, then female identity enters the equation, creating bigger barriers to be overcome both in the UK and back home in Nigeria – because being born male has historically been an unearned privilege and in most parts of the world it remains so.

To this Black, Nigerian female, we could add trans identity, religion, or any of the variables that might go into the identity mix of any one of us. This is why privilege is intersectional – it configures identities and provides both opportunity and disadvantage. Few can claim to be without some privilege, even if it is only being literate and able to use a mobile phone. While there are some whose identity mix is unquestionably privileged especially in a global society which has created higher education systems out of colonial violence.

Colonial conquest brings epistemicide. It's the killing and erasure of knowledge. If you conquer people, you want to impose your own knowledge on them. You put your archives on their archives.

(Toyin Falola, Nigerian historian) (ibid.)

Universities are, for the most part, historic institutions, in which case it would be unrealistic to expect them to erase the privilege which comes with maleness, whiteness, overnight. Moreover, would it even be desirable? Not if one seeks understanding and inclusiveness over ideology. And that understanding must include a recognition that while unearned privilege cannot be undone by an individual, it can be identified and named – and it surely should not be permitted to become the university culture, climate, practice.

If you are reading this and you've never been to university and have no hope of ever doing so, then your likely response is that the whole point of universities is to maintain privilege, especially in social class terms. If you are a white working-class male, living in a depressed suburb of a British city, unemployed and largely deemed unemployable, then it will be difficult for you to recognise what, if any, privileges you enjoy. For you, anyone who attends any university, gets a degree of any description, and certainly works in a university as an academic, is not only privileged, but they are also damned lucky.

If you are North African migrant, hoping against hope to cross the English Channel and start a life in the UK, albeit under the legal radar, then no matter how clever you are, the whole notion of attending a university can be nought but a fleeting dream in a world of very real nightmares. You would risk your life to live in a depressed suburb of an English city – and may well end up doing so.

If you are a 12-year-old girl living in Kabul, Afghanistan, suddenly told by the Taliban in September 2021 that you can no longer attend secondary school, then what hope is there for you attending university anywhere? For you and all those like you, billions of people around the world have unearned privileges but you are not one of them.

Until the day dawns that higher education is universally available at little or no cost to all who would seek it, then so will such discriminations, injustices and violences continue. Though recognising that universal dilemma doesn't let universities off the hook.

Unearned privilege can certainly be challenged by having senior university leaders appointed as VCs in diversity, equity, inclusion and justice, and having systems in place that ensure discrimination is not allowed to flourish and go unchecked. But Total Inclusivity is not expecting universities to overcome centuries of global injustice, masculinism, inequality, colonialism, patriarchy, homophobia and racism overnight. What the Totally Inclusivity university is expected to do is recognise these injustices, challenge them wherever they surface and ensure they do not fester in the institution and thereby become normalised and institutionalised.

Becoming Totally Inclusive means all staff recognising the unearned privileges they enjoy especially those concerned with gender, race and ethnicity. Failure to do so leaves the individual and thereby the institution, incomplete in their journey towards Total Inclusive awareness and understanding. As we discuss in Chapter 12, this is not to corporatise Total Inclusivity, changing it into an imposed ideology, policed by the HR department and which brings its own oppressions and discriminations, but to ensure the institutional climate is comfortable with and able to positively address, the challenges which becoming Totally Inclusive will inevitably raise. Sure, there will be pushback from some quarters, some individuals, but the standpoint adopted by university leaders regarding diversity, equity, inclusion and justice must be unwavering, fair and consistent.

Universities cannot alone erase the unearned privilege which comes with being born white, or middle class or straight, but they can provide environments for mature and growing individuals to reflect on their identity, their power, their agency, and to thereby recognise both the opportunities and the limitations imposed on them by social discourse, culture and the myriad of structural forces at work in any society.

In the recognising, so is progress being made. So does a new sense of identity emerge. So does Total Inclusivity become not only concerned with the other, but also the all.

One place to start is in the personal. Most of us have a story to tell of unearned and earned privilege, whether or not we ever attended a university. Encouraging individuals, students and staff to reflect on their individual stories, journeys, thereby creating a narrative of self which is both enabling and enriching, helps build trust between individuals and the sharing of moments and experiences. We often see our own lives expressed in the words of others.

Many of us have a story to tell of earned and unearned privilege, framed around education and especially higher education. Here is one of them.

A STORY OF PRIVILEGE – EARNED AND UNEARNED

Jose was eight years old when the American mining company representatives arrived in the indigenous Bolivian hilltribe village which was his home. That was 1999. 22 years later, and most of the silver has been extracted, the village has long since disappeared, and so has Jose. He is now known as Dr Jose, a rising civil servant in the Bolivian Ministry of Education. How to get from one place to the other? Only via international higher education, plus luck, providence, and a lot of cultural adaptation and effort.

The villagers may have been unsophisticated and lacking in education, but they were not stupid. In return for access to their land, they did a deal with the US mining company which included several senior executives committing to provide educational sponsorship for the most promising youngsters in the village. Jose was one of the ten youngsters chosen. But the executive sponsoring Jose didn't provide just money, he provided a new home in San Diego, where he lived with his wife and family. When the executive flew back to the US, Jose, with the blessing of his most appreciative mother and father, was accompanying him.

One of the authors of this book first met Jose in South East Asia in 2010, when Jose was attending a study abroad programme at a Thai university. Jose was in the first year of his social science degree at Princeton University. Their tutor/student relationship continued long after Jose returned to the US to complete his degree. Being a positive and engaging person, Jose never lost an opportunity to broaden his social and international network, and his friendship with his ex-tutor was particularly useful when he needed guidance on his next step up the international education ladder; an MA in International Education at East Anglia University, UK. Given financial and emotional support by his American family and being a very determined individual, Jose sailed through the MA and immediately set about looking for a PhD. He loved the UK, so settled on Bristol University for his doctorate.

From the most inauspicious and unlikely beginnings in life, Jose has become a true global citizen, travelling the world, drawing on his indigenous hilltribe language/culture but especially Spanish and English. He has studied in the US, South East Asia and the UK Jose was under 30 years old when he graduated with his doctorate and decided to return to Bolivia to try and put back into the country some of the good fortune he had experienced. At time of writing, Jose's career in the Bolivian Ministry of Education is blossoming, he is married, and a first child is on the way; a girl. Jose and his wife's expectations are that all their children will attend an internationally recognised university.

This is an unusual story, one which can be told with many different emphases not least colonialism, Americanisation, globalisation, class, exploitation and environmental degradation, but whichever aspect one focuses upon, Jose's story signifies familiar patterns of privilege, both earned and unearned.

The *earned privilege* is evident in the determination and effort Jose has applied to his life Whatever Jose has achieved thus far he has worked damned hard for it.

The *unearned privilege* is revealed in a simple statement Jose made to his British course tutor, shortly after they first met, in May 2010.

> I was lucky to be chosen by the village elders to go to the US. I didn't consider myself the brightest eight-year-old in the village though my family were very influential. Only boys were considered for this opportunity. None of the young girls in the village were allowed to go.

Jose didn't choose his parents, he didn't choose to be born in the middle of the Bolivian jungle-clad highlands, and he didn't choose his gender.

And nor did the girls in his village.

No one gets there on their own, no matter how clever, determined and ambitious they may be. We all need some support. Jose is not the beneficiary of Total Inclusivity he is the unlikely beneficiary of capitalism and global economics, plus the love and care both of his birth family and his American sponsoring family. The fact he happens to be male is not incidental to his story but the key to it.

WHAT TO DO ABOUT IT?

Total Inclusivity in a university is not simply the strategic application of certain practices, systems and procedures. To be sure, it does require formalising so that all members of the institution recognise their personal and professional responsibility towards enabling a Totally Inclusive climate and culture and this will need documentation and systems to be in place both for staff and students. But Total Inclusivity goes much deeper than that.

The implementation of Total Inclusivity should be understood and instigated on two levels – the systematic and the subjective, or as we state in Chapter 13, the strategic and the empathetic.

The systematic and systemic application required to create a Totally Inclusive University is discussed in Chapter 12 where we explain the importance of the TI Audit and Continuum. This model provides a template, a guide, for university leaders and stakeholders to work to, helping them identify their personal and institutional positioning on a given continuum or measurement of TI in the institution.

But these systems are of little value unless they are supported by the second level; the subjectivities of all the university's members – all staff and all students.

And here, TI gets much harder to implement, because we are dealing with very likely thousands of unique individuals, each of whom, not unreasonably, sees themselves as the centre of the university indeed the centre of their world. How to get each of these individuals to step outside their intersectional identity mix and start to recognise how unearned privilege has played a part in their lives, has acted in their favour and thereby brought them to the position they now occupy?

To go back to Jose's story. Did Jose recognise the traditional gender/patriarchal dynamics operating in his favour when he flew on the jet plane to start a new and exciting life in the USA?

Of course not. At that age he didn't see gender politics, he just saw male and female.

Many years later, following a BA, MA and PhD, he certainly does see gender politics. His journey has not simply been about acquiring high quality degrees it has been about him opening his eyes to his own identity, history, culture, and thereby gaining a greater empathy and understanding of others.

Which is why when talking to Jose today about his family, and his (yet to be born) children, you will hear a very different account of reality and educational opportunity to that which he was born into, over three decades ago.

I was lucky. But only because I was a male. My children will certainly also be lucky because they are born to two educated, middle-class parents. But

gender won't play a factor in deciding their educational opportunities – at
least not as far as my wife and I are concerned. Whether we have boys and
girls or just boys or just girls, they will be given equal support and equal
opportunity to succeed in their life.

Jose is male, South American, and he still follows the Catholic faith of
his family, but his male identity embraces Total Inclusivity; not exclusivity, discrimination or traditional patriarchal attitudes.

A global higher educational experience has shifted Jose's subjectivity to one whereby he doesn't need to be explained the value of Total
Inclusivity. He gets it. He is now living it. He is embodying it.

To be sure, this is not the only outcome for Jose or for the billions
of people around the world who have also experienced the (self) liberalising possibilities contained in higher education. But it is a most
important outcome for himself and his family. It is also an important outcome for the Bolivian Ministry of Education, because one of
Jose's responsibilities is the development of educational curricula and
opportunities for Bolivia's poor and indigenous peoples.

And this will inevitably involve, for Jose, challenging, and where
possible, dismantling, centuries of gender prejudice against girls and
women, masculinist attitudes, and accompanying stereotypes.

But to get to that position of power and influence and then be able
to turn it into an opportunity for the disenfranchised and marginalised, Jose first had to recognise his unearned privilege as a male.

Every university student, every university employee, must undergo
the same self-reflection, submit themselves to the same critical reflexivity, recognise where and how unearned and earned privilege have
intersected to influence their lives, their opportunities. This may
be reflected in their sex, gender, sexuality, race, ethnicity, class or
ableism. Indeed, all of these will intersect in some way to produce the
individual, their identity. This reflective process is a major part of the
subjective journey that anyone in higher education must be prepared
undertake before they can fully contribute to Total Inclusivity for all.

UNCONSCIOUS BIAS

Shortly before planning for this book took place, one of the co-authors
co-delivered introductory level 'unconscious bias' awareness development and training to the senior management team of a leading

English independent all-girls school.[2] During its 200-year history, the school had taught royalty, as well as the daughters of oligarchs, billionaires, the 'landed gentry', and 'new rich' from most every continent, including Africa. The School Head and her team were dedicated and experienced professionals. However, in early 2020 following the 'Black Lives Matter' global protests, they'd been shocked to receive a number of letters of complaint from ex-students and staff, one signed by 20 alumni, all containing accusations of direct and institutionalised racism in the school.

Hence the need for some rather urgent unconscious bias training.

The first meeting with the school SMT revealed the following: (1) These were not the first such letters/complaints they'd received – they went back at least two decades. (2) There were no Black or Asian teachers on the SMT, only white. The school had around 100 teachers but none who were Black. (3) The school had not commissioned any race awareness/antiracism training in the past. (4) The complaints concerned racial stereotyping by staff and other students; under-representation in the curriculum; under-representation of Black students in committees/leadership.

It should be noted that this school was not the only English independent school to receive such complaints; during 2020 especially, there was a veritable avalanche of accusations directed at some of the most famous names in the English public-school system (see also, Okwanga, 2021; Whitehead, 2022).

Where and how to start making improvements in such a situation?

The school SMT were rather fixated on the concept of 'unconscious bias' and sincerely believed that the priority was to 'fix' this deficit in their operation. In other words, they wanted 'experts' to come along and help them find the 'correct' words/terms to use with those who might otherwise be 'sensitive' to racial bias/stereotypes; find ways to 'celebrate Black identity' in the school; and begin a 'proper reflective process; self-review; and how to work with students in doing so'.

There was unquestionably a genuine desire across the SMT to address the problem of historic institutionalised racism, however when the question was put to them regarding 'white privilege', several senior managers baulked and one influential figure on the SMT openly claimed she 'didn't believe in the concept'.

HOW TO RESPOND?

As we explain above, Total Inclusivity is not impersonal, it is highly personal. It must connect directly to the subjectivity, the very identity, of every member of the school/university, indeed every member of any institution that is committed to this process. Unconscious bias is certainly a valid concept to recognise within the individual and the institution, but it can also be something to hide behind; e.g., 'I am not openly racist/sexist/homophobic, I am simply unaware of my own prejudices. So I need an 'expert' to help me become aware and then I will no longer have a problem.'

But when the first step on that journey to enlightenment requires the individual to recognise their own privilege (white, male, straight, for example), then this step can be too big for many people to take – even highly educated and experienced educationalists.

Recognising one's unearned privilege is essential before any movement can be made towards greater and deeper understanding of how racism, sexism, homophobia, classism operate and thrive in society. Unconscious bias is the inevitable consequence of not realising how and why one is privileged on account of being, for example, white, or male, or straight.

But this can be threatening for people. They look at their own lives, how hard they have worked and struggled, the disadvantages they have had to overcome to get to the professional position they now enjoy, and they truly imagine in it is all about merit and effort. They truly come to believe they are worthy and exceptional and that gender, race, sexuality, class, have played no part in their life journey.

This is a complex if not hidden dimension of the human ego, psyche, sense of self, but it can easily be revealed. All you need do is ask yourself the following questions:

1. How has being a woman/man influenced my career in and experience of higher education?
2. How has being a Black/white person influenced my career and experience of higher education?
3. How has being LGBT+/straight influenced my career and experience of higher education?
4. How has being working/middle class influenced my career and experience of higher education?

Compare your response to these questions with those who exist on the opposite side of the binary to you; e.g., a man compares his answer with that of a woman; a white person compares their answer with that of Black person; a straight person compares their answer with that of an LGBT+ person; and a person of working-class origins compares their answer with that of a middle-class person.

This simple exercise can be undertaken in any university department, school, or institution, anywhere. You can extend it to Asian/Western subjectivities/experiences; the abled and disabled; and to those of different religions.

The outcome is revealing and powerful because it may well expose our own lack of empathy and awareness of 'others'. It can reveal the many ways in which identities, and the powers that hegemonically dominate them, provide opportunity and constraint, advantage and disadvantage.

Without this first simple but powerful raising of self-awareness, there is little chance of the individual embracing Total Inclusivity. And as we are stressing in this book, if the individual doesn't embrace it then TI is not going to happen.

CONCLUSION

Recognising unearned privilege requires us to smell our own ideology. We have to be bold enough to step outside our comfort zone, expose our ego, and face the reality which is that years of social conditioning and lack of self-awareness have combined to create an individual who fails to see the reality of those who are on the receiving end of prejudice and discrimination, whether this takes the form of sexism, misogyny, racism, classism, ableism or homophobia.

Yes, this is challenging. But like the SMT of the English independent school, if you are not prepared to be challenged then all you are doing is paying lip service to diversity, equity, inclusion and justice. At one level you want diversity, equity, inclusion and justice in your institution and society, but you are just not prepared to recognise how you have to personally change in order to bring that about.

And then there is the issue of institutional upheaval. One of the fears which quickly envelops the senior leaders in any university (or school) aiming to bring about TI is 'how many casualties will there be among my staff?' What will this do to the work culture? How much disruption can my institution handle?

Indeed, there may well be 'casualties';' staff who vehemently disagree with the whole concept of TI. But this is part of the process. It cannot be stopped because some people actively resist.

In response to the global outcry for racial justice following the death of George Floyd, many international educational institutions increased their focus on anti-racism and the broader concepts of diversity, equity, inclusion and justice (DEIJ). While some institutions have seen some positive progress, others may be facing open resistance or greater discord from their efforts. Institutions experiencing challenges with their DEIJ efforts must understand that this is part of the process of growth. When diverse perspectives are brought together, disruption and conflict may emerge in the initial stages. However, given time and inclusive leadership, these differences can be leveraged to achieve better performance than that of homogenous groups. Educational institutions must, therefore, remain persistent with their DEIJ initiatives. If we wish to create environments where all identities represented in our communities can thrive, we must stay focused on this work, and it will eventually pay off. DEIJ is not a destination but rather a journey of continuous improvement.

(Nyomi, 2021; also Tapia and Polonskala, 2018)

NOTES

1 See https://ocasio-cortez.house.gov/
2 The training was co-delivered with Viv Grant of Integrity Coaching https://www.integritycoaching.co.uk/about-us

Ten

INTRODUCTION

In this chapter we explore the issue of 'free speech' in universities, and in so doing, raise some provocative questions which, we argue, undermine the key principles of higher education until that is, universities adopt the principles and practices of Total Inclusivity. We start by looking at the opposing positions on free speech now being adopted by various participants in higher education, and their consequences thereof. In reading through this chapter, we would ask you to reflect on your own standpoint in this matter, because as with all the variables impacting Total Inclusivity in Universities, it is necessary to have a standpoint. There is no neutrality.

POSITIONS

What does it mean to be a 'defender of free speech'? Does it mean that you will accept and be prepared to articulate, any words, phrases or communications regardless of their political context or personal impact? Or does it mean you won't? And if you won't where do you draw the line? Which words, phrases or communications are anathema for you, and which are sacrosanct?

These are not simply rhetorical questions, they have very material consequences as well as personal/professional repercussions, not least for those working in supposed bastions of 'free speech' – universities.

One such person who discovered this to be the case is David Miller. At the time of writing, he had just been sacked from his job as a sociology professor at Bristol University. His dismissal followed a high-profile and 'very divisive' investigation by Bristol University leaders into Miller's 'antisemitic tropes in lectures and online' (Hall, 2021a).

The range and depth of Bristol's investigation and the exact reasons for its conclusion remain confidential, though Prof Miller's views on

DOI: 10.4324/9781003277651-12

Zionism were described by some international academics as 'morally reprehensible'.

> We, the undersigned, wholly condemn recent statements by Prof David Miller...Rather than geopolitical theories, some of these are statements directed at Jewish students, UN university Jewish societies and the Union of Jewish students...Prof Miller's views represent a conspiracy theory, and bring great shame on UK academia as well as upon UK political discourse.
>
> (Response to Recent Comments by Prof David Miller, 2021)

> ...Comments by him [Miller] describing Israel as 'the enemy of world peace' and a statement sent to the student news outlet the Tab that described the Jewish Society as an 'Israel lobby group' that had 'manufactured hysteria' about his teacher have further inflamed tensions.
>
> (Hall, 2021a)

Was what Prof Miller said and wrote illegal in the context of UK law? Not according to a QC who found that the comments Miller was alleged to have made 'did not constitute unlawful speech'.

Was what Prof Miller said and wrote acceptable to the leaders of Bristol University and to a good many students and staff? No. The university's disciplinary hearing concluded that he 'did not meet the standards of behaviour we expect from our staff'.

Legal or not, acceptable behaviour or not, Prof Miller's lectures, words and online comments generated a media storm, and divided not only Bristol University, but also many hundreds of academics around the world. Prof Miller received support from a group of eminent lawyers including two former appeal court judges together with an impressive international host of public intellectuals, educators and researchers who made the following statement.

> We oppose antisemitism, Islamophobia and all forms of racism. We also oppose false allegations and the weaponization of the positive impulses of antiracism so as to silence antiracist debate...At a time when the Black Lives Matter movement has invigorated public consciousness about the structural factors entrenching racism, attempts to stifle discourse on Islamophobia and anti-Palestinian racism are particularly repressive and inconsistent with the values University of Bristol represents.
>
> (Support David Miller, 2021)

In the opposing camp were many UK MPs who threatened sanctions against Bristol University if it did not act.

> *Why would you not intervene? Tell Bristol University and the vice chancellor that enough is enough, we're not living in 1930s Germany, and they should deal with this problem and make sure the university is not a hostile environment to Jewish students.*
>
> (Robert Halfon MP, quoted in Hall, 2021b)

> *We need to start sacking people...until we start bringing that kind of scrutiny and action into our university sector, like you would do in primary or secondary schools, these incidents will keep happening.*
>
> (Jonathan Gullis, MP, quoted in Hall, 2021b)

One person very much in support of sacking Prof Miller was Edward Isaacs, the president of the Bristol Jewish Society:

> *The fight against antisemitism is vast, but I hope today's news goes a long way to showing positive change can be made and that we should never settle for anything less than a society free from all forms of hatred.*
>
> (quoted in Hall, 2021a)

YOUR STANDPOINT?

We posed a question above and perhaps you were not able to answer it. Does the 'Miller case' help you? In other words, without knowing the full details of Bristol University's investigation or the precise nature of the case against Prof Miller, which standpoint would you be inclined to adopt – the standpoint of 'free speech' or the standpoint of 'constrained speech'?

There is of course, a third (and overlapping) dimension for universities to consider and that is academic freedom and 'upholding the integrity of academic debate', and we explore this further in the chapter.

A FEBRILE CLIMATE

If universities have ever been the imagined havens of quiet, solitary, intellectually and intensely rigorous but competitive discussion, they are not that today. Currently, they are at the forefront of the so-called 'culture wars' and staff and students are caught up in this like it or not.

There is global evidence for the growing febrile climate in higher education regarding what can and cannot be spoken of and by academics and students.

'New Research confirms free speech crisis at Australia's Universities' (Institute of Public Affairs, 2019).

'The insoluble problem of free speech [on US college campuses]' (Zuckert, 2018).

'The Legal Promise and Sobering Reality of the Fight for Free Speech on [US] Campus' (French, 2020).

'Left-Wing Activists Stifling Free Speech on German Campuses' (Legal Insurrection, 2019).

'Hong Kong University Heads Condemn 'Abuses' of Free Speech' (Redden, 2017).

'Free Speech in Indian Universities under threat: Amnesty International India' (Gohain, 2017).

As for Chinese students, even those studying abroad find free speech is risky. What they say publicly and online is noted by their government with Chinese authorities *'employing a variety of methods to influence academic discussions, monitor overseas students from China, censor scholarship inquiry, or otherwise interfere in academic freedom'* (Sotoudah and Stefano, 2021).

One type of response to this discursive mayhem was signalled in the UK, when in May 2021 the Conservative government published its higher education (freedom of speech) bill. This bill attempts to secure freedom of speech for staff members, students and visiting speakers. Though to what extent protecting 'free speech' at UK universities will be progressed by anyone being able to sue ('bring civil proceedings') where they believe a university or student union has failed to protect free speech, is difficult to say and remains to be seen (Renton, 2021).

As we have discussed elsewhere in this book, in past decades the most hostile debates within university campuses tended to be between Marxists, and those of a different political persuasion – a fairly straightforward political binary. Today, you may well miss such discussions but instead get invited to engage in complex debates concerned trans identity and women (Bristol University);[1] 'celebrating women' as a fixed identity (Oxford University)[2]; the legacy of 'controversial alumnus Cecil Rhodes' (Oxford University)[3] and institutionalised racism in universities (Goldsmiths, University of London).[4]

With academics getting sacked, silenced, blocked and 'no-platformed'[5] from publicly debating these issues, who is to deny that free speech in universities is under threat?

CAN SPEECH EVER BE FREE?

Actually, we deny that free speech is under threat. For the simple reason that free speech never existed in the first place. Well, other than in the minds of those who may mistakenly believe they can exist (work, live, thrive, express themselves) in a social space which has no social dimensions/consequences.

Speech is never free, and certainly not that speech concerned with politics and identities. If you ever imagined it was then you've failed to understand history as well as being uninformed as to the present.

The term 'free speech' is an oxymoron. It has no inherent meaning because it is a contradiction in possibilities. Sure, it is a convenient and instantly recognisable global phrase easily trotted out to enlist for your cause, whatever that might be, but it never has existed and it very likely never will.

Speech carries consequences. What we say matters as much, if not more in some cases, as what we do, especially in the age of 24/7 instant social media.

No one claims that actions do not have consequences. On the contrary, most thinking people will recognise that what they do does have consequences.

So, in what way is speech immune from consequences? Moreover, how can it be?

Words carry multiple meanings and can be deployed both politically and as hate tools. Words can and do engender violence, fear and misinformation. Words count; especially in a university.

There is a particularly disingenuous character to the notion of 'free speech' on university campuses. It is stretching the bounds of reality to imagine that adults (young and old), studying, researching, working in and charged with leading society's most venerable institutes of learning, are somehow unaware of and ignorant as to the effects and impact of their words and phrases.

These HE stakeholders are not innocent children. They have passed that stage whereby they might blunder into saying things without cognisance as to their wider social meanings.

We are not minded to support especially, those academics and students who hide behind phrases such as 'defend my right to free speech', especially when the speech being claimed to be free is a direct attack on an ethnic, religious, racial, gender, or sexual, group. That is not free speech – it as at best divisive, and at worst inflammatory and hateful speech.

We are not, however, claiming a simple 'good and bad' with all words. We do claim this with some words, but it is always worth bearing in mind the multiple meanings contained in language. As Derrida revealed, there is no single, straight, unambiguous and guaranteed correspondence between what is said/written and how it is received by the listener/reader. And this is certainly the case when one uses terms such as 'free speech'. Free to and for whom, one must inevitably ask?

Free speech is a persuasive, appealing, but ultimately meaningless rhetorical device. To attempt to embed it in law as the UK has done, is pointless and doomed to failure.

Moreover, to argue that one must 'self-censor' within universities, because one cannot say what one would like, and that this is dangerous and 'destroys free speech', is another straw man argument.

Why should universities, of all places, be discursive environments where anything can be said to anyone at any time?

What entitles universities to claim the privilege of existing outside society? They are society. Importantly, they should be representing the best of society.

At which point, you may well ask; 'so what do we mean by 'best', and how do we define it?'

TOTALLY INCLUSIVE SPEECH

The opening question to this chapter is, we admit, rather misleading. We've presented it as a simplistic choice between total or 'constrained' free speech. Unless you are a libertarian, content to have no constraints at all on language or content, then your standpoint will veer towards some measure of control. At which point you must be forced to recognise, as we argue above, that the very term 'free speech' is itself part of the problem. And even if you are a libertarian then you'll still be constrained by the laws of the land.

In their book, *Freedom of Speech in Universities*, Scott-Bauman and Perfect (2021a), indirectly reinforce our point about speech never being entirely 'free', and nor should it be.

> **Reciprocity is the key.** *Instead of viewing freedom of speech as either an absolute right (which can lead to a disregard for other people's rights) or only through the lens of risk management (which can lead to risk aversion), we see it as something requiring reciprocity...Instead of the monologic outcome of speaking freely without considering how the exercise of my right affects others, or the silence that comes from risk aversion, we must communicate reciprocally, where everyone involved in a conversation acknowledges they have obligations to everyone else.*
>
> (p. 7, original emphasis)

Scott-Baumann and Perfect go on to list three options available to universities:

1. Liberal (where free speech on any topic is upheld so far as lawfully possible, but the most offensive language is avoided).
2. Guarded liberal (where some restrictions may be in place).
3. No-platforming (where particular ideas or speakers are denied a platform).

They suggest that '*universities should take the liberal approach by default, although it might occasionally be reasonable to use different approaches for particularly controversial topics*' (Scott-Bauman and Perfect, 2021b).

Recognising and generally supporting the strong argument put forward by Scott-Baumann and Perfect, we would opt for their 'guarded liberal' position as default. The reason being; speech is not the most important element of university life, safety is. Which is why our definition of Total Inclusivity is as follows:

> **Total Inclusivity means recognising, valuing, protecting and nurturing diverse identities, including those of race, gender, sexual orientation, class, disability, age, religion and language.**

Speech, and indeed, research, teaching and learning, all come secondary to these core principles at the heart of which is the sanctity of individual identity.

Which is why there will be situations where certain speakers *must be no-platformed*. Examples would be any speaker promoting holocaust denial, Islamophobia, antisemitism, incel movements, white supremacy, homophobia, violence and hatred against any group of people.

We would advise university leaders, in consultation with staff and students, to draw up their own list of topics which are not permitted to be given platforms within the university.

Who is fair game under these 'guarded liberal' conditions? Any government or political group, philosophy or ideology. To publicly criticise the Israeli government is not antisemitic, any more than it would be racist to criticise the Kenyan government, Islamophobic to criticise the Saudi Arabian government, or orientalist to criticise the Chinese government. Nor should criticism of feminist theories/positions, for example, be withheld, though personally directed and abusive criticism of individual feminists would not be acceptable. Just as it would be entirely valid to criticise the concept of Total Inclusivity without getting into a personal attack on us two authors on the basis of our individual identity mix.

There is no place in universities for antisemitism, homophobia, sexism, misogyny, racism, ableism, classism, transphobia, or the promotion of violence and hatred towards individuals or groups. Reciprocity does not extend to those who would destroy universities and the values they represent.

This is what we mean by the 'best of society' and we have no qualms in identifying and labelling it. Indeed, it is encapsulated in the very concept of Total Inclusivity.

So, how might we test this Total Inclusivity standpoint with, say, one of the most contentious 'freedom of speech' issues currently being played out (or more accurately 'fought over') in universities today, especially in the West: That is, does trans woman = woman?

Universities have long had to deal with highly contentious debates on campus, but few have matched the ferocity around gender identity issues. Privately, many vice chancellors say this is the most difficult issue on campus that they have had to manage.

(Jeffreys, 2021a)

TRANS WOMEN ARE WOMEN?

Many UK academics have, unwittingly or not, found themselves caught in the trans/women debate, including Professor Kathleen Stock of Sussex University, who at time of writing was facing calls to be sacked over her views on gender identification, which she admits are "at odds" with a large section of academics.

The depth of animosity towards Prof Stock comes not only from 'queer, trans and non-binary students', but also from her peers and colleagues. In January 2021, hundreds of academics criticised the decision to give Prof Stock an OBE for services to higher education in the New Year honours list. (Badshah, 2021)

At the core of this issue is identity. The protection of identity for some (trans women) but possibly at the expense of others ('biological' women).

One argument put forward by 'biological' women is that by allowing trans women to be legally recognised as women puts women at physical risk of violence or abuse (e.g., trans women using women-only toilets).

One argument put forward by trans women is that to deny they are women is to deny their existence, renders them excluded, and cancels their identity.

Unfortunately for both parties, this is another false dualism.

There is no simple dualism of male or female, and nor has there ever been in human society.

Both sex and gender are social constructs.

Even mainstream public opinion is now starting to embrace the reality of endless multiplicity to gender identity performance. And while there may be less multiplicity to sex identity, the idea that there are only male and female is a falsification of the biological facts.

A sex identity (male or female) is assigned to us at birth, based on genitalia. However, even this apparently objective assessment is fraught with risk. For example, there are at least six biological sexes as identified by chromosomes. XX is the most common form of female and XY is the most common form of male, but approximately 1 in 3,000 people have just an X, 1 in approximately 750 have an XXY, 1 in 1,000 have an XYY, and 1 in 20k–50k have an XXXY. There are tens of millions of us who are neither male nor female.

(Kennon, 2021)

And then there are the 1 in 1,500 of us who have no typical genitalia; the intersexed.

Complicated? Yes. But in the not-too-distant future, we are all going to have to get our heads around the truth of the matter, which is that the male and female binary is a convenient illusion; at least, convenient for some: mostly straight males and men in power.

For the organisers of the Olympic Games, this will mean having more than two sex categories of competitor.

For governments around the world, it will mean issuing passports for more than two sex categories.

And for universities it will mean embracing human diversity in all its fascinating and sometimes confusing, reality.

Many universities and organisations are already well on the way to achieving this objective; others are stuck in a 1950s time-warp.

In terms of Total Inclusivity, we claim that individuals should not be discriminated against on account of their identity mix, even while recognising identity is always in process and never fixed. In so doing, we seek to protect and safeguard the individual. With this principle in mind, we must therefore come down on the side of the trans women: They are entitled to see themselves as women and be treated by society and the legal system, as women. Any research which attempts to 'prove' otherwise should not be supported nor given a platform. Why? Because it is a direct attack on the identity integrity of individuals. It is not, therefore, an attack on a particular feminist theory or psychological theory but on the possibility of people enjoying a legitimate existence which they can only do in a society not befuddled by simplistic gender/sex binaries.

Woman is certainly a political category, but so is trans. You cannot prioritise women over trans women by virtue of claiming that women are a biological sex; the implication being that trans women are not. The reality is that there are a number of biological sexes, not just two.

Inevitably, this comes down to politics and power, not biology. And in terms of politics and power, both women and trans women should be united as feminists. Just as women and LGBT+ should be united as feminists. Because the threat to their existence, security, safety and identity comes not from each other, but from those men who would define them as the 'other' and thereby deny them their existence, security, safety and identity.

As we explored in Chapter 7, all identities are intersectional, not simple categorisations which remain exclusive of other variables and influences. Entwined within this intersectionality and identity mix is power, notably gender power. But gender power is not and never has been held by women nor by LGBT+ people. Both are the designated 'other' within this historical gender (masculinist) power regime. In which case it is worth recognising that that which unites them is more important than that which divides them.

So how should universities approach this issue in terms of allowing such debates to take place on their campuses?

Of course, allow these debates. But in so doing, stick with the gender and sex realities, not with political posturing or adherence to outdated notions of identity. One cannot and should not be permitted to deny trans identities on the basis that doing so does not suit one or other of the binary.

So, safety first, but that doesn't mean silence first. Here, we concur with the notion of 'reciprocity' but protected by a guided liberal approach. This aim shouldn't be beyond the capabilities of university stakeholders who follow a Totally Inclusive agenda.

Ideally, the people who should be most encouraged to speak up on these matters, regardless of their particular standpoint, should be those who are academically research active in this field, not 'celebrity names' who may just attract participants out of curiosity.

In the final reckoning, only history will tell which was the 'right side to be on' regarding LGBTQ+ rights (Siddique, 2021).

We are confident that history is on the side of Total Inclusivity.

ACADEMIC FREEDOM?

In our above discussion of the case of Prof David Miller, we made a reference to the open letter signed by a host of recognised public intellectuals and researchers in support of his case.

The letter is forthright and articulate, and the range of signatories, impressive. However, it's argument and position are weakened by its contradictions.

...we urge you to vigorously defend the principle of academic freedom and the rights to free speech and to evidence-based & research-informed

public discourse. We hope that you will uphold the integrity of academic debate.

(Support David Miller, 2021)

As we have argued above, it is not possible to defend 'free speech' without first clarifying what you mean by free and by speech. And as soon as you do that, unless you adopt a libertarian position, then the speech is no longer free – it is automatically constrained by social/political discursive limitations and impositions. We believe this constraint to be appropriate in certain circumstances, and for the reasons given.

Then there is the phrase 'integrity of academic debate'. At first glance perhaps a most worthy cause to be defending. But what precisely is meant by 'academic debate'? Do we mean debate based on a clear evidential base or do we mean political discourse? For most universities, debates will be supported by evidence, not political propaganda and rhetoric.

To be sure, there is a place for pure political debate and certainly universities can be that place, but should universities open their doors to any and all types of political debate? Hardly, for the simple reason that some such debates are intended to sow discord between people on the basis of identity; e.g., gender, religion, sexuality and race.

A similar unbridgeable contradiction exists between the notion of 'academic freedom' and that of 'evidence-based and research-informed public discourse'. The two are most definitely not the same thing.

To put it another way, what is the point of the Ethic Committees which now exist in most any institution claiming the title of 'university'? The point, we suggest, is to monitor potential and existing research to ensure it does not breach moral and ethical positions; in particular, that it does not engender the physical and emotional *safety* and *wellbeing* of participants and respondents.

This is not 'academic freedom' in the libertarian sense of the term. An academic cannot simply go out and undertake 'evidence-based' research without first addressing any ethical and moral issues which might subsequently arise.

For example, would it be right and proper to permit research which aimed to 'prove' that Donald Trump did not lose the 2020 Presidential election? Would it be right and proper to permit research into child sex abuse which had a methodology of one-on-one qualitative interviews with abused children? Would it be right and proper to undertake research which had an inherent intention to 'prove' social stereotypes of any given group, e.g., Jews, gays, lesbians, Blacks, Asians?

Of course not, which is why such research would not be permitted to proceed by any university or reputable funding body.

Our intention here is not to condemn the said letter in support of Prof Miller, or those who signed it, but to expose the rhetorical persuasiveness of terms such as 'free speech' and 'academic freedom' and set them against the reality. These two terms are not universally understood and accepted. They are, and must be, qualified by other more important factors. Universities have a responsibility primarily to the safety and wellbeing of their community of learners and the wider society within which they exist.

Universities should aim to explore and define reality, reflect the best of it with regards to their community of learners and social responsibilities, and avoid slippage into popularist but ultimately meaningless phrases which do nothing more but inflame passions and polarise positions.

Following which, we would have to take issue with Prof Adam Tickell, the vice chancellor of Sussex University who, in coming to the defence of Prof Kathleen Stock, accused of 'transphobia', stated:

> *Everyone in the university has the right to be free from harassment and intimidation. We cannot and will not tolerate threats to academic freedoms and will take any action necessary to protect the rights of our community.*
>
> (Badshah, 2021)

> *It is absolutely clear that all of our staff have an untrammelled right to say and believe what they think, so we take it very seriously indeed if people try to prevent that right from being exercised.*
>
> (Lawrie, 2021)

Within these emotive and compelling phrases, which is the standout one for you?

For us, it is '*untrammelled right to say…what they think*'.

Actually, university staff do not have that right and nor does anyone else. This libertarian approach is not an automatic right of anyone, least of all university professors. Certainly, professors have the right to undertake research which follows ethical guidelines and to do so without being subjected to harassment and intimidation. But they do not have the right to free speech.

It is just too easy and simplistic for any of us, but especially higher education professionals, to unthinkingly enlist emotive terms such as 'free speech' and 'academic freedom' and use them as blunt instruments to garner public and professional sympathy. Those universities and its stakeholders which seek to be Totally Inclusive should avoid these terms because they create more than a misunderstanding; they erect a screen, behind which can lurk deliberate provocation to discrimination, intolerance and hatred.

We suggest *totally inclusive speech* and *totally inclusive research*, more accurately reflect the contexts and limits for what is permissible to be said and undertaken in the name of higher education teaching, learning and research. And it is the responsibility of each university to establish what these precise contexts and limits are but always returning to the fundamental values of Total Inclusivity.

LAMENTING A 'SIMPLER AGE'?

The social problem of the divergence between the universal interest and the particular interest, the interests of particular individuals, is what goes to make up the problem of morality.

That was written by Theodor Adorno over 50 years ago (quoted in Butler, 2005: 5): And to 'morality', one could add 'free speech' and 'academic freedom' because both terms speak of privileging the epistemology and ontology of the individual.

In his writing Adorno was exploring the tensions between the universal and the singular, the communal and the individual, even the very notion of what it means to have an identity, an 'I'. These dilemmas have inspired philosophers down the ages. In which case, while we might look upon this century with some concern if not fear, and subsequently lament a simpler age, the reality is that there never was a simpler age.

What we did have in ages past was ignorance as to the diversity of human society enabled by non-recognition of that diversity by the majority or at least a powerful minority.

Today, thanks in part to globalisation and the massification of further and higher education, ignorance is no longer an excuse, not least because non-recognition has pretty much disappeared. We are all shouting to be recognised, and in the shouting so are we exposing and condemning the historic conditions (of class, patriarchy, colonialism, especially) which denied not only all the voices, but also the very possibility of identity for anyone deemed 'the other' by those with hegemonic power over culture, language – and higher education.

Sure, in writing that statement Adorno was not thinking of 21st century culture wars and identity politics all fuelled by social media. Though the contemporary relevance is clear. Today, a multitude of voices are raising a lot of noise with each claiming its right to 'an authentic self', a 'protected identity', to be seen, heard, validated as part of the inclusive community while being respected for its uniqueness.

On the face of it, the gap between the existential needs of the 'I' and the search for a universal morality seems as unbridgeable as ever.

Or perhaps not.

> [Adorno] cautions against the error to be found in the opposite position, when the 'I' becomes understood apart from its social conditions, when it is espoused as a pure immediacy, arbitrary or accidental, detached from its social and historical conditions – which, after all, constitute the general conditions of its own emergence.
>
> (Butler, 2005: 7)

One of the central tenets of Total Inclusivity is the recognition that no individual exists outside the social conditions of their own identity production. Within Total Inclusivity, there is no authentic 'I' even while Total Inclusivity respects the needs and desire of the individual to embrace and express an 'authentic self' and to have that sense of self protected, nurtured, valued.

The point being that no one is unique outside the circumstances of their existence. This is not a new recognition arrived at by Western philosophers. In South Africa, the ancient spiritual concept of 'ubuntu', globalised by the late Archbishop Desmond Tutu, basically means 'I am because we are'.

The universal not only diverges from the particular, but this very diver-
gence is what the individual comes to experience...We must ask, however,
whether the 'I' who must appropriate moral [and social] norms in a living
way is not itself conditioned by norms, norms which establish the viability
of the subject.

(ibid: 9)

Gay, lesbian, woman, man, female, male, trans, Black, white, Asian, Jew, Christian, Muslim, Buddhist, Hindu, Chinese, English, Welsh, Republican, Democrat, African, Scandinavian...the list goes on. And within each of these overlapping categories of social identity so an individual voice emerges and asks for 'freedom of speech'. And why not? Each of these voices should be permitted to speak, to announce itself to the world and in so doing announce itself to its self – self-validate.

But what none of these voices can achieve is separation from their history, their circumstances of being and becoming, their inevitable and irrevocable connection to the universal.

There are no sovereign individuals – only discursive subjects narrated into existence through the devices of epistemology, an epistemology which the subject does not own, which does not belong to them alone but which they borrow, adapt, display in the moment.

The 'I' can neither tell the story of its own emergence nor the conditions
of its own possibility without bearing witness to a state of affairs to which
one could not have been present, which are prior to one's own emergence
as a subject who can know, and so constitute a set of origins that one can
narrate only at the expense of authoritative knowledge.

(ibid: 37)

We fully respect the rights of individuals to tell their story, to speak, to express themselves. But this is not an unqualified right.

It doesn't become automatically conferred on individuals at birth or upon adulthood.

There is something more important here, bigger than the self, and that is the historic conditions which have rendered the self into being as a social actor.

We all have origins and we all therefore have associations and responsibilities to those associations.

There is no authentic voice that can legitimately and without qualification claim to speak for its owner without recognition of its obligations to all voices.

There is no authentic voice that rises above the mass of voices and can claim uniqueness, exclusiveness, individuality beyond the mass.

There is no narrative of self that is itself not also a narrative of its production and the contribution to that production made by other voices, selves, narratives.

Who we are and the voice we present is not ours alone, not solely the 'I'. We are all entwined within our selves and with others, and in ways we can barely fathom.

Intersectionality is the currently favoured term for this condition, but the reality of intersectionality goes deeper than simply a complex mix of entwined, reinforcing, overlapping, and power-related, identities.

We have to recognise the roots of those identities, even if we are unable to unpick them, separate them and distinguish our selves from them.

In other words, there can be no individual outside of the social, exclusive to society, the communal, **because the social, society, communal, now and down through its unfathomable and distant past, is present within each and every one of us.**

When we speak, we speak not only for ourselves but for the whole. Because we each of us belongs to the whole, we represent it. We exist only because it exists.

There is no 'freedom' from that obligation and there never could be.

NOTES

1 https://legalresearch.blogs.bris.ac.uk/2018/12/sex-gender-and-the-trans-debate/

2 https://www.bbc.com/news/uk-england-oxfordshire-51737206

3 https://www.wsj.com/articles/oxford-union-set-to-debate-the-future-of-rhodes-statue-1453222242

4 https://www.theguardian.com/education/2019/mar/20/students-occupy-goldsmiths-in-protest-at-institutional-racism

5 https://www.theguardian.com/education/2020/jan/14/sacked-silenced-academics-say-they-are-blocked-from-exploring-trans-issues

Eleven

It is rare to find the word 'love' in any analysis of contemporary university life. Indeed, you'd be hard pushed to find a discussion of love in any analysis of any organisation, anywhere (Whitehead, 2022).

Yet as one commentator notes, love is an HE variable, it exists if only to signal how little we have of it:

> The writer Loudon Wainwright Jr called Christmas "the annual crisis of love". A university is a permanent crisis of love. But crises are what we struggle through because it's worth getting to the other side – and because a university is a community or it's nothing.
>
> (Moran, 2021)

A more cynical (realistic?) view of universities would claim something rather different:

> [the modern university] is just a series of individual faculty entrepreneurs held together by a grievance over parking.
>
> (Clark Kerr, 2001)

As we've explored in this book, once you introduce managerialism, casualisation, performativity, funding crises, and unmanageable workloads into HE, and mix it with whiteness, masculinism and elitism, then there can be no surprise if 'the language of corporate togetherness rings hollow' for a great number of staff and students.

Total Inclusivity requires the element of love in order to make it real. Why? Because all communities, including the TI one, need at least a touch of love if they are to enable belonging. Love born not of desire, but love born of empathy, unity and understanding. The recognition that 'I am because we are' – Ubunto (Chapter 10). This requires the collective act of believing in the worthiness of the

DOI: 10.4324/9781003277651-13

community, indeed of the human story, not simply for survival but for advancement.

Challenges to the values and ethos espoused by a Totally Inclusive education and especially higher education, exist everywhere. And one reason for this is that community does not arise without some effort and declared intent by and on behalf of all its members.

Community requires not just the 'Tinkerbell effect' to survive – keep believing and it will become real – it requires '*the incremental wealth of small gestures – weaving the wider fabric that binds us*' (Katherine May, quoted in Moran, 2021).

That fabric can only be woven and rendered strong if there is intent to protect the community against all those who would endanger it. And the first step is to recognise that if a few are unsafe, all are unsafe. If a few are violated, all are violated. The university must protect the one in order to protect everyone. Which is why, as we discussed in Chapter 10, the binary of individuals v communality is, in truth, a false one. Because individuality can only flourish where there is a community to protect and enable it.

That protection may be legislated for in university policies and in public law. It may well be enforced through HR departments and their policies, management systems, and various performance indicators. But in the end, those who constitute the institution have to care enough to put all this into practice.

There has to be a sprinkling of love.

How much love is there right now in global higher education?

WELLBEING AND SAFETY INDICATORS

To try and answer that question, we examine contemporary discussions and research into three key aspects of university life, each of which directly connects with Total Inclusivity:

1. Employment Conditions.
2. Mental Health.
3. Violence.

1. Employment Conditions

One of the first lessons any academic, or aspiring one, learns is to recognise 'what counts in terms of career progression?' And what they learn is not 'teaching', and nor is it 'the students'. Across the Western world (USA, Canada, UK, Europe, Australasia), the performative-driven focus on research output results in the marginalisation of teaching and tutoring, which inevitably results in the marginalisation of the students. Teaching, and particularly tutoring, is now increasingly relegated to junior or hourly paid people. One result is that the tenured academics often don't know the students they are supposed to be responsible for. This situation is compounded by the rapid casualisation occurring in academia. Even wealthy universities, such as Oxford and Cambridge, are embracing this practice, with 77.2% of Oxford staff now on casualised or precarious contracts, and nearly half of Cambridge undergraduate tutorials delivered by staff who lack proper contracts (Hall, 2021c; Oxford Anti-Casualisation Network, 2021).

If the likes of Oxford and Cambridge are putting profit before wellbeing (of both staff and students), then what chance of near-bankrupt universities deciding not to? No chance according to the research.

The casualization of academic work is a deepening problem at UK universities. From the late 1990s, the number of academics working on non-permanent non-full-time contracts has skyrocketed, even as student fees have increased at an exponential rate.

(Parfitt, 2018)

The logic of rampant casualisation in Australian universities is exposed... less skilled, less professionally equipped and less secure teaching staff, fewer inputs from up-to-date research, compromised academic and professional integrity...These findings expose a grim outlook of Australia academia.

(Lama and Joullie, 2015; also Hommel and Hommel, 2020)

The influence of neoliberalism and higher education's uptake of corporate organizational models have furthered the reliance on non-tenure track {US} academic labor...A 2016 study from the American Association of University Professors (AAUP) found that 70% of all faculty in higher education worked off the tenure track.

(McConnell, 2018)

There is a place for casualised work in academia, but it is becoming so widespread that talent is being driven away, and both staff and students suffer...Universities are using casual contracts to put profit before people.

(Andrews, 2016)

The rise in precarity in global higher education should not surprise anyone as it is an inevitable result of market forces; it is worth noting that where universities are part of the civil service the proportion of those on precarious contracts is much less – roughly a quarter in France (Bataille et al., 2017).

Inevitable or not, the rise of precarious contracts is a loud warning to universities that any 'sense of community' they might aspire to is being badly damaged through toxic working conditions, and that is before we explore the equally important issue of the persistent gender pay gap.

The Athena Swan Charter (see also Chapter 5) was introduced in 2017 and is one of a number of global initiatives aiming to support and transform gender equality in higher education. It includes an obligation on each university to report their gender pay gap. According to the Charter data, since 2017 UK universities have reduced their individual gender pay gap by an average of 3%. However, for the year 2020–21, a median pay gap of 14.7% between male and female employees persisted and *'while gradual improvements have been made, universities are still reporting structural barriers to closing the pay gap fully...in particular, there remains a higher proportion of men than women in higher paid roles at universities'* (Pinsent Masons, 2021).

As one UK vice-chancellor put it, commenting on the combined impact of Covid, staff wellbeing, universities finances, and reflecting on her five years as a VC.

I probably wouldn't start with finances now, I would turn to them pretty quickly, but I think we have to build communities. I think people are deep, deep tired now and they need a bit of compassion. They need to feel they are part of a community. To make the big changes and tackle the big challenges, you have to do that from the base of a strong community and if I go back five years, there were times when it was pretty tough and pretty lonely and it would have been easier to have done things if I'd had the full backing of a really strong, empowered community and think that's what the sector is looking for now.

(Prof Cara Aitchison, quoted in Baker, 2022a)

As this VC is tacitly acknowledging, any leader, whether or not of a university, has to have a hard heart if they are to implement working conditions which put profit before people, indeed, in the case of universities, which put profit before their 'clients' wellbeing. Not least because these leaders are only too well aware that a great many of their clients (students) are going into heavy indebtedness for the privilege of this 'exclusive learning experience'. Sure, HE leaders can attempt to justify this on the basis of institutional 'economic realities', though not in the case of Oxbridge and the like. To put it starkly, someone (a senior manager) has chaired a meeting in the university and agreed to increase the ratio of casualised to permanent staff, including academics. Have they then experienced a sleepless night, anguishing over this decision, this act of hard-hearted managerialism? We cannot know. But we do know such decisions do not arise from an act of love; they run counter to the wellbeing of staff, the wellbeing of students, and indeed, to the wellbeing of higher education generally. As one of us as written elsewhere, such casualised workers are the 'Expendables':

The Expendable worker symbolises, as it has always done, exploitation...It should not be necessary to make the point that socially responsible organisations must have a higher aspiration than the bottom line, but unfortunately, the reality requires such a point to be made and consistently.

(Whitehead, 2022)

If universities haven't the strength of leadership necessary to become model 'socially responsible organisations', then where do we look for such examples? Amazon? Google? Apple? Facebook/Meta? As we have stressed in this book, universities should be bold enough to present themselves as, and exemplify, model organisations, which translates as meaning they should be learning communities. As Moran (2021) observes above, 'a university is a community, or it is nothing.'

147   **A Crisis of Love**

HE leaders should seek to build communities not simply for financial expediency nor in order to be able to get tough decisions supported by staff, but from a base of compassion and empathy. However, with Oxford, Cambridge and a host of other big-name universities (and even more lesser-named ones) 'operating a gig economy like Deliveroo' (Gazzotti, quoted in Hall, 2021c), and staff being treated badly as a result, is there a link here to the next 'HE love variable' we look at – mental health?

2. Mental Health

Since the turn of this century, a veritable globalised wellbeing industry has emerged, driven not least by the recognition that paid employment brings both positives and negatives for individuals.

> *The quality of our lives is marked by our experience of work as a source of wellbeing but also malaise, blessings and curses, emancipation and alienation, and success and failure, of healthy effects and pathological consequences.*
>
> (Oacha and Blanch, 2019: 4)

And that was written before the word 'Covid' passed anyone's lips. Stress, fear, anxiety, burn-out, loneliness, grief, sleep-loss and exhaustion, are all symptoms of the global pandemic, though it also needs to be recognised these conditions were becoming more common among the global workforce long before humans began succumbing to the virus (Pfeffer and Williams, 2021).

Mental health issues is a can of worms which has, since Covid, been well and truly cracked open. Politicians, popstars, celebrities, British royalty, the known and the unknown across society are now opening up about their very personal, and painful, mental health experiences in ways which not that long ago would have been impossible, not least due to the cultural sanctions which demanded those suffering from, say, depression and PTSD, stay silent at all costs.

Not surprisingly, work and organisations find themselves at the forefront of this mental health tsunami. A 2020 McKinsey survey of approximately 1,000 employers found that 90% reported that the Covid-19 crisis was affecting the behavioural health and often productivity of their workforce (Pfeffer and Williams, 2021).

By way of example, at time of writing, prominent Scottish politician, Lady Ruth Davidson, revealed her own struggles with mental health:

I almost didn't run for leader of the Scottish Conservatives in 2011 in case my mental health history became known. I was diagnosed with depression about 20 years ago, while at university, and it was very shameful. I didn't want anyone to know.

(BBC News, 2022)[1]

If we add into this equation substance use disorder and suicide then the scale of the problem becomes staggering (Pfeffer and Williams, 2021).

- One in four Americans has a mental or substance use disorder.
- The US suicide rate increased 35% between 1999 and 2018 and has been increasing at 2% per year since 2006.
- Suicide is now the 10th leading cause of death in the USA.
- Depression increases suicide risk – about 60% of people who die by suicide have had a mood disorder.
- Covid is predicted to result in a 50% increase in behavioural health conditions in the USA.
- A 2019 USA study revealed that almost 60% of the 1,500 employed respondents sampled across all types of organisations, reported symptoms of a mental health condition in the previous year.

Crucially for universities, they are more likely to see mental health conditions than almost any other organisation, largely because of their client demographic.

Young adults between the ages of 18 and 25 had the highest prevalence of any mental illness.

(Pfeffer and Williams, 2021)

One tragic outcome of such mental health conditions among students is suicide:

- One UK student dies of suicide every four days.
- Around 10% of Spanish university students have experienced suicidal thoughts.

- 12% of US college students report the occurrence of suicide ideation during their first four years in college.
- 24,000 college students attempt suicide each year in the USA.
- Since 1996, suicide has been the top cause of death among Japanese university students.

Global academic research into the mental health of university students over the past decade certainly tells of a crisis – one not brought on by Covid but undoubtedly exacerbated by it.

> There are increasing concerns globally about the mental health of students. In the UK, the actual incidence of mental health disturbance is unknown, although university counselling services report increasing referrals...Second year students reported the most significant increases in psychiatric problems.
>
> (Macaskill, 2012)

> With increasingly severe psychopathology of [college and university] students, psychiatric services must be enhanced. Clinicians who support and treat the most troubled students and who can assess and manage psychiatric emergencies are needed.
>
> (Schwartz and Kay, 2009)

> ...students who self-identified having a mental health problem [showed] that the "silence" surrounding mental health problems permeates the university environment and impacts on help seeking behaviours. Universities must decrease stigma and foster social inclusion to build self-esteem in people who have mental health problems.
>
> (Wynaden et al., 2014)

> We might expect students in higher education to have better mental health than the general population. Strong social networks and better employment prospects are two of the many benefits of going to university. Yet survey data repeatedly show that, on average, students are less happy and more anxious than non-students, including other young people.
>
> (Brown, 2022)

To take just one country, Ireland, as an example, these are the statistics for severe mental health problems amongst its students (https://usi.ie/chatsforchange/).

- 48.4% experiencing severe levels of anxiety.
- 29.9% experiencing depression.
- 32.2% had a formal diagnosis of a mental health difficulty at some point in their lives.

There are many myths surrounding higher education but perhaps one of the most insidious yet pervasive is the notion of using the experience to 'grow up', emerge comfortably into adulthood. Hundreds of thousands of young people go, literally overnight, from being schoolchildren, parented 24/7, to living on their own, albeit on or near campus, alongside other young adults similarly catapulted into 'independence.' This life transformation can itself be traumatic enough but when we add in serious indebtedness, borderline or actual poverty, exam stress, study skill issues, intensified competition for jobs, socialisation anxieties, drink, drugs, sex, together with every possible relationship connotation, then to expect HE students NOT to have mental health problems is to fail to recognise the demands society is placing on these young people.

Take, by way of example, the increased incidence of students working in the sex industry. While this is not new – first reports of British students selling their bodies for payment surfaced in the mid-1990s (Barrett, 1997) - the growing phenomenon of sex work among students is evidenced now in many countries, including Norway, UK, Canada, USA and Sweden. A German study revealed that 7% of respondents (HE students) are or have been involved in sex work (Betzier et al., 2015). A recent British survey put the figure at 10% (Petter, 2018), while a study by Roberts et al in 2010, reported that 16.5% of UK students would be willing to engage in sex work to pay for their education (Roberts et al., 2010).

Indeed, so commonplace (if not accepted) is student sex work, that two UK universities, Durham and Leicester, now offer 'training to support students working in the sex industry' and a 'student sex work toolkit' (Barncroft, 2021; University of Leicester, 2021).

If Durham and Leicester, both globally prestigious universities, are responding in an open and responsible way to the growth in student sex workers, then is there any university leadership anywhere that can claim this is not happening in their institution? And recognising such, what are they doing to support students engaged in sex work?

Being realistic, it is unlikely that any university leadership can claim sex work is not part of at least some of their student's activities. What is even more unlikely is that student's parents envisaged their children 'growing up' in quite this way when they received their offer letters.

Whatever one's view as to sex work, and we are not suggesting that being a sex worker is a mental health problem in and of itself, the point remains that higher education is not simply about advanced learning, it is also a place of risk for young people and as we explore below, one major risk is gender-based violence, inevitably heightened for those who pursue sex work.

Sure, risk is inevitable, indeed some level of stress can be beneficial, but the global data on student's mental health confirms an altogether more worrying situation, with anxiety, depression, suicidal feelings and isolation, occurring at pandemic levels in universities. And this before Covid raised it all by several notches.

To summarise, as global research is now showing, 'mental health problems' covers a multitude of conditions, all of which can be quickly exacerbated by the financially insecure and highly intense HE experience especially for young adults many of whom are living away from home and thereby removed from relative domestic security for the first time in their lives. There can be little doubt that many students are on the edge, physically and mentally. A few may find a level of remittance by earning money in the sex industry, but for all students the conditions of higher education are not inevitably and always safe, secure, positive, benign and productive.

As one of the academic studies into HE student mental health states, 'fostering social inclusion' is a 'must' for universities if they are serious about addressing this problem.

3. *Violence*

Is there a correspondence between student mental health and gender-based violence? We certainly believe so. Take just one example; the mental health statistics for students in Ireland, referred to above.

A survey of the sexual experiences of students in Ireland, completed by 6,026 undergraduate and postgraduate students at Irish Higher Education Institutions during February to April 2020, revealed the following:

> *29% of females, 10% of males, and 28% of non-binary students reported rape (i.e., non-consensual penetration by incapacitation, force or threat of force)...The vast majority of female students (98%) reported that the perpetrator was a man...Approximately three in ten of the survey participants said the perpetrator was a student at their college.*
>
> (Sexual Experiences Survey, 2020: 15)

When this level of gender-based violence is apparent in higher education, and in individual universities, how could there not be a corresponding link to student mental health?

Which is why an obvious measure of Total Inclusivity for any organisation, be it a car wash or a university, is the level and types of violences which occur within it. By violences we refer to:

- That which is or involves the use of force physical or otherwise, by a violator or violators.
- That which is intended to cause harm.
- That which is experienced, by the violated, as damaging and/or violation.
- The recognition of certain acts, activities or events as 'violent' by a third party, for example, a legal authority.

(Hearn, 1998: 16)

Violence is more likely to occur where there are imbalances of power and equality; where those in powerful positions feel a sense of entitlement; and where certain parties/individuals either feel immune from justice or are oblivious to the violent effects of their actions. This could be in a family setting, or it could be in a place of higher education. For example, any university which has a clear hierarchical positioning that renders students and certain staff at the lowest level increases the potential vulnerability of such students and staff to violence of all kinds, especially gender-based violence (O'Connor et al., 2021).

Which could explain why the report into sexual violence in UK universities undertaken by the University and College Union and informed by an extensive survey of 4,000 university staff (UCU, 2021) confirmed;

> *...encounters with sexual violence are "commonplace" within universities and colleges. One in 10 respondents said that they had directly experienced sexual harassment or abuse within the past five years, yet half of them did not report it to their employers.*
>
> (Grove, 2021)

The report goes on to note that 'an obsession with reputational damage...is impacting on how universities deal with this' (ibid).

What the report also clearly states is that 'predatory male academics' are the primary cause of this violence and that 'staff on non-permanent contracts are 1.3 times more likely to experience sexual violence' (ibid).

The toxic mix which emerges is one where a culture of masculinism prevails, sustained by hegemonic/toxic masculine identities, and where entitlement, opportunity, inequality and vulnerability create an environment which is as far from being a community of learning as it is possible to get.

Is this, then, a problem unique to the UK HE sector?

Not according to numerous studies (Strid, 2021). What emerges from research into gender-based violence in academia across Europe, America, Australia and host of other countries, are the same conditions and manifestations as apparent in UK higher education (see, for example, Bondestam and Lundqvist, 2020; O'Connor et al., 2021; Husu, 2001; SWG GRI, 2020).

> *Universities and research organisations, especially universities, have a distinct organisational structure with specific implications for gender-based violence: a senior layer of permanent positions, dominated by men; a middle layer of more gender-equal permanent and non-permanent researchers and lecturers, supported by administrative and professional services staff; and a lower level of students, where women tend to outnumber men in a number of disciplines. This can create hierarchies of power that are structured by gender and age, and which can underpin violence.*
>
> (Strid, 2021)

This argument is supported by research which identifies the key organisational characteristics that facilitate gender-based harassment and violence in higher education (GBHV):

1. Male-dominated hierarchies.
2. Neoliberal managerialist ethos.
3. Gender/Intersectional Incompetent leadership.

(O'Connor et al., 2021)

To this institutionalised gender-based violence which many academics and students are subjected to, can be added the wider online violence experienced by researchers.

According to European research of almost 2,500 researchers in five Finnish universities and published the same month as the UCU study (Upton, 2021)...

Overall, three in 10 respondents reported being harassed online during the past six months, with one in 20 reporting monthly attacks and just over one in 100 describing it as a weekly occurrence...2.8% said they had received violent threats, and 1% reported receiving death threats.

(ibid)

While this online violence and intimidation is increasingly common, especially for those academics who appear regularly in the media, what is also common is the reluctance of victims to report it, with only 16.3% reporting any form of online harassment to their supervisors, and just 3.3% reporting it to police. Indeed, 45% of those threatened with violence did not report it to the police, a result described by authors of the study as 'remarkable'.

And one reason for this under-reporting?

The 'competitive culture and lack of community within universities' (Upton, 2021) where victims do not wish to 'appear more vulnerable' (especially to senior managers and supervisors) than they already are.

This is evidence of the masculinist culture at work in higher education, where results, output, male-dominated leadership, performativity and an intensely competitive silo-work mentality, diminish the possibility for community, belonging, safety and empathy between staff and between staff and students.

Not surprisingly, when female students experience the worst effects of male violence and report it, they can quickly find their university unwilling to act, with managers often citing guidance which states 'there should be no duplication of the criminal process, save for any precautionary measures'. In the case of a female student violently stalked by a male student (at Oxford Brookes University during 2020) this resulted in 'the university's failure to swiftly act, leaving her terrified: of the stalker' (Jeffreys, 2021b).[2]

The Oxford Brookes University example is merely the tip of the violence iceberg in universities. A 2021 report by *Al Jazeera's Investigative Unit* examined data from all 164 UK universities on the total number of sexual misconduct cases made against students and staff members between 2017 and 2020 and found that out of over 1,400 sexual misconduct cases reported, most are not investigated and 'complaints against staff and students habitually do not result in disciplinary action'.

A telling example of how far-removed university leaders can be from the violent realities experienced by their students, in 2021, Skidmore College in New York, banned a young female student from campus after she posted online about her experiences of sexual violence (Donegan, 2021). This resulted in a mass protest by students on the campus.

None of this is new, however. In 1990, students at Brown University in the USA wrote of their experiences of rape and sexual assault on the wall of a women's bathroom stall, and condemned the university's incompetence and indifference in handling sexual assault cases (Schmich and Chicago Tribune, 1990).

As one woman scribbled on the loo wall: 'Rich white boys can do whatever…they want on this campus.'

That was written over 30 years ago. Unfortunately, too little has changed.

THE INVISIBLE STUDENT

Hierarchies are inevitable in all organisations. There are the managers and there are those who are managed. There are those who make decisions and are responsible for them and those who follow the decisions. This reality is not going to disappear any time soon, either in universities or anywhere else.

But this reality also makes the need for Total Inclusivity even more vital. TI is not intended to remove all hierarchies, but it is intended to remove completely the idea that the top of a hierarchy is untouchable, entitled, invulnerable, protected, and therefore enabled to act in any way it chooses.

Universities need to avoid at all costs situations where they can be accused of this:

The behaviour of Durham University speaks to the toxic atmosphere that so many students and staff must live with at universities up and down the country. Students and staff must join forces to dismantle this culture of permissiveness towards bullying, harassment and misogyny.

(Halliday, 2021)

And where this can be said of male professors at the world's leading universities:

His academic reputation was high, his personal reputation was as an alcoholic and a sexual predator.

(Prof Catherine Karkov, quoted in
Davies and Al Jezeera Investigative Unit, 2021)

One clear safeguard in this respect is to ensure the hierarchy is diverse. That means the powers of leadership of any university must not be solely invested in men. From all the evidence into violences of all types in universities (and elsewhere), one clear major risk factor is having an unrepresentative, male-dominated leadership (O'Connor et al., 2021).

That must end if universities and colleges are serious about student and staff wellbeing and safety. Gender violence stems primarily from the violences of men and those men who enact violence in universities will feel protected if other men are their enablers either by default or intent.

At the root of all this is, of course, the invisible student. Which is ironic given that universities are expected to operate in some quasi-liberal capitalist marketplace which purports to put the needs and welfare of its paying clients (the students) first and foremost.

That is clearly not happening. Which suggests that when it comes down to it, gender power trumps capitalist economic rationalities.

Which is why there must be an active intervention, not just rhetorically, but in reality. And that intervention must be Total Inclusivity.

And at the heart of Total Inclusivity in Universities is the student. They are the beginning and the end of it.

Making the student visible requires listening to them, acknowledging their needs, learning from them, protecting them first and foremost from any form of violence no matter where and from whom it might originate, thereby ensuring their days in higher education are memorable for all the right reasons.

That is where the love starts.

NOTES

1 Lady Davidson became Scottish Conservative leader in November 2011, and a peer in 2021.
2 The stalker was subsequently successfully prosecuted and banned from the university.

What Next for Universities?
Part Three
Stephen Whitehead

Twelve

INTRODUCTION

In this book, we have engaged with concepts and theories, explored debates, and given real-world examples to underpin our arguments. All fine, but in the end, there has to be a clear relationship to practice otherwise we just end up talking to each other about where we would like an organisation such as a university to be heading in terms of becoming Totally Inclusive.

This chapter is where we put the debates and the theory aside to focus on the practice and the tool, we use is our Totally Inclusive University Audit.

The TI University Audit (TIUA) is essentially a means of assessing where your institution is placed on the continuum (or journey) towards becoming Totally Inclusive. In using it you should be able to identity the strength and weaknesses of your institution in terms of meeting its obligations to all its stakeholders regarding diversity, equity, inclusion and justice.

Although we term it an 'audit', it is not intended to be purely objective and nor do you have to be a skilled auditor to apply it. There is an element of the subjective in this process. In other words, where do you feel your university is located on this continuum? When you reflect on your job and your work/academic relationships, does it feel to you like you are working in a community or in an anonymous and remote institution? Of course, where you are positioned in the institution, your role, status, history, will have a bearing on your assessment, nevertheless, none of that diminishes the importance of your opinion. Your assessment is as valid as anyone else's regardless of your organisational responsibilities.

DOI: 10.4324/9781003277651-15

In that respect, it matters not whether you are the Vice Chancellor or a first-year undergraduate. If you are a stakeholder in the university, whether student, casual lecturer, Dean or the person who cleans the Dean's offices out every morning, your perspective counts.

That said, one section of the university which can and should use the TIUA to full effect is HR. Human Resource managers can readily use the TIUA in order to acquire a more precise understanding of what has been achieved and what more needs to be achieved. They may approach this task by a quantitative methodology – asking all stakeholders to answer questions on the TIAU, and/or via a more qualitative approach – e.g., individual in-depth interviews with representative stakeholders plus focus groups.

HR can then disseminate that information/data through the institutional system, and in such a way that all stakeholders identify the areas of progress, spot the gaps and recognise where they can make positive contributions.

Note that the structure and content of the TIUA is very similar to that which we've devised for schools and other work organisations, albeit tailored to the realities of higher education. All such audits operate along the same key stages/levels (see, Whitehead, 2022; Aow, Hollins and Whitehead, 2022).

The Six Stage Totally Inclusive Continuum

1. **Actively discriminatory** – a failing university.
2. **Tokenistic** – a rhetorically correct university.
3. **Reflectively unsettled** – a contradictory university.
4. **Tentative** – working to become a learning university.
5. **Rebuilding** – a transformative and advancing university.
6. **Totally Inclusive** – a Totally Inclusive University.

While your sense and feel for your institution is valid and important, we are now starting to clarify a little more clearly just where it might be located in respect of how close it is to being Totally Inclusive.

These six stages of development provide the markers for the journey a university needs to be undertaking, supported by all the stakeholders. This won't be achieved by simply having good policy documents, or relying on the efforts of the HR department and some good-willed individuals. It will only happen if the university is operating as a learning community; which means listening to all its members, being open to change, and not pretending that it has reached the end of the road as regards TI when clearly it hasn't.

Like any journey, the TI one takes physical action as well as fine words. Though applied positive leadership at all levels will be key in ensuring there is consistency, fairness and intent.

CONTINUUM ON BECOMING A TOTALLY INCLUSIVE UNIVERSITY

THE SIX STAGES:

1. **Actively discriminatory (a failing university)**
   o Intentionally and publicly excludes or segregates by race, ethnicity, gender, sexual orientation, class, language, disability, age and religion. This includes discriminations over marital status, pregnancy, health needs.
   o Intentionally and publicly enforces a monocultural, masculinist status quo throughout institution.
   o Institutionalisation of racism, sexism and homophobia, includes formal policies, practices, and decision-making on all levels.
   o Openly maintains and encourages a white, male, heterosexual dominated leadership.
   o Employment and recruitment systems and policies designed to identify 'others' as undesirable.
   o Views privilege (especially white, straight, male) as entitlement and seeks to substantiate it in all policies and practices.
   o Actively resisting liberalisation and progressive attitudes.
   o Leadership actively resistant to LGBT+ identities at all levels of the organisation
   o Leadership and management teams actively support each other both covertly and overtly in maintaining a discriminatory climate.
   o Employees treated as 'resources' to be exploited to maximise 'efficiency' and profit.
   o Employees have no opportunity to participate in the decision-making process.
   o Employees controlled by performative measures.
   o Sexual harassment and other forms of gender violence are commonplace across the institution and embedded in the masculinist, male-dominated, managerialist culture.
   o Staff at all levels experience bullying and intimidation

o Hierarchical, top-down model of leadership and management with lower levels having minimum input and working to strictly regimented systems and imposed targets, while being made fully accountable for success or failure.

o No professional development opportunities for staff or managers beyond that which serves to reinforce the discriminatory, performative work culture.

Summarising the actively discriminating, failing university

*Given the mission and values which define global higher education it would be unusual, if not tragic, to find any university had systems and culture that matched **all** of the above criteria. But it would not be unusual to find universities around the world that had several of these criteria in operation. So for a good many institutions, like it or not, this is their starting point. At the same time, it will be very difficult for those university leaders to recognise this fact. But if your assessment has placed you at this first stage then you must be strong and determined enough to say so, to admit it, and to take some responsibility for moving the institution forward. Languishing at this stage is not only unacceptable it is damaging people – students and staff alike – not only is it putting individuals at risk, but the university is also not fulfilling its obligation to stakeholders and society. To progress out of this stage don't be afraid to face reality but neither be quick to apportion blame to individuals and groups. It is important to maintain organisational unity and that will require all individuals reflecting on their mindsets, languages, behaviours. Leaders will need to take responsibility for the systems they may have inherited, designed and/or upheld and not be fearful of recognising inequalities. Will it be a comfortable experience for everyone? No. But that only tells you how important it is to go through it. Because the first thing to recognise is that this is a dangerous place to work and a dangerous university to study in.*

Examples of next step initiatives include:

- Begin having open conversations across the university about DEIJ and which involve all staff and students.
- Analyse current policies using a DEIJ lens and identify all terms and concepts requiring shared understanding.

- Introductory workshops to raise levels of understanding about; power and privilege, culturally responsive learning, implicit bias, safeguarding and safe reporting pathways, courageous conversations, 'guarded liberal' speech protocols and more.
- Ensuring that open conversations are protected spaces for individuals to share their experiences of, for example, bullying, sexual harassment, sexual violence, intimidation and aggression.
- Leadership to acknowledge past DEIJ failings and publicly declare responsibility for changing the institutional culture towards TI.
- Begin identifying TI Advocates from within the staff and student body. Provide them with support and training.
- Begin full training of HR department in Total Inclusivity values and systems using HR as one of the vehicles for extending this knowledge throughout the institution.

2. **Tokenistic (a rhetorically correct university)**
   - o Tolerant of a limited number of 'token' Black (BAME) people, LGBT+ people, women, but not in positions of authority or power.
   - o Uses progressive rhetoric in public presentation of organisation but systems and culture remain unchanged and discriminatory.
   - o Uses notion of 'meritocracy' to justify filtering and excluding thereby ensuring continuation of existing power groups (e.g., white men)
   - o Decision-making processes and recruitment practices remain under the control of an unrepresentative and self-sustaining cohort.
   - o Has adopted anti-discriminatory policies due to legal requirements to do so and for whatever presentation value it is considered they may offer to students and staff.
   - o Leadership covertly discourages discussion of diversity and inclusivity (e.g., prohibits use of words such as 'racist', 'sexist', 'feminist', 'white privilege')
   - o Leadership overtly resists liberalising measures by prohibiting professional development in diversity and inclusivity on the grounds of cost and priority.
   - o Continues to intentionally maintain white/male power and privilege through its formal policies, practices and decision-making on all levels of institutional life.

o Key individuals often declare, "We don't have a problem."
o Monocultural norms, policies and procedures of dominant culture viewed as the 'right way' and 'business as usual'
o Engages issues of diversity and social justice only on 'club' member's terms and within their comfort zone.
o Professional development for staff in areas of inclusivity and diversity are actively discouraged and PD remains unreflective, monocultural, exclusionary and orientated towards biological determinism.
o Key actors within the organisation deny terms such as 'white privilege' and 'unconscious bias'.
o Little or no attempt to relate to identities, politics and concerns of staff.
o Attempts to shut down staff complaints of discrimination, either past or present.
o Leadership adopts an instrumental approach to diversity and inclusivity.
o Operational (management and leadership) systems and culture mirror those of the 'discriminatory' level, albeit with more effort to appear inclusive and democratic.

Summarising the tokenistic, rhetorically correct university

Universities at this stage have a 'business as usual' attitude towards DEIJ. They may well present themselves as DEIJ aware and this discourse will be present in marketing and promotional material, but the change process is slow, resisted and minimalistic. Often, having activated some of the initiatives indicated in Stage 1, university leaders may be complacent, assuming 'all is well' and that there 'are no DEIJ' problems. However, this complacency can come crashing down when, for example, students and staff continue to complain of institutionalised racism, sexual harassment, gender-based violence, bullying and discrimination. At which point the organisation hurriedly tries to minimise public fall-out and show it is 'dealing with the issues, and has learned from the experience'. The sense of shutting the stable door too late is paramount. In short, universities at this stage are aware of their DEIJ responsibilities and rhetorically at least, all looks good. But the practices, systems, and work culture have not adequately progressed while some sections of the institution will be either uncooperative or actively resisting – so there is a large gap between rhetoric and reality. The tokenistic approach prevails, encouraged by leaders suggesting that 'now is not the right time for major cultural changes in the institution.' The key actors at this stage are the TI Advocates, whether they be students or staff, as they are most likely to speak truth to power thereby encouraging the institution not to stagnate but to move into the 21st century.

Examples of next step initiatives include:

- Creating opportunities for interactive participation where voices are valued in decision-making and learners (students and staff) can ask questions, make mistakes and co-construct meaning without fear (Right Question Institute, 2020).
- Decentralise decision-making by empowering students and staff to make informed choices.
- Facilitate intercultural understanding workshops that shifts understanding from token surface level actions (flags, foods, fashion, festivals, etc) to a deeper understanding of how individuals attend to difference (Hall, 1976)
- Create up to date and inclusive policies collaboratively with all stakeholders.
- Seek the help of DEIJ experts who can expand thinking and help inform how to be a more effective ally.
- Engage in deep reflection and actions that have been co-constructed with various stakeholders.
- Ensure there is a strong and open feedback loop from the TI Advocates and other TI supporters to the institutional leadership and that public commitments are made by leaders to further progress and address issues.
- Begin strategic planning for TI implementation across the institution within agreed timeframes.
- Implicit bias training that includes exploration of micro-aggressive behaviours that marginalises cross sections of the university's population.

3. **Reflectively unsettled (a contradictory university)**

- o Makes official policy pronouncements regarding multicultural values, and embracing of diversity regards sexual orientation, gender, religion, class, language, race, ethnicity, disability, language, age.
- o Leadership see itself heading an inclusive institution with open doors to Black (BAME), LGBT+, women.
- o Carries out intentional inclusiveness efforts, e.g., recruiting 'someone of colour' on committees and at middle management level.
- o Expanding view of diversity includes other socially oppressed groups, especially LGBT+.
- o A minority of staff and leaders begin their own reflective journey towards Total Inclusivity, both personally and professionally.
- o A minority of staff and leaders begin to recognise their own privilege and how this has fed into a sense of entitlement.
- o Women leaders emerge in the organisation but are pressured to adopt masculinist styles of leadership.
- o Women leaders and aspiring leaders experience being patronised and told to 'not push too hard for change'.
- o The minority BAME and women leaders experience schizogenic identity – meeting dominant cultural expectations while trying to maintain an authentic self.
- o BAME and LGBT+ staff experience toleration rather than acceptance.
- o BAME and LGBT+ staff experience bullying and discrimination.
- o Open dissent towards the organisational leadership is actively discouraged and 'those who make waves' marginalised.
- o Little or no contextual change in culture, policies and decision-making.
- o Gender-based violence and harassment remains a problem but is hidden behind the culture of male privilege and managerialism.
- o The majority of staff remain relatively unaware of continuing patterns of privilege, paternalism and control.
- o Token placements in staff positions: must assimilate into organisational culture – no attempt to encourage 'authentic selves' at work.

o Diversity and inclusivity training is limited and restricted to overcoming 'unconscious bias'.
o Key organisational actors continue to resist progressive change but do so covertly.
o Organisational leadership attempts to retain control and overall direction of the progression towards full inclusivity and not fully recognise diverse views and experiences.
o Staff diversity and inclusivity forums are allowed to exist but remain separate from the primary workplace processes and therefore have little influence on the organisational climate.
o Leaders may genuinely believe the organisation is totally inclusive but have failed to audit the reality of this and have failed to undergo training in order to recognise the contradictions and tensions inherent in the organisation.
o Leaders accept the need for inclusivity but reluctant to engage in this process personally, certainly if it results in what they see as a diminution of their power and authority.
o Employees sense the contradictions between (inclusive) rhetoric and (exclusive) reality, but may well accept the organisational leadership is attempting to improve.

Summarising the reflectively unsettled, contradictory university

This is the point at which a university, or indeed any institution, starts to move from its blinkered comfort zone regarding DEIJ into a greater honesty and awareness of what stakeholders are actually experiencing and feeling. The tokenism has mostly been put aside in favour of a much more active and strategically reinforced push towards Total Inclusivity and at all levels of the organisation. There is energy and growing optimism, but there is also tension. Indeed, a hallmark of this stage is disruption – individuals and groups feeling unsettled, perhaps even threatened especially those who have been reluctant to recognise how their behaviour and attitudes might have contributed to problems in the past. But the tension is important and should not be avoided or dismissed. Staff and students will want to bring about positive change though there will still be pockets of resistance so expect it to get rather heated and noisy at times. Overcoming this resistance isn't easy and will require determined and committed leaders and advocates. Part of the problem is simply ignorance about Total Inclusivity – and this can be overcome by suitable professional development and training, especially of the leaders. The other key problem is that some identities (e.g., male, white, straight) will recognise they won't necessarily be beneficiaries of the changes in climate and culture which are starting to bubble under the surface. This is why no organisation can get through this stage on its own. It needs help and no matter what resistances are expressed (especially by those who feel threatened by the process) then this stage must see the development of a powerful momentum towards a Totally Inclusive community.

Examples of next step initiatives include:

- Commitment from all senior post-holders to actively engage in learning about patterns of privilege, paternalism, protection-ism and control and how to be culturally proficient and equity focused.
- Strategic implementation which is committed to sustainable development over time and reinforced by DEIJ training and awareness across the university.
- Prioritising and funding initiatives related to DEIJ work, especially research and teaching and learning.
- Establishing ways to measure growth over time and holding all stakeholders to account for planned initiatives.
- Greater transparency and democratic decision-making where reasons for decisions provide legitimacy, the process of decision-making is transparent and visible to all. People who are impacted by decisions have opportunities for participation and play a role in the process (Right Question Institute, 2020).
- Work to overcome resistance, overt or covert, by making it clear that a totally inclusive, equitable and just institution is now inevitable and won't be compromised. Examples of tools that can be used to achieve clarity include; the university's mission, guiding statements, strategic plan of actions, policies, professional/academic expectations, student behavioural expectations, community agreements, code of ethics, safeguarding policies and more.
- Hold all university members to account for behaviours and actions that are not aligned with totally inclusive beliefs and values.

- Introduce DEIJ achievements into staff appraisals/assessments and promotion systems so that all academics are fully aware that their career pathways within the institution must now align with TI.

4. **Tentative (working to become a learning university)**
   o Leadership have begun to strategise diversity and inclusivity into the training, professional development, systems, planning, and recruitment processes.
   o Intersectional (DEIJ) leadership standards are clearly identified and expected.
   o Growing understanding of racism, homophobia, sexism, gender-based violence, harassment, bullying, masculinism, classism, as barriers to effective diversity.
   o Develops analysis of systemic racism and all forms of discrimination.
   o Sponsors programmes of diversity and inclusivity training.
   o New consciousness of institutionalised gendered white power, privilege, entitlement.
   o Develops intentional identity as a totally inclusive institution.
   o Begins to develop accountability to oppressed communities, socially/economically/racially disenfranchised communities.
   o Increasing commitment to dismantle racism and eliminate inherent white male advantage
   o Actively recruits and promotes members of groups which have been historically denied access and opportunity.
   o Totally Inclusive Advocates within the organisation now work within a Totally Inclusive Committee containing staff, management, administration representatives.
   o Institutional structures and culture that maintain white male power and privilege still intact and relatively untouched with evidence of continued resistance by some staff at different levels of the organisation.
   o Workplace and management culture remains performative, and target driven, with outcomes privileged over processes.
   o Staff and students still experience bullying, racism, discrimination, gender-based violence and harassment.
   o Senior Management Teams now starting to work towards Total Inclusivity and with genuine intention but also having to counter covert negativity, ignorance and resistance at different levels.

This is a realistic and achievable continuation of the TI process so long as the energy and commitment are maintained by leaders and key organisational players. Staff and students must be much more involved and the process less reliant on the enlightened leadership of a few. All voices are being heard and this increased input brings enhanced perspectives on how to address systemic discrimination and inequalities. However, resistance is likely to remain and if not challenged will be a major hurdle to the institution moving forward, depending on where the resistance is located in the management/leadership hierarchy. To what extent this resistance is overcome and ends up diminishing and much less rooted in the emergent organisational culture, depends to a large extent on the quality of leadership. If there is a visible commitment to institutional transformation at the top of the institution (e.g., intersectional leadership standards) then the force for change will grow. One danger is in addressing TI through policy initiatives only and not reaching the hearts and minds of the staff. If this happens then the gap between what leaders perceive is going on in their organisation and the reality for the typical employee can still be quite large. Problems may remain in recruitment, promotion, language, training and retention of staff. Many organisations will need outside help to get through this important transitional stage. So long as the leaders remain open-minded, and are prepared to be guided by experts both within and outside the university, then the organisation can look forward to an upward turn in its culture as the sense of community and belonging starts to emerge across the institution.

Examples of next step initiatives include:

- Differentiated professional learning opportunities across the university related to DEIJ impact on research, teaching and learning.
- Require all stakeholders, students and staff, to commit to the university's TI policy and practices.
- HR and all leadership are ensuring that there are safeguarding measures in place for all staff and students.
- Coaching, mentoring, sponsoring and supporting diverse advocates for DEIJ initiatives.

- Actively and regularly measuring TI impact in specific areas, working out the best method for data collection and establishing baseline measures to track growth.
- Continuously engage in professional inquiry to seek understanding and to co-construct equitable practices via staff and students.
- Engage in systems and design thinking to spark new ideas and to stimulate disruption where needed.
- Begin to create a critical mass of DEIJ/TI aware leaders at various levels of the organisation.
- The establishment of a 'Respectful Speech' committee which is tasked with identifying subjects/topics which should not be given a platform in the university (see Chapter 10).

5. **Rebuiilding (transformative and advancing)**
   o Commits to process of intentional institutional restructuring, based upon Total Inclusivity values, ethics, aims and objectives.
   o Audits and restructures all aspects of institutional life to ensure full participation of Black (BAME), LGBT+, women, and different social and economic groups, including their worldview, culture and lifestyles.
   o Strategically and openly pursuing a vision of an institution and wider community that has overcome systemic racism and all other forms of oppression.
   o identifies where masculinism continues to linger in the institution and addresses it.
   o Where any instances of gender-based violence and harassment occur, they are immediately dealt with, and sanctions applied.
   o Implements structures, policies and practices with inclusive decision-making and other forms of power sharing on all levels of the institutions life and work.
   o Commits to struggle to dismantle racism, discrimination, prejudice in the wider community, and builds clear lines of accountability to all oppressed communities.
   o Total Inclusive intercultural diversity becomes an institutionalised asset which is understood, accepted, recognised and practiced by all staff and managers.
   o Redefines and rebuilds all relationships and activities in society, based on antiracist, Totally Inclusive commitments.

- o Professional Development and Training in Total Inclusivity is strategic, progressive, and led by trained internal Advocates.
- o Professional development and learning processes support the voices of the community and all its members.
- o Organisational leadership is committed and engaged in creating a Totally Inclusive community and this agenda is supported and understood by all staff.

Summarising the rebuilding, transformative and advancing university

This stage is more than simply a marker on a TI journey, it is a period of total transformation. The university is now in a process of doing nothing less than redefining itself. It has moved far beyond TI rhetoric and into TI understanding and practice. The difference within the work culture is positive, engaging, exciting and energetic. The sense of community is tangible, and the momentum is only in one direction – towards Total Inclusivity. This can be an exciting time to be associated with the university – there will be a lot of positive energy around, a feeling of progress and togetherness, and any staff who previously worked in less advanced organisations will appreciate having their voices heard and the feeling of commitment this generates for them. There may still be some minor pockets of resistance and the leaders will have to take care to ensure progress is maintained especially by careful hiring processes and ongoing training and development. But overall, there are few barriers to stopping the organisation moving to the final stage, a Totally Inclusive Community. However, if leaders and staff treat this stage of development as one where revisions to existing structures and systems are enough, then the university may be at risk of regressing or stagnating. The institution must recognise that rebuilding is essential to ensure that Total Inclusivity becomes its first defining principle.

Examples of next step initiatives include:

- Community visioning to build shared understandings of the DEIJ agenda and what a liberated institution looks like, including clear definitions of terms, roles and responsibilities.
- Identifying where discrimination continues and addressing it as an institution.

- Modelling, valuing and highlighting behaviour and practices that provide learning stories for growth and affirmation that a liberated state is achievable.
- Professional learning opportunities led by trained internal advocates who can contribute to sustaining learning over time in the institution.
- Continuing to actively reach out to all stakeholders and valuing diverse voices and their contributions to decision-making processes.
- Continuing to advocate for and develop new initiatives to meet the needs of marginalised identities.
- Continuing to hold individuals to account for their behaviours and the institution to account for staff and student's sense of belonging and success.

6. **Totally Inclusive University**
   o Institution's life and culture reflects full participation and shared power with diverse racial, sexual, gender, cultural and economic groups fully participating and represented equitably.
   o Leadership and staff work in harmony in ensuring a Totally Inclusive mission, structure, constituency, policies and practices.
   o Gender-based violence has disappeared from within and across the university, and is no longer experience by any members – staff and students.
   o Members across all identity groups are full participants in decisions that shape the institution, and inclusion of diverse cultures, lifestyles and interests.
   o A sense of restored community and mutual caring.
   o Allies with others in combating all forms of social oppression.
   o Actively works in larger communities (regional, national, global) to eliminate all forms of oppression and to create intercultural organisations.
   o Ensures Total Inclusive agenda, principles and values are embedded in the community and regularly monitored for effectiveness.
   o The community has confidently and openly identified its present and future as a Totally Inclusive organisation and regularly imparts this reality to all stakeholders.

o Community undertakes regular Totally Inclusive audits to ensure all aspects of the community maintain alignment with these aims.

o The leadership and staff are fully familiar with Total Inclusivity and ensure this value permeates and informs all practices and behaviours.

o Community climate ensures the wellbeing and safety of all, regardless of sexual, racial, class, ethnic, gender identity.

o Leaders and staff actively support feminist (inter-sectionalist) understandings, values and principles.

o Where appropriate, professional development actively promotes understanding of intersectional identity as a means of appreciating and valuing diversity.

o The community recognises and accepts that diversity is a fact, a right and an important resource.

o The pursuit of Total Inclusivity takes precedence over all other aspects of the operation and defines the mission.

o A Totally Inclusive community has been established which is therefore able to act as a model for other organisations to follow.

o The physical and mental wellbeing of all Community members is held paramount and this includes ensuring a healthy work-life balance and protection of employment rights (e.g., paternity and maternity rights).

o Employees and work teams develop their own project and work objectives with support and guidance from leaders.

o Intersectional leadership is the standard, expectation and template throughout the university.

Summarising the totally inclusivity university

If you are working in a Totally Inclusive university community then you won't need this assessment device to confirm it. You will know for yourself. It will be evident in the systems, vision and especially in the climate. As an employee you won't feel like an employee you'll feel like an equal part of a thriving educational institution, where humanistic values prevail and take priority over any other factor. There will be no need to discuss efficiency, because a Totally Inclusive Community is, by definition, operating at maximum. How? Through having enabled and developed the unique skills and attributes of all its members. Empathy, support, trust, respect and all the intelligences combine to make such organisations not only strong but great adaptors, able to weather whatever changes emerge in their professional field. To sustain this stage individuals should feel comfortable to be their authentic selves. An institution at this stage requires a dynamic and cyclical approach to refining one's systems and structures so that continuous evolution into better versions of itself is possible.

Examples of sustaining practices:

- Honest and open feedback mechanisms.
- Evaluation protocols to monitor progress and to recalibrate for continuous university improvement and at all levels.
- Ensuring that decision-making is research-informed. Research is defined broadly to encompass academic publications, educator experiences and collection of data ranging from student learning evidence to community perception surveys.
- Quality assurance protocols are selected for their embedded DEIJ values. These are chosen to help guide, monitor and evaluate growth.
- Deep implementation across systems, structures and policy is evident through consistency of practice, collective efficacy, skill development and continuous reflection (Jacobs and Alcock, 2017).
- Intersectional leadership models encourage voice, choice and ownership of learning. Rigid hierarchical leadership structures have been dismantled.
- Maintains a reputation for being a totally inclusive university and is able to act as a model for other universities to follow.

Where is your university on the totally inclusive continuum?

Despite having read and understood the various stages on the continuum, you still may not be able to answer the above question with any degree of confidence and certainty. The reason being, your university seems just too big to get an accurate evaluation done, to undertake a single and realistic assessment. You may be daunted by the potential complexity of the TIUA and/or you lack insight into the multiple systems and cultures operating in different parts of the university, many of which you are not personally familiar with.

This is why the first department which should be charged with oversight of the TIUA is Human Resources, though they need to be clear as to their objectives, trained to undertake the TIUA, and be supported by TI Advocates from across the university who are experienced, confident and determined enough to ensure the process is transparent, fair and fully implemented.

If you are not able to confidently place your university at a particular stage on the continuum, then you should try and place your department/section – the working environment which employs you, structures your activities, appraises you, and largely determines your responsibilities.

Doing the assessment at a more local level has the advantage of having your personal and professional experience and insights applied – so it is a little more objective and accurate.

The process of TIUA implementation we suggest universities should follow is this:

1. **University level**: organised by the HR department and undertaken with a mix of quantitative and qualitative methods.
2. **Department level**: organised within individual departments by TI Advocates and undertaken with a mix of quantitative and qualitative methods.
3. **Student level**: TI Advocates within the student body (not academics) undertake a mix of quantitative and qualitative research methods.

The key principles of data collection and subsequent processes would be as follows:

1. All methodologies are undertaken under anonymised conditions unless the individual respondent agrees otherwise.
2. University-wide data and information is collated by HR and made available to all stakeholders. HR in this respect must act as a neutral

professional entity and not be co-opted into leadership narratives and agendas.

3. TI Action committees are created across the university and within the student body tasked with taking the university to the next stage of the TI continuum.

Within most universities, regardless of where they are positioned on the TI Continuum, there will be individuals who are fully committed to Total Inclusivity though they may not necessarily be in positions of power and authority. In which case, it is important to identify and then enlist the help of these individuals, providing them with the professional support and training which will enable them to become TI Advocates, trainers and mentors of others.

Additionally, you may find it useful to link the application of the TI continuum with other ongoing or potential DEIJ university-wide initiatives. An example is the EU Gender Equality Plans (GEPS), the implementation of which is required for HORIZON funding (European Commission, GEPS, 2021). There are common elements to the TI Continuum and GEPS, not only in the 'typical steps of a GEP life-cycle' (audit, planning, implementation, monitoring/evaluation)' but also in terms of developing strategies designed to engage the whole organisation. It is worth noting that the HORIZON Europe eligibility criterion for universities requires that 'the GEP be a formal document published on the institution's website and signed by the top management'. The very same public and institutional commitments required for the GEP should be made if an organisation is declaring itself committed to Total Inclusivity. These include:

1. Publication of the TI Commitment on the institution's website.
2. Be signed by the senior leadership.
3. Be actively communicated within the institution.
4. Be accompanied by regular TI progress reports.
5. Commit dedicated resources to TI.
6. Establish a dedicated TI function (structure or team).
7. Utilise staff skills from across the institution.
8. TI budgeting as a management strategy.

9. Continuous data collection, monitoring and analysis.
10. DEIJ awareness-raising and training – ongoing and long-term.

This institutional-wide TI learning/change process is no different from any professionalisation process. At first it may feel unfamiliar, be viewed with some cynicism, and co-opting academics especially may prove difficult, but so long as it is persisted with, then over time it will become part of the university culture, climate, systems and expectations. It is especially important that new staff appointments at any level are fully engaged with TI and committed to it.

Universities are complex, multi-layered organisations inhabited by some of the world's cleverest people, academically. These institutions are not going to turn wholesale to TI overnight. It will take time, vision and resolve. Many academics may well speak out against TI with conviction and in a compellingly discursive manner. But every university, no matter where it is located must put the safety and well-being of all its members, and future members first. That single principle cannot be watered down and as such it demands nothing less than Total Inclusivity.

This level of resolve will require sanctions being applied to those staff and students whose behaviour continues to be incompatible with the values and practices of a Totally Inclusive university. It must be for the individual university to decide at what point sanctioning is appropriate and the nature of such, but as a starting point we advise a zero-tolerance position on any proven instances of racism, homophobia, LGBT+ discrimination, bullying, gender-based violence and harassment.

A question that will immediately be asked by any institution intent on moving towards TI will be 'who is going to drive it?' We explore this in more detail in the final chapter.

While each university will have those who are uncomfortable with changing the power status quo, each university will also have some individuals who can be the spark for TI. They may be tenured professors, administrators, and/or students. Find out who they are and get them working together. That is the best start any university can make on its TI journey.

In terms of strategic implementation, the 'cascade model of strategy' (Goal Atlas, 2021), can be highly effective. This strategy will enable the university to define its...

...desired future state, identifies the benefits of achieving it and proposes the core methods needed to get there. Strategic mapping is the technique that can be used to build the cascade of connections between strategic goals that is required to bring about strategic success. A strategy map presents strategic goals in a prioritised, validated logic diagram that can be used to manage and track the performance of strategy, assess strategic risks and ensure systemic strategy adoption, whilst helping to identify missing goals and opportunities for innovation.

(Goal Atlas, 2021)

Finally, consider this Total Inclusive University Audit to be a template. It is to some degree adaptable, flexible and is therefore available to being adjusted to reflect the particular needs of an institution at a particular time. What is immutable is the fact that your university, as an institution, will be situated on the TI Continuum somewhere. Use this as the opportunity to find out where and take action accordingly.

What Next for You?

Thirteen

One aspect of this book which will be apparent is its critical, in places accusatory, perspective on what is currently happening across global higher education in respect of diversity, equity, inclusion, justice and, relatedly, staff and student wellbeing and safety. We make no apologies for that. The evidence is clear and unambiguous; universities need to change, and our recommendation is that they change to adopting and embracing Total Inclusivity both as a foundational philosophy and set of practices.

Merely having the policies in writing, supported by the best intent of a few students and staff is not enough. There has to be a fundamental shift in the character of higher education and that requires a fundamental recognition that everyone involved in HE is a part of that change. There are no exceptions. Total Inclusivity is everyone's responsibility, and everyone has to be held to account for achieving it.

In this final chapter, we continue with the criticality, though we also acknowledge evidence of good practice in two universities, offering them by way of examples for other institutions, staff and students, to follow. This then, is the framework within which we ask 'what next for you?'

MALE DOMINANCE

It may or may not be beyond the power of university leaders to persuade governments to adopt an HE funds system which is inherently equal and inclusive. Not one, as we state in Chapter 8, '*where managerialism rules, performativity defines ability and value, students are weighed down by insecurities and facing a life of indebtedness*'.

But whether or not political leaders become enlightened as to the real potential of higher education to change the world into a much more positive, safe and inclusive place, and accordingly make higher

DOI: 10.4324/9781003277651-16

education free for all who can benefit from it, the onus on university leaders remains.

Because what university leaders can do is instigate change from within their institutions. They can be encouraged to do this by state and systemic initiatives, for example, by linking state funding to specific developments, such as the gender profile of senior positions, and they can be encouraged to do so by pressure and raised expectations from staff and students.

But we suggest that regardless of the original impetus for change, the Total Inclusivity University Audit, identified and explained in detail in the previous chapter, is the starting point. This mechanism offers at least the possibility of an objective analysis taking place, informed by individual subjectivities, and which draws on the views, opinions, and experiences of all staff and all students.

Universities may not always be demonstrably expert in teaching and learning, but they are generally recognised to have expertise in carrying out research. In which case, executing the Total Inclusivity University Audit should not present a major challenge.

But what is going to be a major challenge is changing the gendered work culture of universities.

One word which crops up throughout this book is 'masculinism' – and the reason is that this term names and defines the major hurdle which universities must overcome if they are to have any hope of becoming Totally Inclusive. Because, for sure, they cannot become Totally Inclusive if they remained numerically dominated by men and culturally dominated by a value system which is infested with hegemonic masculinity and is, therefore, essentially patriarchal.

Masculinism is the ideology that justifies and naturalises male domination, as such it is the ideology of patriarchy. Masculinism takes it for granted that there is a fundamental difference between men and women, it assumes that heterosexuality is normal, it accepts without question the sexual division of labour, and it sanctions the political and dominant role of men in the public and private spheres.

(Brittan, 1989; quoted in Whitehead, 2002: 97)

As we discussed in Chapter 6, masculinism feeds male entitlement and privilege. It is, consequently, the instigator and enabler for gender violence and harassment; homophobia; transphobia; misogyny; racism and white supremacy; and the fact that universities are not yet places of wellbeing, safety, inclusion, justice, equity and diversity.

Masculinism is a relatively recent concept within sociology and in critical gender studies, but it has a long history. One can reasonably speculate that masculinism has informed higher education since the first university got built, several centuries ago. It is certainly visible today.

In which case, how to get rid of it?

INTERSECTIONAL LEADERSHIP

There is a growing literature and evidential base on the ways in which intersectionality links with and can support a more inclusive leadership approach. For example:

> ...leadership for diversity can be developed by shifting towards a more radical and transversal politics that challenges social and political structures that enable intersectionality or interlocking oppressions. This challenge relies on critical alliances negotiated across multiple intellectual, social and political positions and enacted through flexible solidarity to foster a collective ethical responsibility and social change. These forms of alliance-based praxis are important for advancing leadership for diversity.
>
> (Pullen et al., 2021)

One of the first steps on this journey towards an intersectional (feminist) leadership approach in universities is to cease idolising leadership and cease putting leaders on pedestals of exclusivity, entitlement and privilege. As we now discuss, leaders are not heroes, nor are they the 'best of us'.

No 'love song' to leadership

Anyone who takes on a leadership role in a university (or indeed in any organisation) should do so by first acknowledging their primary obligation – which is to staff and students. All else, must be secondary. So leadership ceases being a 'love song to imperialism, whiteness and patriarchy' (Helena, 2020), where leaders (of whatever gender) deliberately or by default 'fashion themselves after fantasies of white [hegemonic] masculinity' (ibid). Instead, an intersectional feminist practice of leadership would follow the following principles (from Helena, 2020; also Liu, 2021c).

1. Advance the aims of ending all discrimination, oppression and exploitation.
2. Centre marginalised people, especially women, Black, minority ethnic people, LGBTQ+ people all of whom have been traditionally side-lined from leadership roles.
3. Use the power and authority invested in leadership to listen, learn, collaborate, coordinate, empower, and instigate social and organisational change and development.
4. Prioritise the university as a learning community rather than as a vehicle for the individual heroic narrative.
5. Move from silo mentalities where the individual is heroized to collective communities where power is distributed, shared, dispersed and community belonging is prioritised.
6. Flatten the hierarchical rise. Diminish the 'command and control' approach to leadership, reinforced by performative appraisal.
7. Strategically and actively appoint leaders to ensure that leadership across the university represents intersectional identities and is therefore not dominated by cisgender, straight, able-bodied, white, middle-class men.
8. Ensure that demonstrable experience of promoting a gender/intersectional agenda is criterion for appointment to all line management positions.

What does intersectional feminist leadership feel like?

1. **It is non-hierarchical** – Power is shared as much as possible.
2. **It is humanising** – it allows and encourages the individual to demonstrate their authentic self.
3. **It is relational** – non-violent, respectful, supportive and protects the dignity of all.
4. **It is politically aware** – e.g., it recognises that patriarchy and white supremacy are destructive and violent wherever and whenever they appear within the organisation.
5. **It is reflective** – all university members are encouraged to be critically self-aware and seek the decolonisation of the mind.

6. **It seeks social and global transformation** towards Total Inclusivity.

What can you do as an TI advocate to advance intersectional leadership? Ask yourself these questions:

1. When you make decisions, whose interests are taking precedent and why? Whose voices are being heard. Is the notion and reality of university as community being protected?
2. How is the university reproducing performative, cis-gender, white, male normative assumptions and practices? Am I complicit in this reproduction of oppressive and discriminatory behaviours?
3. Are all students living and learning in a safe, caring, healthy environment?
4. Are all staff working in a safe, caring, healthy environment?
5. When I exercise power am I doing so in way which is non-oppressive?

Overcoming masculinism across universities and the toxic values which accompany it, will not be achieved only by appointing more women to leadership positions, though that is most definitely a start. Masculinism is a deeply rooted value system and only by reflective action on the part of the individual (woman and man) supported by strong intersectional feminist leadership values and practices, can it be dismantled.

> So much of leadership is tacit, non-reflective and non-conscious; impro-
> vised through the mundane day-to-day interactions between people,
> intersectional feminist leadership requires practice-based training that
> explores the subtler aspects of leadership.
>
> (Helena, 2020)

As we have detailed, evidenced and discussed in this book, the global template for university leadership is currently most definitely not intersectional. It is masculinist, reinforced by the numerical dominance of men in leadership positions and the hegemonic dominance of a work culture rooted in managerialism, individuality, competitiveness, aggression, fear, insecurity, casualisation, bullying and violences.

This type of leadership marginalises and excludes from leadership positions, women, Black, ethnic minority and LGBT+ people. In many cases it does so deliberately and with intent. In more cases it does so as a consequence of unreflective practice and traditional adherence to patriarchal managerialist values.

University leadership, which is perceived to be solely about results-based competences, charisma, vision and output, will fail to deliver Total Inclusivity. As we detailed in Chapter 12, the Totally Inclusive University Audit will expose this so long as it is undertaken across the institution and carried out with resolution.

In short, if you are a university leader, or aspiring to be one, then you only have one thing to recognise, which is that you are a leader solely because you seek to bring about social transformation. And that starts with you and your role.

EXAMPLES OF TOTAL INCLUSIVITY-APPROACHES IN ACTION

While we've made very clear that universities worldwide have some way to go before they can claim to be Totally Inclusive, it is also true that there are examples of good practice regards DEIJ. Indeed, it is probably fair to say that many universities are working hard to ensure that their whole strategic and cultural approach is one which puts staff and student wellbeing first and foremost while encouraging intersectional leadership styles, though more likely one will find ad-hoc pockets of good practice in universities rather than a fully implemented, Totally Inclusive workplace culture.

This book is not so much intended to show where good practice is taking place regarding DEIJ, but rather to challenge all universities and their members to adopt good practice at every level of the institution. However, when asking the question 'What next for you' (and your university), it is helpful to demonstrate what that might mean in reality.

Basically, there are two approaches to take regards implementing Total Inclusivity. The first is the strategic, described in detail in our Totally Inclusive University Audit (Chapter 12). The second is the empathetic, referred to in many places in this book. For TI to work both the strategic and the empathetic must be dominant across the university.

Below we give examples of both approaches in action[1]:

1. *The Strategic* — *Manchester University* (submitted by Alexander Gardner-McTaggart, 2022).[2]

First of all, the University of Manchester was the first British University to set social responsibility as a core goal. It was also ranked globally as number 1 in the 2022 Times Higher Education for social and environmental impact aligning with the UN's sustainable development goals. The way it manages this is through its strategic approach and I would point primarily towards the University's core values: Knowledge, Wisdom, Humanity, Academic Freedom, Courage and Pioneering Spirit.[3]

Its stated purpose being '*To advance education, knowledge and wisdom for the good of society*'.[4]

With a strategic focus at policy level that is centred around 'Our People, Our Values', and looks like this:

Our people, our values: From life-saving research to life-changing teaching, from gold medals to green spaces, everything we do at our University has people, our students, colleagues and alumni, at its heart.

Together we will achieve great things, working collectively towards our shared goals. Priorities at a glance:

- *Great people doing great things.*
- *Wellbeing.*
- *Equality, diversity and inclusion.*
- *An environment and facilities to support our people.*
- *Our values.*

So, this is how the university articulates itself at the top level and correspondingly these priorities are written into how we produce curricula, implement pedagogy, advance professional colleagues, and work with our student body. Now I will turn to the example of the Manchester Institute of Education (MIE) and relay my own personal experience here.

At school level, there is an associate Dean of EDI, and at departmental level, we have a director of EDI. These are significant positions, and they work together at faculty and school level to promote EDI with initiatives designed to improve teaching and learning[5] and ensure that EDI is consistently upheld as a component part of the system of administration at the University.

In my own experience of MIE I was able to initiate an antiracist teaching group, which I have since moved on from, but which is thriving, promoting such initiatives as this recent book launch,[6] and continues to explore student centred ways of making our teaching and learning, and our institutional spaces more inclusive.

I have now talked at length with Dr Susie Miles, Assoc. Dean of EDI. One thing she mentioned sticks in my mind. When talking to Prof Mel Ainscrow, she asked how one might achieve a truly inclusive University environment. Mel paused for quite a while (uncharacteristic of Mel), and then replied: '*If you want real inclusivity, you have to listen. You have to foreground the student voice.*'

I think this is a very good, practical, educator's view on inclusion, and one I find myself and my team profiting from. I am Programme Director of the Award-Winning Best Humanities Programme 2022. It is award winning, and I have received much kudos and attention because this is a student award, and our nomination was a result of listening to students. Initiatives like this are powerful reminders of who we are here for, and how to listen when we make the student the central component of our work.

2. *The Empathetic – Cambridge University* (submitted by Alec Letten, 2022)[7]

I realised I was transgender in my first year of sixth form, when I was 17. When you finally piece it together it feels like an awakening and you're desperate to grasp that newfound clarity to your life and take action, but the reality of transitioning is very scary especially when surrounded by people who you're certain won't support you. After a few attempts to come out to my parents, which ended in arguments and me scurrying back to the closet, I had in my mind that I could start living as male at university and it would be a fresh start. Cambridge University began and as I introduced myself to new people living in my halls, my parents were stood beside me, I couldn't be truthful, so in the closet I remained. The next plan of action was to wait until after university – transitioning is expensive so whilst it was a horrible prospect it was the 'logical' decision to wait until I was employed.[8]

However, I wasn't at Cambridge university long before I met someone I really liked, and she had to know before I could pursue any kind of relationship with her. I was scared this would change our friendship in some way and I realised if one person knows I would have to tell the rest of our friends soon. My fears were unfounded – she smiled and nodded and asked me what my name was, and I felt this huge weight lift from my shoulders. She was the first person to properly listen and to make me feel completely seen, and she's continued to be my biggest advocate for the three years we've been together so far.

Once I'd told her, I began the process of coming out properly. I started with my closest friends and eventually built up the courage to send out the stock email I'd drafted to all my university supervisors, because it was vital that this all happened at the same time – the thought of a supervisor still using my birthname when I'm surrounded by my peers who now know me as 'Alec' was hideous. All considering, the staff at Cambridge were fantastic. Most supervisors simply thanked me for telling them and asked if they could do anything further to support me, a couple of the staff would say things they thought were kind but were actually hurtful. I can't blame them for not fully understanding though, I was grateful they were listening at all.

It was tackling the Cambridge university online system that was the real problem. Emails received from the university are all personalised, taking the names off several databases within the system, and so receiving around five emails a day with my birthname on it quickly became intolerable. I spoke to several supervisors, emailed multiple admin teams etc. and it transpired nothing could be changed without an official deed poll certificate. Changing my name officially was always the plan, but I was at a point in my transition where this didn't feel possible, as my family back home were still completely unaware. Eventually, I gave up and found a Google extension that finds and replaces text, so every time my birthname was written, my screen would show 'Alec', which was a lifesaver, but it shouldn't have been necessary.

When I realised I was trans, I hadn't been immersing myself in queer theory, and I would have scoffed at the idea of gender differing from assigned gender not long before. After coming to terms with myself it was then I began learning about gender as a social construct, the fluidity of gender and sexuality etc and you start to realise that all these rules you'd been taught were meaningless. None of these concepts matter, and so long as we're not hurting each other, everyone should be allowed to do and be what they want. It was with this doctrine in mind that I was faced with the university refusing to change my name, it made me very angry for a time, I felt I was fighting a war for my existence, but it wasn't their fault. There are rules they have to follow about students' personal information, so their hands were tied, and you come to realise that our whole society is structured so it's not easy for people like me to fit into it. We would need a complete overhaul of every system to make names and gender markers unimportant (obviously there are some instances where they are important). One day things will change but we're centuries away from that, and unfortunately there are more pressing matters.

Waiting until university to come out was definitely the right decision. You're exposed to so many new people, and ideas and thoughts on life that it inspires you and fills you with the confidence that you can do this, and it will be okay. However, when you go home for the long holidays, everything is exactly as it was throughout your childhood and suddenly that confidence has vanished. There was about a year where I was out at uni, but closeted at home. It was horrible having to go back to being called the wrong name, being referred to in the wrong way and perceived incorrectly – it felt like the progress I'd made at uni had been a wonderful dream. Living some kind of double life was scary whenever both worlds happened to collide; trying to keep my parents and friends apart whenever they would visit, being unable to show them mundane things like the uni portal because my name would be there etc. I felt like I was deceiving people, like I was being dishonest when at the heart of it I was endeavouring to be as honest as possible whilst trying not to lose the love of my parents. Equally you worry your friends are judging you and their belief in your identity may falter the longer you go without beginning your medical transition. In the end, Covid struck, and I was sent home for the last term of my second year. With the prospect of 6 months at home I knew I had to talk to my parents, and we did talk a lot. There were endless conversations, and arguments and tears but we've come out the other side of it and the relationships with my close family have really healed.

Despite the problems I faced with transitioning at uni, I wouldn't change the way it all happened. In that first year of uni you grow into yourself, so I would never have had the maturity to navigate those difficult conversations if I'd have tried to do it any younger. Cambridge University gave me a space to be unapologetically myself and nobody would question it. I remember when I was in the early stages of coming out to my peers, we were having a few drinks one night, and everyone there was calling me by my name, but I hadn't had the chance to tell half of those people yet that I was trans. They had heard what others were saying and just switched immediately to what would clearly make me most comfortable, they never questioned me once, it was magical.

At the time of writing, I've been out at uni for two and a half years and have been on testosterone for 7 months. Being trans was such a huge part of my identity for so long, and I would spend my time dreaming of reaching the point I've finally reached. As a result, in these last few months I've found myself wondering who I am outside of that, now I've got the time and space to think about other things, I find my sense of self has relied heavily upon this one aspect. If I've learned anything over my first three years at uni though, it's that there's room for me to experiment and the people at Cambridge University will provide me with unwavering support.

STRATEGY AND EMPATHY NEED EACH OTHER

The examples offered above by Alex and Alec are not presented as objective assessments of Total Inclusivity in action in the University of Manchester or in Cambridge University. Neither university is Totally Inclusive. For example, the University of Manchester is not the highest placed UK university in terms of the gender and race profile of its professoriate,[9] while it is clear from Alec's account that Cambridge University was ill-prepared to handle the transitional requests and needs of one of its students. Both universities still have a long way to go before they can claim to be Totally Inclusive.

However, what the two examples do reveal is firstly, the importance of an holistic strategically implemented approach to Total Inclusivity led by institutional leaders and embedded in a vision as well as systems, procedures and data recording. This commitment is demonstrated in the University of Manchester and acknowledged by one of its academic staff.

Second, the vital issue of empathy and understanding is fully demonstrated in Alec's vignette. This account does not validate the DEIJ credentials of Cambridge University, but it does validate the importance of individual action by institutional members. In other words, where an institutional response is weak and inadequate, this can be partly ameliorated by the care, empathy and consideration offered by individual students and staff.

What both accounts underline is that Total Inclusivity requires cognitive nurturing in any organisation. Assuming the best of people won't be enough. There have to be policies, strategies and enlightened, intersectional leadership to ensure that diversity, equity, inclusion and justice are prioritised. The university strategy and vision must clearly state and commit to 'advance education, knowledge and wisdom for the good of society' though inevitably, whether or not that statement becomes more than rhetoric requires every individual in the institution being prepared to recognise and accept their role in that process and enacting it.

Alexander feels impassioned that his employer, The University of Manchester, is demonstrably committed to a DEIJ agenda. He knows that this strategy both safeguards and empowers him, as it does his colleagues and students.

Alec encountered empathy from his friends and supervisors at Cambridge University and that made the difference between his experience of higher education being an empowering and validating journey rather than a total nightmare.

There isn't a university in the world which does not have its Alec's and its Alex's. Which is why kindness, compassion and humanity must be the cornerstones for Total Inclusivity, reinforced by strategies, policies and practices that put the safety, security, care and wellbeing of the individual at the centre.

Yes, this is a challenge for any university and its leadership, but they are not undertaking this task alone. There is much good practice and support already available; from 'How to make campuses and courses more compassionate'[10] to 'available support for LGBTQIA+ university students'.[11] What all university leaders are well aware of, or should be, is that their institutions are not automatically safe havens for all. Indeed, the extent of student mental health problems in universities, often stemming from gender-based violence and discrimination and magnified by Covid-19 lockdowns, etc, is apparent not only in the Western world (Krantz, 2022) but also now in the East (Liu, 2021b).

Partial solutions are no solutions. So, when answering 'what next for you?', it must be to recognise the essentialness of Total Inclusivity and commit to it in your personal and professional practice.

No single book can nor should attempt to set out the best and precise process towards Total Inclusivity for every single university, but what we have attempted is to explain why TI is needed now across global higher education and given guidance for implementation.

You may already be a committed DEIJ Advocate. You may already be an intersectional leader who embraces all aspects of DEIJ in their professional and personal ethos and practice. Or you may be neither of these.

For us, the time for Total Inclusivity has come. In which case please use this book as a guide, a text to support the implementation of TI across your university, all universities.

Because for Total Inclusivity to be real it requires you, all of us, to commit to it. We believe that history is on the side of TI, but getting there will still require strategy, empathy, determination and commitment.

NOTES

1 Both contributors (Alex and Alec) offered their respective accounts to the authors without reservation and in the spirit of promoting Total Inclusivity in global higher education.

2 Dr Alexander Gardner-McTaggart is Academic Lead at University of Manchester Worldwide and lecturer in Educational Leadership at The University of Manchester.

3 https://www.manchester.ac.uk/discover/vision/

4 https://www.manchester.ac.uk/discover/facts-figures/0086-UoM-Facts-and-Figures-2021-500kb-edited-220421.jpg

5 'Thinking About Things Differently'. Inclusive Teaching Workshops at the School of Arts, Languages and Cultures, The University of Manchester.

6 See Joseph-Salisbury, R. and Connelly, L. (2021) *Anti-Racist Scholar-Activism*. Manchester University Press.

7 At time of writing, Alec Letten was a fourth year undergraduate at the University of Cambridge. He studied medicine, having intercalated in Biological Anthropology and Ethics and Law in Clinical Medicine. His research interests are in mental health, specifically in the field of obstetrics and gynaecology, and LGBTQ+ healthcare. https://www.linkedin.com/in/alec-letten-1b78a6212

8 Whilst the British NHS can fund your medical transition, this is only possible if you're able to wait several years. All British trans people have had to 'live in their chosen gender' for at least two years before they can receive a diagnosis of gender incongruence, and this is easily done since the waiting list for the first appointment at an NHS gender clinic is three years. Waiting times for further psychiatry appointments, hormones and surgery are then even longer and so many trans people resort to pursuing private treatment. Every private consultation will set you back between £150–£400, and surgery costs begin at around £6,000, with the more complex surgeries costing up to £100,000.

9 University of Manchester's Annual (HR) Performance Review (2018/2019) shows its proportion of women Professors at 25.5%, slightly above the UK's Russell Group average of 24.1%. The University of Liverpool had in the year 2017/2018, the highest proportion of women Professors at 29.1%. The proportion of ethnic minorities among Professors, Russell Group Institutions for the year 2017/2018, shows the University of Manchester at 9.6%, slightly above the Russell Group average of 7.9%. Queen Mary University of London had the highest percentage of ethnic minority Professors at 11.4%. (Annual Performance Reviews 2019; University of Manchester).

10 https://www.timeshighereducation.com/campus/collections/teaching-compassion?utm_source=newsletter&utm_medium=email&utm_campaign=campus-weekly&mc_cid=1f93d830a5

11 https://www.timeshighereducation.com/student/blogs/what-support-available-lgbtqia-university-students?utm_source=newsletter&utm_medium=email&utm_campaign=student-newsletter&mc_cid=5e581f50f9

AACE (Asian American Coalition for Education) (2015) https://asianamerican foreducation.org/en/issue/discrimination-on-admissions/. Accessed 20th July, 2021.

Aow, A., Hollins, S., and Whitehead, S. (2022) *Creating A Totally Inclusive School*. London: Routledge.

Abbott, A. (2019) "Max Planck Conducts Huge Bullying Survey." *Nature* 571: 14–15.

Acker, J. (1990) "Hierarchies, Jobs, Bodies: A Theory of Gendered Organizations." *Gender and Society* 4 (2): 139–158.

Acker, J. (2006) "Inequality Regimes: Gender, Class and Race in Organizations." *Gender and Society* 20 (4): 441–464.

Adams, R. (2020) https://www.theguardian.com/education/2020/jan/22/senior-uk-academics-protest-over-pay-and-working-conditions. Accessed 18th November, 2021.

Adams, R. (2021) https://www.theguardian.com/education/2021/sep/11/tuition-fees-uk-students-fail-to-cover-costs-undergraduate-courses-ucl?CMP=Share_iOSApp_Other. Accessed 15th September, 2021.

Agócs, C. (1997) "Institutionalised Resistance to Organisational Change: Denial, Inaction and Repression." *Journal of Business Ethics* 16 (9): 917–931.

Ahlqvist, V., Andersson, J., Hahn Berg, C., Kolm, C., Söderqvist, L., and Tumpane, J. (2013) "Jämställdhetsobservationer i ett urval av vetenskapsrdets beredningsgrupper 2012 [Observations on Gender Equality in a Selection of the Swedish Research Council's Evaluation Panels]." Vetenskapsrådet. www.vr.se/nyheterpress/nyheter2013/jamstalldhetsobservationerietturvalavvetenskapsradets beredningsgrupper2012.5.7e727b6e141e9 ed702b2b90.html. Accessed 14th March, 2014.

Al Jazeera Investigative Unit and Howlett, A. (2021) *Degrees of Abuse*. 26 October.

Allen, M. and Castleman, T. (2001) "Fighting the Pipeline Fallacy." In A. Brooks and A. Mackinnon (eds.) *Gender and the Restructured University Changing Management and Culture in Higher Education*. Buckingham: The Society for Research into Higher Education and Open Press University, pp. 151–165.

Alvesson, M. (2019) "Waiting for Godot: Eight Major Problems in the Odd field of Leadership Studies." *Leadership* 15 (1): 27–43.

Alvesson, M. and Spicer, A. (2014) "Critical Perspectives on Leadership." In D. V. Day (ed.) *The Oxford Handbook of Leadership and Organisations*, pp. 40–56. Oxford: Oxford University Press.

Amery, F., Holden Bates, S., McKay, S., Miller, C., Pflager Young, Z., Billings, T., Hayton, R. et al. (2019) "Why Do UK Universities Have Such Large Gender Pay Gaps?" www. psa.ac.uk/psa/news/why-do-uk-universities-have-such-large-gender-pay-gapss

Andrews, K. (2016) https://www.theguardian.com/commentisfree/2016/nov/17/ universities-casual-contracts-casualised-work-profit-academia-staff-students. Accessed 12th January, 2022.

As, B. (2004) "The Five Master Suppression Techniques." In B. Evengård (ed.) *Women in White: The European Outlook*, pp. 78–83. Stockholm: Stockholm City Council.

Badshah, N. (2021) https://www.theguardian.com/education/2021/oct/07/university-defends-academic-freedoms-after-calls-to-sack-professor?CMP=Share_iOSApp_ Other. Accessed 8th October, 2021.

Bagilhole, B. and Goode, J. (2001) "The Contradiction of the Myth of Individual Merit, and the Reality of a Patriarchal Support System in Academic Careers: A Feminist Investigation." *European Journal of Women's Studies* 8 (2): 161–180.

Baker, S. (2020) https://www.timeshighereducation.com/news/covid-19-crisis-could-bankrupt-dozen-uk-universities-ifs-warns. Accessed 21th November, 2021.

Baker, S. (2021) https://www.timeshighereducation.com/news/why-investment-higher-education-not-payingoff-women?utm_source=newsletter&utm_ medium=email&utm_campaign=editorial-daily&mc_cid=ed9a28535c. Accessed 23th September, 2021.

Baker, S. (2022a) https://www.timeshighereducation.com/news/tackle-precarity-or-lose-sense-community-says-v-c?utm_source=newsletter&utm_medium=email&utm_ campaign=editorial-daily&mc_cid=c1563a3180&mc_eid=6de1e590f3. Accessed 12th January, 2022.

Baker, S. (2022b) https://www.timeshighereducation.com/depth/cash-king-uk-universities-shore-finances?mc_cid=d8e61e815e. Accessed 24th January, 2022.

Bangkok Post (2022) https://www.bangkokpost.com/world/2246835/58-of-americans-believe-us-democracy-in-danger-of-collapse-poll. Accessed 15th January, 2022.

Barnard, S. (2017) "The Athena SWAN Charter: Promoting Commitment to Gender Equality in Higher Education Institutions." In K. White and P. O'Connor (eds.) *Gendered Success in Higher Education: Global Perspectives*, pp. 155–174. London: Palgrave Macmillan.

Barncroft, H. (2021) "Durham University Offers Training for Students Working in Sex Industry." https://www.independent.co.uk/news/uk/home-news/sex-work-durham-university-students-b1956484.html. Accessed 5th January, 2022.

Barnett, R. (2011) *Being a University*. Abingdon: Routledge.

Barrett, D. (1997) "Students on the Game." *The Times Higher Education Supplement*, 18th July.

Bataille, P., Le Feuvre, N., and Kradolfer, S. (2017) "Should I Stay or Should I Go? The Effects of Precariousness on the Gendered Career Aspirations of Post Docs in Switzerland." *European Educational Research Journal Special Issue* 16 (2–3): 313–331.

BBC News (2022) https://www.bbc.com/news/uk-scotland-scotland-politics-60017599. Accessed 19th January, 2022.

de Beauvoir, S. (1949/2009) *The Second Sex*. London: Vintage.

Bencivenga, R. and Drew, E. (2020) "Towards a Gender Sensitive University". In E. Drew and S. Canavan (eds.) *The Gender Sensitive University: A contradiction in Terms?* 177–182. Oxfordshire: Routledge.

Bencivenga, R. and Drew, E. (2021) "Promoting Gender Equality and Structural Change in Academia through Gender Equality Plans: Harmonising EU and National Initiatives." *GENDER – Zeitschrift für Geschlecht, Kultur und Gesellschaft,* 13 (1): 27–42. https://doi.org/10.3224/gender.v13i1.0.

Bennett, J. (2009) "Policies and Sexual Harassment in Higher Education: Two Steps Forward and Three Steps Somewhere Else." *Agenda* 23 (80): 7–21.

Benschop, Y. (2021) "Sheep with Five Legs: Gender and Excellence." Keynote at EWORA seminar on *Excellence and Gender,* 18th October.

Benschop, Y. and Brouns, M. (2009) 'The Trouble with the Glass Ceiling: Critical Reflections on a Famous Concept'. In J. W. Cox, T. G. Letrent-Jones, M. Voronov, and D. Weir (eds.) *Critical Management Studies at Work: Negotiating Tensions Between Theory and Practice,* pp. 259–270. Cheltenham, UK: Elgar.

Betzier, F., Kohler, S., and Schlemm, L. (2015) "Sex Work among Students of Higher Education: A Survey-Based, Cross-Sectional Study." https://www.researchgate.net/publication/271443846_Sex_Work_Among_Students_of_Higher_Education_A_Survey-Based_Cross-Sectional_Study

Bilton, I. (2018) https://www.studyinternational.com/news/record-high-numbers-women-outnumbering-men-university-globally/. Accessed 10th February, 2021.

Blackmore, J. (2002) "Globalisation and the Restructuring of Higher Education for New Knowledge Economies: New Dangers or Old Habits Troubling Gender Equity Work in Universities." *Higher Education Quarterly* 56 (4): 419–441.

Blackmore, J. (2011) "Bureaucratic, Corporate/Market and Network Governance: Shifting Spaces for Gender Equity in Education." *Gender, Work and Organization* 18 (5): 443–465.

Blackmore, J. (2013) "A Feminist Critical Perspective on Educational Leadership." *International Journal of Leadership in Education* 16 (2): 139–154.

Blackmore, J. and Sachs, J. (2007) *Performing and Reforming Leaders: Gender, Educational Restructuring and Organisational Change.* Albany: State University of New York.

Blackmore, J. and Sawers, N. (2015) "Executive Power and Scaled-up Gender Subtexts in Australian Entrepreneurial Universities." *Gender and Education* 27 (3): 320–337.

BMI Global (2017) https://bmiglobaled.com/Market-Reports/Vietnam/education. Accessed 16th November, 2021.

Bokova, I. (2010) *A New Humanism for the 21st Century* | United Nations Educational, Scientific and Cultural Organization. unesco.org. Accessed 17th August, 2021.

Bondestam, F. and Lundqvist, M. (2020) "Sexual Harassment in Higher Education – A Systematic Review." *European Journal of Higher Education* 10 (4): 379–419.

Brittan, A. (1989) *Masculinity and Power.* Oxford: Basil Blackwell.

Brooks, L. (2021) https://www.theguardian.com/society/2021/sep/02/protesters-against-transgender-rights-changes-boo-nicola-sturgeon. Accessed 10th September, 2021.

Brower, A. and James, A. (2020) "Research Performance and Age Explain Less than Half of the Gender Pay Gap in New Zealand Universities." *PLoS One* 15 (1): 1–13.

Brown, P. (2022) https://www.hepi.ac.uk/wp-content/uploads/2016/09/STRICTLY-EMBARGOED-UNTIL-22-SEPT-Hepi-Report-88-FINAL-1.pdf. Accessed 18th January, 2022.

Brownstein, R. (2020) https://www.theatlantic.com/politics/archive/2020/10/millennials-and-gen-z-will-soon-dominate-us-elections/616818/. Accessed 26th October, 2021.

Burkinshaw, P. and White, K. (2017) "Fixing the Women or Fixing Universities: Women in HE Leadership." *Administrative Science* Special Issue 7 (3): 1–14.

Butler, J. (1990) *Gender Trouble: Feminism and the Subversion of Identity*. New York: Routledge.

Butler, J. (2005) *Giving an Account of Oneself*. New York: Fordham University Press.

Butler-Bowden, T. (2017) *50 Philosophy Classics*. London: Nicholas Brealey Publishing.

Butrymowicz, S. (2020) https://www.nbcnews.com/news/education/crisis-looming-u-s-colleges-not-just-because-pandemic-n1235338. Accessed 20th November, 2021.

Campbell, P. (2018) "Editorial." *Nature* 554: 403–404.

Carvalho, T. (2011) "Shaping the "New" Academic Profession: Tensions and Contradictions." In G. Neave and A. Amarak (eds.) *Higher Education in Portugal 1974–2009: A Nation, A Generation*. Amsterdam: Springer.

Carvalho, T. and Machado, M. (2011) "Senior Management in Higher Education." In B. Bagilhole and K. White (eds.) *Gender, Power and Management: A Cross Cultural Analysis of Higher Education*, pp. 90–109. London: Palgrave Macmillan.

Carvalho, T. and de Lourdes Machado-Taylor, M. (2017) "The Exceptionalism of Women Rectors." In K. White and P. O'Connor (eds.) *Gendered Success in Higher Education: Global Perspectives*, pp. 111–132. London: Palgrave Macmillan.

Clark, R. (2020) https://www.spectator.co.uk/article/university-challenge-the-next-education-crisis. Accessed 18th November, 2021.

Cockburn, C. (1991) *In the Way of Women: Men's Resistance to Sex Equality in Organisations* London: Macmillan.

Collier, S. (2021) https://www.topuniversities.com/student-info/student-finance/how-much-does-it-cost-study-europe. Accessed 20th November, 2021.

Collinson, D. L. (2019) "Critical Leadership Studies: Exploring the Dialectics of Leadership." In R. E. Riggio (ed.) *What's Wrong with Leadership? Improving Research and Practice*, 260–278. Abingdon, Oxon: Routledge.

Connell, R. W. (1994) "The State, Gender and Sexual Politics: Theory and Appraisal." In H. L. Radke and H. J. Stam (eds.) *Power/Gender*, pp. 136–173. London: Sage.

Connell, R. W. (1995) *Masculinities*. Cambridge: Polity Press.

Connell, R. W. (2002) *Gender*. Cambridge: Polity Press.

Connell, R. W. (2005) *Masculinities*, 2nd ed. Cambridge: Polity.

Cooper, R., Baird, M., Foley, M., and Oxenbridge, S. (2020) "Normative Collusion in the Industry Ecosystem: Explaining Women's Career Pathways and Outcomes in Investment Management." *Human Relations*, 10th August. DOI: 10.1177/0018726720942826.

Crenshaw, K. (1991) "Mapping the Margins Intersectionality, Identity Politics, and Violence against Women of Color." *Stanford Law Review* 43: 1241–1299.

Davies, D. and Al Jezeera Investigative Unit (2021) https://www.aljazeera.com/news/2021/10/19/oxford-professors-abused-position-with-sexist-and-drunken-conduct. Accessed 19th January, 2021.

DeLaquil, T. (2021) https://www.universityworldnews.com/post.php?story=20210719134249610. Accessed 30th December, 2021.

Deleuze, G. and Guattari, F. (1988) *A Thousand Plateaus*. Trans. B. Massumi. London: Athone.

Deloitte Global Millennial and Gen Z Survey (2021) https://www2.deloitte.com/xe/en/pages/about-deloitte/articles/millennialsurvey.html. Accessed 22nd October, 2021.

De Vries, J. and Binns, J. (2018) *Sponsorship: Creating Career Opportunities for Women in Higher Education*. Canberra, Australia. https://www.universitiesaustralia.edu.au/UAEW/SponsorGuide.

De Vries, J. and Van Den Brink, M. (2016) 'Transformative Gender Interventions: Linking and Extending Theory and Practice using the "Bifocal Approach"'. *Equality, Diversity and Inclusion: An International Journal* 35 (7–8): 429–448.

Donegan, M. (2021) https://www.theguardian.com/commentisfree/2021/oct/31/sexual-assault-us-colleges-officials-must-listen?CMP=Share_iOSApp_Other. Accessed 20th December, 2021.

Eagly, A. H. and Carli, L. E. (2007) "Leadership." *Harvard Business Review*, September, pp. 63–71.

EC (2021a) *She Figures, Policy Briefs*. KI0721083ENN.en.pdf. Accessed 7th December 2021.

EC (2021b) *She Figures 2021 Gender in Research and Innovation Statistics and Indicators*. KI0221406ENN.en(1).pdf. Accessed 7th December 2021.

EC (2021c) *Horizon Europe Guidance on Gender Equality Plans*. KI0221806ENN.en (1).pdf. Accessed 3rd December 2021.

Educate Inspire (2019) https://educateinspirechange.org/how-many-people-of-the-world-have-a-college-degree/. Accessed 13th November, 2021.

Edwards, L. (2018) https://www.heritage.org/progressivism/commentary/what-americans-must-know-about-socialism. Accessed 30th October, 2021.

El-Alayli, A., Hansen-Brown, A. A., and Ceynar, M. (2018) "Dancing Backwards in High Heels: Female Professors Experience More Work Demands and Special Favour Requests." *Sex Roles* 79 (3–4): 136–150.

Equality Tribunal Report (2014) DEC-E2014-078. https://www.workplacerelations.ie/en/Cases/2014/November/DEC-E2014-078.html

Esterman, T. Pruvot, E. B., Kupriyanova, V., and Stoyanova, H. (2020) *The Impact of the Covid-19 Crisis on University Funding in Europe*. Brussels: European University Association.

European Commission (2021) Horizon Europe Guidance on Gender Equality Plans (GEPs), Brussels: EU.

Feng, J. (2021) https://supchina.com/2021/08/26/a-chinese-university-seems-to-be-making-a-list-of-lgbt-students-no-one-knows-what-it-will-do-with-the-information/. Accessed 27th August 2021.

Ferber, A. L. (2018) "Are You Willing to Die for This Work? Public Targeted Online Harassment in Higher Education." *Gender and Society* 32 (3): 301–320.

Ferguson, K. E. (1984) *The Feminist Case Against Bureaucracy*. Philadelphia: Temple University Press.

Ferlie, E., Musselin, C., and Andresani, G. (2008) "The Steering of Higher Education Systems: A Public Management Perspective." *Higher Education* 56: 325–348.

Ferretti, F., Guimaraes Pereira, A., Vertesy, D., and Hardeman, S. (2018) "Research Excellence Indicators: Time to Reimagine the 'Making of'." *Science and Public Policy* 45 (5): 731–741.

Filardo, G., da Graca, B., Sass, D. M., Pollock, B. D., Smith, E. B., and Martinez, M. A. M. (2016) "Trends and Comparison of Female First Authorship in High Impact Medical Journals' (1994–2014)." *British Medical Journal* 352: 1.i847.

Fitzgerald, D. (2012) "Education and Irish Economic Development." Paper presented at Investment in Education Fifty Years on, Joint Seminar by School of Education, TCD and Economic and Social Research Institute, TCD, Dublin.

Fitzgerald, T. (2018) "Looking Good and Being Good: Women Leaders in Higher Education in Australia and New Zealand." *Education Sciences: Special Issue Gender and Leadership* 8 (2): 54. DOI: 10.3390/educsci8020054.

Fitzgerald, D. and Black, G. (2020) https://www.wsws.org/en/articles/2020/10/23/soci-o23.html. Accessed 10th September, 2021.

Foley, M., Oxenbridge, S., and Cooper, R. (2020) 'I'll Never Be One of the Boys': Gender Harassment of Women Working as Pilots and Automotive Tradespeople'. *Gender, Work and Organisation* doi:10.1111/gwao.12443.

Foucault, M. (1984) *The History of Sexuality: Vol 1. An Introduction*. London: Penguin.

Foucault, M. (1991) "On the Geneology of Ethics: An Overview of Work in Progress." In P. Rabinow (ed.) *Technologies of Self: A Seminar with Michel Foucault*. London: Tavistock.

Franzway, S., Court, D., and Connell, R. W. (1989) *Staking a Claim; Feminism, Bureaucracy and the State*. Sydney: Allen & Unwin.

French, D. (2020) https://frenchpress.thedispatch.com/p/the-legal-promise-and-sobering-reality. Accessed 10th September, 2021.

French, H. W. (2021) https://thefrontierpost.com/chinas-culture-wars-are-just-getting-started/. Accessed 20th September, 2021.

Fuller, K. and Stevenson, H. (2018) "Global Education Reform: Understanding the Movement." *Educational Review* 71 (1): 1–4.

Galant, M. and Agarwala, T. (2021. "Silencing Women's Voices: An Ethnographic Perspective from India and the UAE." In P. O'Connor and K. White (eds.) *Gender, Power and Higher Education in a Globalised World: Where to Now?* 117–138. Cham, Switzerland: Palgrave Macmillan.

Gallagher, M. (2012) *Academic Armageddon*. Dublin: Liffey Press.

GCPEA (2014) https://protectingeducation.org/news/soldiers-in-schools-the-impact-of-military-occupations-on-education/. Accessed 15th November, 2021.

Giroux, H. A. (2002) "Neoliberalism, Corporate Culture and the Promise of Higher Education: The University as a Democratic Public Sphere." *Harvard Educational Review* 72 (4): 425–463.

Giroux, H. A. (2011) "Beyond the Swindle of the Corporate University." In M. Bailey and D. Freedman (eds.) *The Assault on Universities*, pp. 145–156. London: Pluto.

Gohain, M. P. (2017) https://timesofindia.indiatimes.com/city/delhi/free-speech-in-indian-universities-under-threat-amnesty-international-india/articleshow/57296421.cms. Accessed 20th September, 2021.

Goldin, C. and Rouse, C. (1997) "Orchestrating Impartiality: The Impact of 'Blind' Auditions on Female Musicians NBER Working Paper No. 5903." http://www.nber.org/papers/w5903

Goal Atlas (2021) https://goalatlas.com/cascade-model-of-strategy/. Accessed 12th November, 2022.

Graham, G. (2008) *Universities: The Recovery of an Idea*, revised ed. Exeter: Imprint Academic.

Graves, A., Rowell, R., and Hunsicker, E. (2019) *An Impact Evaluation of the Athena Swan Charter*. Ortus: Loughborough University. www.ecu.ac.uk/wp-content/uploads/2019/08/Athena-SWAN-Impact-Evaluation-2019.docx

Grint, K. (2011) "A History of Leadership." In A. Bryman, D. Collinson, K. Grint, B. Jackson, and M. Uhl-Bien (eds.) *The Sage Handbook of Leadership*, pp. 3–14. London: Sage.

Grove, J. (2021) "UCU: Sexual Harassment is Rife as UK Universities 'Protect Predators'." *Times Higher Education*, 22nd December.

Grummell, B., Lynch, K., and Devine, D. (2009) "Appointing Senior Managers in Education: Homosociability, Local Logics and Authenticity in the Selection Process." *Educational Management, Administration and Leadership* 37 (3): 329–349.

Gunter, H. (2010) "A Sociological Approach to Educational Leadership." *British Journal of the Sociology of Education* 31 (4): 519–527.

Hall, E. (1976) Beyond Culture. New York: Anchor Books Doubleday.

Hall, R. (2021a) https://www.theguardian.com/education/2021/oct/09/cambridge-colleges-accused-exploiting-gig-economy-tutors. Accessed 9th October, 2021.

Hall, R. (2021b) https://www.theguardian.com/education/2021/oct/01/bristol-university-sacks-professor-accused-of-antisemitic-comments?CMP=Share_iOSApp_Other. Accessed 1st October, 2021.

Hall, R. (2021c) https://www.theguardian.com/uk-news/2021/apr/27/conservative-mps-call-bristol-university-a-hotbed-of-antisemitism. Accessed 9th August, 2021.

Hall, R. (2021d) https://www.theguardian.com/education/2021/oct/09/cambridge-colleges-accused-exploiting-gig-economy-tutors?CMP=Share_iOSApp_Other. Accessed 11th January, 2022.

Hall, B. and Tandon, R. (eds.) (2021) *Socially Responsible Higher Education: International Perspectives on Knowledge Democracy*. Leiden, The Netherlands: Koninklijke Brill NV.

Halliday, J. (2021) https://www.theguardian.com/education/2021/sep/28/students-staff-durham-university-apathy-complain-bullying?CMP=Share_iOSApp_Other. Accessed 15th October, 2021.

Haringsma, P. (2021) https://www.universityworldnews.com/post.php?story=20210908100721929. Accessed 10th September, 2021.

Hartmann, H. (1981) "The Unhappy Marriage of Marxism and Feminism: Towards a More Progressive Union". In L. Sargent (ed.) *Women and Revolution*, pp. 1–41. Boston: South End Press.

Harvard University (2021) https://finance.harvard.edu/financial-overview. Accessed 2nd November, 2021.

Hazelkorn, E. (2015) *Rankings and the Reshaping of Higher Education: The Battle for World Class Excellence.* (2nd ed.). Basingstoke: Palgrave Macmillan.

Hazelkorn, E. (2018) "Introduction: The Geopolitics of Rankings." In E. Hazelkorn (ed.) *Global Rankings and the Geopolitics of Higher Education*, pp. 1–20. London: Routledge.

HEA (2016) *Report of the Expert Group: HEA National Review of Gender Equality in Irish Higher Educational Institutions.* http://hea.ie/assets/uploads/2017/04/hea_review_of_gender_equality_in_irish_higher_education.pdf. Accessed 15th January, 2017.

Hearn, J. (1998) *The Violences of Men.* London: Sage.

Hearn, J. (2021) "Men and Masculinities in Academia: Towards Gender-sensitive Perspectives, Processes, Policies and Practices." In E. Drew and S. Canavan (eds.) *The Gender Sensitive University: A Contradiction in Terms*, pp. 97–109. Oxon: Routledge.

Heijstra, T. O'Connor, P., and Rafnsdottir, L. G. (2013) "Explaining gender inequality in Iceland: What Makes the Difference?." *European Journal of Higher Education*, 3(4): 324–331.

Heijstra, T. M., Einarsdóttir, Þ., Pétursdóttir, G. M., and Steinþórsdóttir, F. S. (2017) "Testing the Concept of Academic Housework in a European Setting: Part of Academic CareerMaking or Gendered Barrier to the Top?" *European Educational Research Journal* 16 (2–3): 200–214.

Helena (2020) https://disorient.co/intersectional-feminist-leadership/. Accessed 29th January, 2022.

Herschberg, C., Benschop, Y., and van den Brink, M. (2019) "The Peril of Potential: Gender Practices in the Recruitment and Selection of Early Career Researchers." In A. Murgia and B. Poggio (eds.) *Gender and Precarious Careers*, pp. 111–142. Oxon: Routledge.

HESA (2021) https://www.hesa.ac.uk/news/19-01-2021/sb259-higher-education-staff-statistics. Accessed 2nd November, 2021.

Hewett, S. A. (2013) *Forget a Mentor, Find a Sponsor: The New Way to Fast-Track Your Career.* Harvard: Harvard Business School Publishing.

Higher Educational Authority (Ireland) (2021) *HEA Institutional Staff Profiles by Gender 2021* https://hea.ie/assets/uploads/2019/07/Higher-Education-Institutional-Staff-Profiles-by-Gender-2021.pdf. Accessed 15th January 2022.

Hill Collins, P. and Bilge, S. (2020) *Intersectionality* (2nd ed.). Cambridge: Polity.

Hodgins, M., MacCurtain, S., and Mannix MacNamara, P. (2020) "Power and Inaction: Why Organisations Fail to Address Workplace Bullying." *International Journal of Workplace Health Management* 13 (3): 265–290.

Hodgins, M. and O'Connor, P. (2021) "Progress, But at the Expense of Male Power? Institutional Resistance to Gender Equality in an Irish University." *Frontiers of Sociology* July, 6: 696446.

Hommel, M. J. and Hommel, U. (2020) https://www.universityworldnews.com/post.php?story=20201211110620766. Accessed 15th December, 2021.

Husu, L. (2001) *Sexism, Support and Survival in Academia*. Helsinki: Helsinki University.

Husu, L. (2021) "Gender and Excellence in the Research Funding Landscape." Keynote speaker at EWORA Webinar, 18th October.

Hutton, W. (2021) https://www.theguardian.com/commentisfree/2021/dec/26/which-philosphy-helps-us-confront-crises-that-beset-us. Accessed 12th January, 2022.

Ibarra, H., Carter, N., and Silva, C. (2010) "Why Men Still Get More Promotions Than Women." *Harvard Business Review* 126: 80–85.

Igiebor, O. T. (2021) "Gender Equity Policy and Women in Academic Positions in Nigeria." PhD thesis submitted to the University of Auckland, New Zealand.

Institute of Public Affairs (2019) https://ipa.org.au/publications-ipa/opinion/new-research-confirms-free-speech-crisis-at-australias-universities. Accessed 10th September, 2021.

IRC (Irish Research Council) (2018) "Policies and Practice to Promote Gender Equality and the Integration of Gender in Research." http://research.ie/assets/uploads/2016/06/final-_progress_report_on_gender.pdf. Accessed 20th July, 2018.

Jacobs, H. H. and Alcock, M. H. (2017) Bold Moves for Schools. London: ASCD.

Jeffreys, B. (2021a) https://www.bbc.com/news/education-58841887. Accessed 9th October, 2021.

Jeffreys, B. (2021b) https://www.bbc.com/news/education-59587275. Accessed 20th December, 2021.

Jones, O. (2021) https://www.theguardian.com/politics/2021/sep/20/eat-the-rich-why-millennials-and-generation-z-have-turned-their-backs-on-capitalism?CMP=Share_iOSApp_Other. Accessed 20th September, 2021.

Kennon, J. (2021) https://www.joshuakennon.com/the-six-common-biological-sexes-in-humans/. Accessed 17th July, 2019.

Kerr, C. (2001) The Uses of the University, (5th Edition). Cambridge: Harvard University Press.

Khan, J. (2021) https://nowthisnews.com/videos/politics/activist-janaya-future-khan-on-redefining-privilege. Accessed 16th January, 2021.

Knights, D. and Willmott, H. (1990) *Labour Process Theory*. London: Macmillan.

Krantz, L. (2022) https://www.bostonglobe.com/2022/01/30/metro/mental-health-top-concern-colleges-students-return-spring-semester/?et_rid=961390994&s_campaign=todaysheadlines:newsletter. Accessed 30th January, 2022.

Lama, T. and Joullie, J.-E. (2015) 'Casualization of Academics in the Australian Higher Education: Is Teaching Quality at Risk?' *Research in Higher Education*, 28: 1–11.

Lamont, M. (2009) *How Professors Think*. Cambridge: Harvard University Press.

Lawrie, E. (2021) https://www.bbc.com/news/education-58841887. Accessed 9th October, 2021.

Learmonth, M. and Morrell, K. (2017) "Is Critical Leadership Studies 'Critical'?" *Leadership* 13 (3): 257–271.

Lee, J. (2018) 'Passive Leadership and Sexual Harassment'. *Personnel Review* 47 (3): 594–612.

Le Feuvre, N., Bataille, P., Kradolfer, S., del Rio Carral, M., and Sautier, M. (2019) "The Gendered Diversification of Academic Career Paths in Comparative Perspective." In A. Murgia and B. Poggio (eds.) *Gender and Precarious Research Careers: A Comparative Analysis*, pp. 50–80. London: Routledge.

Legal Insurrection (2019) https://legalinsurrection.com/2019/09/left-wing-activists-stifling-free-speech-on-german-campuses-says-leading-professors-association/. Accessed 12th September, 2021.

Lemert, C. (1997) *Postmodernism Is Not What You Think*. London: Blackwell.

Levy, B.-H. (2003) *Sartre: The Philosopher of the Twentieth Century*. Cambridge: Polity.

Li, J. (2021) https://qz.com/2051550/china-will-teach-xi-jinping-thought-to-schoolchildren/. Accessed 25th August, 2021.

Lidington, D. (2019) https://www.gov.uk/government/news/universities-must-do-more-to-tackle-ethnic-disparity. Accessed 20th July, 2021.

Linkova, M., Atay, O., and Zulu, C. (2021) "Making the Right Choice: Discourses of Individualised Resonsibility in Higher Education." In P. O'Connor and K. White (eds.) *Gender, Power and Higher Education in a Globalised World: Where to Now?* pp. 71–92. Cham, Switzerland: Palgrave Macmillan.

Lipinsky, A. and Wroblewski, A. (2021) 'Revisiting Gender Equality Policy and the role of University Top Management'. In *Gender, Power and Higher Education in a Globalised World: Where to Now?*, pp. 163–186. London: Palgrave Macmillan.

Lipton, B. (2020) *Academic Women in Neoliberal Times*. Cham: Palgrave Macmillan.

Liu, J. (2021a) https://www.timeshighereducation.com/news/chinese-universities-ticked-ideological-education-gaps. Accessed 16th September, 2021.

Liu, J. (2021b) https://www.timeshighereducation.com/news/china-makes-mental-health-courses-compulsory-undergraduates. Accessed 10th January, 2022.

Liu, H. (2021c) *Redeeming Leadership: An Anti-Racist Feminist Intervention*. Bristol: Bristol University Press.

Lorin, J. and Kochkodin, B. (2020) https://www.inquirer.com/education/china-funding-us-colleges-universities-trade-tensions-20200207.html. Accessed 16th November, 2021.

Lumby, J. (2019) "Leadership and Power in Higher Education." *Studies in Higher Education* 44 (9): 1619–1629.

Lynch, K. (2006) "Neo-liberalism and Marketisation: The Implications for Higher Education." *European Educational Research Journal* 5 (1): 1–17.

Lynch, K. (2013) "New Managerialism, Neoliberalism and Ranking." *Ethics in Science and Environmental Politics* 13 (2): 141–153.

Lynch, K. (2014) "New Managerialism: The Impact on Education." *Concept* 5 (3): 1–11.

Lynch, K., Grummell, B., and Devine, D. (2012) *New Managerialism in Education: Commercialisation, Carelessness and Gender*. Basingstoke: Palgrave Macmillan.

Macaskill, A. (2012) "The Mental Health of University Students in the United Kingdom." *British Journal of Guidance and Counselling* 41 (4): 426–441.

Machin, D. and Whitehead, S. (2020) *International Schooling: The Teacher's Guide*. Bangkok: Pedagogue.

Mackay, F. (2011) "Conclusion: Towards a Feminist Institutionalism." In M. L. Krook and F. Mackay (eds.) *Gender, Politics and Institutions*, pp. 81–196. London: Palgrave Macmillan.

Mackay, F., Kenny, M., and Chappell, L. (2010) "New Institutionalism Through a Gender Lens: Towards a Feminist Institutionalism." *International Political Science Review* 31 (5): 573–588.

MacKinnon, C. A. (1989) *Towards a Feminist Theory of the State*. Harvard: Harvard University Press.

Manfredi, S., Grisoni, L., Handley, K., Nestor, R., and Cooke, F. (2014) *Gender and Higher Education Leadership: Researching the Careers of Top Management Programme Alumni*. London: Leadership Foundation for Higher Education.

Marginson, S. (2007) "The Public/Private Divide in Higher Education: A Global Revision." *Higher Education* 53: 307–333.

Martin, P. Y. (2003) "'Said and Done' versus 'Saying and Doing': Gendering Practices, Practicing Gender at Work." *Gender and Society* 17 (3): 342–366.

Martin, P. Y. (2006) "Practicing Gender at Work: Further Thoughts on Reflexivity." *Gender, Work and Organization* 13 (3): 254–276.

McConnell, K. (2018) "Labored Speech: Reconsidering How Communication Studies Works." *Review of Communication* 18 (2): 67–84.

McKay, R. and Fratzl, J. (2011) "A Cause of Failure in Addressing Workplace bullying: Trauma and the Employee." *International Journal of Business and Social Science* 2 (7): 13–27.

McNay, L. (2000) *Gender and Agency*. Cambridge: Polity.

Meyer, J. W., Ramirez, F. O., Frank, D. J., and Schoffer, E. (2007) "Higher Education as an Institution." In Gumport (ed.) *Sociology of Higher Education*, pp. 187–221. Baltimore, Maryland: John Hopkins University Press.

Miner, K. N., January, S. C., Dray, K. K., and Carter-Sowell, A. R. (2019) "Is It Always This Cold? Chilly Interpersonal Climates as a Barrier to the Well-Being of Early-Career Women in STEM." *Equality, Diversity and Inclusion: An International Journal* 38 (2): 226–245.

MIT Facts (2021) https://facts.mit.edu/operating-financials/. Accessed 2nd November, 2021.

Montes López, E. and O'Connor, P. (2019) "Micropolitics and Meritocracy: Improbable Bed Fellows?" Educational Management Administration and Leadership 47 (5): 678–693.

Mooney, G. (2021) https://thetab.com/uk/2021/01/22/the-governments-neglect-of-students-has-made-university-unbearable-i-wish-i-never-came-191472. Accessed 10th November, 2021.

Moran, J. (2021) https://www.timeshighereducation.com/depth/university-really-community?utm_source=newsletter&utm_medium=email&utm_campaign=editorial-daily&mc_cid=dee4782bcd. Accessed 18th December, 2021.

Moratti, S. (2021) "A Woman's Place is in the 'Home'? Gender-specific Hiring Patterns in Academia in Gender-equal Norway." *Journal of Sociology* 57 (4): 916–934.

Morley, L. (1999) *Organising Feminisms: The Micropolitics of the Academy*. New York: St Martin's Press.

Morley, L. (2005) "Sounds, Silences and Contradictions: Gender Equity in British Commonwealth Higher Education." *Australian Feminist Studies*, 20 (46): 109–119.

Morley, L. (2013) "The Rules of the Game: Women and the Leaderist Turn in Higher Education." *Gender and Education* 25 (1): 116–131.

Morley, L. (2014) "Lost Leaders: Women in the Global Academy." *Higher Education Research and Development* 33 (1): 114–128.

Morrison, N. (2021) https://www.forbes.com/sites/nickmorrison/2021/02/09/uk-universities-face-financial-loss-as-brexit-hits-eu-student-numbers/?sh=15a15569e2a8. Accessed 10th November, 2021.

Moss-Racusin, C. A., Dovidio, J. F., Brescoll, V. L., Graham, M. J., and Handelsman, J. (2012) "Science Faculty's Subtle Gender Biases Favor Male Students." *Proceedings of the National Academy of Sciences* 109 (41): 16474–16479.

Murgia, A. and Poggio, B. (eds.) (2019) *Gender and Precarious Research Careers: A Comparative Analysis*. London: Routledge.

Myklebust, J. P. (2015) https://www.universityworldnews.com/post.php?story=20150313224103532. Accessed 15th October, 2021.

Myklebust, J. P. (2017) https://www.universityworldnews.com/post.php?story=20170908102945748. Accessed 15th October, 2021.

Naezer, M., van den Brink, M., and Benschop, Y. (2019) "Harassment in Dutch Academia: Exploring Manifestations, Facilitating Factors, Effects and Solutions." https://www.lnvh.nl/uploads/moxiemanager/Scientific_Harassment_LNVH_presentatie_Marieke_van_den_Brink.pdf.

Neate, R. (2021) https://www.theguardian.com/business/2021/oct/09/oxford-colleges-wealth-boost-exposes-academia-haves-have-nots?CMP=Share_iOSApp_Other Accessed 2nd November, 2021.

Nielsen, M. W. (2016) "Limits to Meritocracy? Gender in Academic Recruitment and Selection Processes." *Science and Public Policy* 43 (3): 386–399.

Nietzsche, F. (1973) *Beyond Good and Evil*. Harmondsworth: Penguin.

Ni Laoire, C., Linehan, C., Archibong, U., Picardi, I., and Uden, M. (2021) "Context Matters: Problematising the Policy-practice Interface in the Enactment of Gender Equality Action Plans in 'Universities'." *Gender, Work and Organization* 28: 575–593.

Nyomi, N. (2021) "Strengthening the Impact of International Education upon the Pillars of Access, Diversity, Equity, Inclusion, and Justice." *Educational Digest International*, 25th June.

Oacha, P. and Blanch, J. M. (2019) "Psychosocial Wellbeing at Work: Reasons to Invest in Healthy Employees and Workplaces." In P. Oacha, M-T. Lepeley and P. Essens (eds.) *Wellbeing for Sustainability in the Global Workplace*. London: Routledge.

O'Brien, K., Selboe, E., and Hayward, B. M. (2018) "Exploring Youth Activism on Climate Change: Dutiful, Disruptive and Dangerous Dissent." *Ecology and Society* 23 (3). https://www.ecologyandsociety.org/vol23/iss3/art42/

O'Connor, P. (2012) "Reflections on the Public Intellectual's Role in a Gendered Society." In M. P. Corcoran (ed.) *Reflections on Crisis: The Role of the Public Intellectual*, pp. 55–73. Dublin: Royal Irish Academy.

O'Connor, P. (2014) *Management and Gender in Higher Education*. Manchester: Manchester University Press.

O'Connor, P. (2015) "Good Jobs - but Places for Women?" *Gender and Education* 27 (3): 304–319.

O'Connor, P. (2018) "Gender Imbalance in Senior Positions in Higher Education: What Is the Problem? What Can Be Done?" *Policy Reviews in Higher Education* 3 (1): 28–50.

O'Connor, P. (2020) "Why Is It So Difficult to Reduce Gender Inequality in Male dominated Higher Education Organisations? A Feminist Institutional Perspective." *Interdisciplinary Science Reviews* 45 (2): 207–228.

O'Connor, P. (2022) "Probationary Citizens and the Patriarchal Bargain in Science, Technology, Engineering and Mathematics in a Case Study Irish University."

O'Connor, P. and Barnard, S. (2021) "Problematising Excellence as a Legitimating Discourse." In P. O'Connor and K. White (eds.) *Gender, Power and Higher Education in a Globalised World*, 47–69. Cham, Switzerland: Palgrave Macmillan.

O'Connor, P. and Goransson, A. (2015) "Constructing or Rejecting the Notion of Other in Senior University Management: The Cases of Ireland and Sweden." *EMAL* 43 (2): 323–340.

O'Connor, P. and O'Hagan, C. (2016) "Excellence in University Academic Staff Evaluation: A Problematic Reality?" *Studies in Higher Education* 41 (11): 1943–1957.

O'Connor, P., O'Hagan, C., Myers, E. S., Baisner, L., Apostolov, G., Topuzova, I., Saglamer, G., Tan, M. G., and Caglayan, H. (2019a) "Mentoring and Sponsorship in Higher Educational Institutions: Men's Invisible Advantage in STEM?" *Higher Education Research and Development* 39 (4): 1–14.

O'Connor, P., Hodgins M., Woods D. R., Wallwaey, E, Palmen R., Van Den Brink, M., and Schmidt, E. K. (2021) "Organisational Characteristics that Facilitate Gender Based Violence and Harassment in Higher Education?" *Administrative Sciences* 11: 138. DOI: 10.3390/ADMINSCI11040138.

O'Connor, P., Martin, P. Y., Carvalho, T., O'Hagan, C., Veronesi, L., Mich, O., Saglamer, G., Tan, M. G., Caglayan, H. (2019b) "Leadership Practices by Senior Position Holders in Higher Educational Research Institutes: Stealth Power in Action?" *Leadership* 15 (6): 722–743.

O'Connor, P., Montes López, E., O'Hagan, C., Wolffram, A., Aye, M., Chizzola, V., Mich, O., et al. (2020) "Micro-political Practices in Higher Education: A Challenge to Excellence as a Rationalising Myth?" *Critical Studies in Education* 61 (2): 195–211.

O'Connor, P. and White, K. (2021a) "Power, Legitimating Discourses and Institutional Resistance to Gender Equality in Higher Education." In P. O'Connor and K. White (eds.) *Gender, Power and Higher Education in a Globalised World*, pp. 187–207. London: Palgrave Macmillan.

O'Connor, P. and White, K. (2021b) "Gender Equality in Higher Education: The Slow Pace of Change." In P. O'Connor and K. White (eds.) *Gender, Power and Higher Education in a Globalised World* pp. 1–23. London: Palgrave Macmillan.

OECD (2012) *Closing the Gender Gap: Act Now!*. Available at www.oecd.org/gender/closingthegap.htm/. Accessed 19th December, 2012.

OECD (2021) *Education at a Glance 2021.* https://www.oecd.org/education/education-at-a-glance/. Accessed 1st December, 2021.

O'Hagan, C. O'Connor, P., et al. (2019) "Perpetuating Academic Capitalism and Maintaining Gender Orders through Career Practices in STEM." *Critical Studies in Education* 60 (2): 205–225.

Okwanga, M. (2021) https://inews.co.uk/news/long-reads/eton-privilege-nurtured-uk-power-structures-systemic-racism-forged-952620. Accessed 12th February, 2022.

O'Leary, M. and Wood, P. (2018) "Reimagining Teaching Excellence: Why Collaboration, Rather than Competition, Holds the Key to Improving Teaching and Learning in Higher Education." *Educational Review* 71 (1): 122–139.

O'Meara, K., Kuvaeva, A., Nyunt, G., Waugman, C., and Jackson, R. (2017) "Asked More Often: Gender Differences in Faculty Workload in Research Universities and the Work Interactions That Shape Them." *American Educational Research Journal* 54 (6): 1154–1186.

O'Mullane. M. (2021) "Developing a Theoretical Framework for Exploring the Institutional Responses to the Athena SWAN Charter in Higher Educational Institutions - A Feminist Institutional Perspective." *Irish Journal of Sociology* 29 (2): 215–235.

Ovseiko, P. V., Pololi, L. H., Edmunds, L. D., Civian, J. T., Daly, M., and Buchan, A. M.. (2019) "Creating a More Supportive and Inclusive University Culture." *Interdisciplinary Science Reviews* 44 (2): 166–191.

Oxford Anti-Casualisation Network (2021) https://twitter.com/oxfordantics. Accessed 10th January, 2022.

Parfitt, S. (2018) "Academic Casualisation in the UK." *International Labor and Working-Class History* 93: 221–227.

Parker, M. (2002) "'The romance of lonely dissent': intellectuals, professionals and the McUniversity." In M. Dent and S. Whitehead (eds.) *Managing Professional Identities.* London: Routledge.

Perez-Encinas, A. and Rodriguez-Pomeda, J. (2018) "International Students' Perceptions of Their Needs When Going Abroad: Services on Demand." *Journal of Studies in International Education* 22 (1): 20–36.

Peterson, M. W. (2007) "The Study of Colleges and Universities as Organisations." In P. Gumport (ed.) *Sociology of Higher Education*, pp. 147–186. Baltimore, Maryland: John Hopkins University Press.

Peterson, H. and Jordansson, B. (2017) "Gender Equality as a Core Academic Value: Undoing Gender in a 'Non-Traditional' Swedish University." In K. White and P. O'Connor (eds.) *Gendered Success in Higher Education: Global Perspectives*, pp. 27–48. London: Palgrave Macmillan.

Petter, O. (2018) "More than 10% of Students 'Use their Bodies' to Pay for University Fees When Facing Emergency Costs, Study Claims." https://www.independent.co.uk/life-style/students-sell-sex-money-university-fees-costs-photos-online-a8451241.html. Accessed 3rd January, 2022.

Pfeffer, J. and Williams, L. (2021) https://www.mckinsey.com/industries/health-care-systems-and-services/our-insights/mental-health-in-the-workplace-the-coming-revolution?cid=other-eml-alt-mip-mck&hdpid=17550184-5e75-49bb-aa4e-692da090b94b&hctky=12628122&hlkid=880f7bfb9fea490e946b458180f3f604. Accessed 10th December, 2021.

Philstar (2021) https://www.philstar.com/headlines/2021/09/27/2130322/young-female-activists-driving-gender-equality-asia-pacific-report. Accessed 1st October, 2021.

Phipps, A. (2020). "Reckoning Up: Sexual Harassment and Violence in the Neoliberal University." *Gender and Education* 32 (2): 227–243.

Pinsent Masons (2021) https://www.pinsentmasons.com/out-law/analysis/universities-tackling-gender-pay-gap-local-global-levels#:~:text=The%20universities%20which%20have%20reported,Statistics%20(ONS)%20in%202020. Accessed 13th January, 2022.

Power, A. (2021) "Understanding Leadership in Higher Education as a Tool for Change in Gender Relations." In E. Drew and S. Canavan (eds.) *The Gender Sensitive University: A Contradiction in Terms*, pp. 140–153. Oxon: Routledge.

Pullen, A., Rhodes, C., McEwen, C., and Liu, H. (2021) "Radical Politics, Intersectionality and Leadership for Diversity in Organisations." https://www.emerald.com/insight/content/doi/10.1108/MD-02-2019-0287/full/html. Accessed 12th November, 2021.

Ramazanoglu, C. (ed.) (1993) *Up Against Foucault: Exploration of Some Tensions between Foucault and Feminism*. London: Routledge.

Redden, E. (2017) https://www.insidehighered.com/quicktakes/2017/09/18/hong-kong-university-heads-condemn-%E2%80%98abuses%E2%80%99-free-speech. Accessed 12th September, 2021.

Renton, D. (2021) https://www.theguardian.com/commentisfree/2021/may/22/the-free-speech-law-will-make-university-debate-harder-not-easier?CMP=Share_iOSApp_Other. Accessed 25th July, 2021.

Response to Recent Comments by Prof. David Miller (2021) https://recentstatementsbyprofdavidmillerconcerningbristoluniversity.wordpress.com/. Accessed 15th October, 2021.

Right Question Institute (2020) https://rightquestion.org/. Accessed 2nd December 2020.

Roberts, R., Sanders, T., Myers, E., and Smith, D. (2010) "Participation in Sex Work: Student's Views." *Sex Education* 10 (2): 145–156.

Roser, M. and Ortiz-Ospina, E. (2013) https://ourworldindata.org/tertiary-education. Accessed 18th November, 2021.

Ross, J. (2021) https://www.timeshighereducation.com/news/pandemic-job-losses-accelerating-australia?utm_source=newsletter&utm_medium=email&utm_campaign=editorial-daily&mc_cid=998bcab546. Accessed 13th September, 2021.

Ryan, M. and Haslam, S. (2007) "The Glass Cliff: Exploring the Dynamics Surrounding the Appointment of Women to Precarious Leadership Positions." *The Academy of Management Review* 32 (2): 549–572.

Sainato, M. (2021) https://www.theguardian.com/education/2021/feb/24/us-universities-protests-cuts-tuition-right-to-unionize. Accessed 25th February, 2021.

Sanz-Menéndez, L., Cruz-Castro, L., and Alva, K. (2013) "Time to Tenure in Spanish Universities: An Event History Analysis." PLoS ONE 8 (10): e77028.

Sarrouh, M. (2021) https://www.thestar.com/news/gta/2021/08/19/report-details-covids-devastating-financial-effects-on-canadian-universities-and-colleges.html. Accessed 25th November, 2021.

Sarup, M. (1993) *Post-Structuralism and Postmodernism* (2nd ed). London: Harvester-Wheatsheaf.

Schein, V. E., Mueller, R., Lituchy, T., and Liu, J. (1996) "Think Manager-Think Male; a Global Phenomenon?" *Journal of Organizational Behaviour* 17: 33–41.

Schmich, M. T. and Chicago Tribune (1990) https://www.chicagotribune.com/news/ct-xpm-1990-12-09-9004110950-story.html. Accessed 23rd January, 2021.

Schwartz, V. and Kay, J. (2009) "The Crisis in College and University Mental Health." *Psychiatric Times*, July 2009. https://www.researchgate.net/profile/Victor-Schwartz/publication/265182028. Accessed 15th January, 2022.

Scott, C. (2018) https://www.universityworldnews.com/post.php?story=20180411071640489. Accessed 15th September, 2021.

Scott-Bauman, A. and Perfect, C. (2021a) *Freedom of Speech in Universities: Islam, Charities and Counter-Terrorism*. London: Routledge.

Scott-Bauman, A. and Perfect, C. (2021b) "Free Speech on Campus: Universities Need to Create 'Safe But Critical' Spaces for Debate – Here's How They Can Do It." *The Conversation*. https://theconversation.com/free-speech-on-campus-universities-need-to-create-safe-but-critical-spaces-for-debate-heres-how-they-can-do-it-157013. Accessed 12th October, 2021.

Sexual Experiences Survey (2020) *The Active* Consent/Union of Students in Ireland Sexual Experiences Survey 2020*. Union of Students in Ireland.

Sharma, Y. (2019) https://www.universityworldnews.com/post.php?story=20190712071639621. Accessed 15th September, 2021.

Shepherd, S. (2017) "Why are there So Few Female Leaders in Higher Education: A Case of Structure or Agency." *Management in Education* 31 (2): 82–87.

Siddique, H. (2021) https://www.theguardian.com/society/2021/jun/05/stonewall-trans-debate-toxic-gender-identity. Accessed 3rd August, 2021.

Sidelil, L. T. (2020) "Gender Inequality in the Science and Technology Universities of Ethiopia: Policy Representations and the Experiences of Women." PhD thesis submitted to RMIT, Australia.

Sinclair, A. (2013) "A material dean." *Leadership* 9 (3): 436–443.

Sinclair, A. (2014) "A Feminist Case for Leadership." In J. Damousi, K. Rubenstein, and M. Tomsic (eds.) *Diversity in Leadership: Australian Women, Past and Present*, pp. 17–38. Canberra: ANU Press. Access at http://press.anu.edu.au/titles/diversity-in-leadership/

Slaughter, S. and Rhoades, G. (2010) *Academic Capitalism and the New Economy: Markets, States and Higher Education*. Baltimore: John Hopkins University Press.

Smail, A. and Waye, F. (2019) *Changing the Culture: Tackling Gender Based Violence, Harassment and Hate Crime: Two Years on. Results of a Sector Wide Survey to Review Progress.* Universities UK. Changing the culture: two years on. universitiesuk.ac.uk.

Smircich, L. and Morgan, G. (1982) "Leadership: The Management of Meaning." *Journal of Applied Behavioural Science* 18: 257–273.

Smyth, J. (2017) *The Toxic University. Zombie Leadership. Academic Rock Stars and Neoliberal Ideology.* London: Palgrave.

Sotoudah, N. and Stefano, E. (2021) https://eurasianet.org/free-speech-risky-as-china-keeps-close-tabs-on-its-overseas-students. Accessed 2nd October, 2021.

Statista (2019) https://www.statista.com/statistics/721304/oxford-university-annual-income/. Accessed 3rd November, 2021.

Steinporsdottir, F., Smidt, T. B., Petursdottir, G. M., Einarsdottir, P., and Le Feuvre, N. (2018) "New Managerialism in the Academy: Gender Bias and Precarity." *Gender, Work and Organization* 26: 124–139.

Strid, S. (2021) https://unisafe-gbv.eu/blog/on-the-importance-of-addressing-gender-based-violence-in-universities-and-research-organisations/. Accessed 23rd January 2021.

Study.eu (2020) https://www.study.eu/article/study-in-europe-for-free-or-low-tuition-fees. Accessed 19th March, 2021.

Sümer, S., O'Connor, P., and Le Feuvre, N. (2020) "The Contours of Gendered Academic Citizenship." In S. Sümer (ed.). *Gendered Academic Citizenship: Issues and Experiences*, pp. 1–36. Cham: Palgrave Macmillan.

Support David Miller (2021) https://supportmiller.org/educators-and-researchers. Accessed 15th October, 2021.

SWG GRI. (2020) *Sexual Harassment in the Higher Education Sector. National policies and measure in EU Member States and Associated Countries.*

Tapia, A. and Polonskala, A. (2018) *The 5 Disciplines of Inclusive Leaders: Unleashing the Power of All of Us.* Los Angeles: Korn Ferry.

Tepe, F. F. (2019) "Women's Discrimination in Engineering Faculties: A View From Turkey." *Anemon* 7 (3): 199–209.

THE (2020) The UN Impact Ratings. Accessed 15th November, 2021 https://www.timeshighereducation.com/rankings/impact/2020/overall#!/page/0/length/25/sort_by/rank/sort_order/asc/cols/undefined

THE (2021) *University Impact Ratings - United Nations Sustainable Development Goals* Impact Rankings 2021 | Times Higher Education (THE).

The Guardian (2019) https://www.theguardian.com/education/2019/jul/05/uk-universities-condemned-for-failure-to-tackle-racism. Accessed 5th July, 2021.

The Guardian (2021) https://www.theguardian.com/artanddesign/2021/may/29/ai-weiwei-on-colonialism-and-statues-churchill-china-and-covid. Accessed 29th May, 2021.

Tiernan, A. and O'Connor, P. (2020) "Perspectives on *Power Over* and *Power To*." *Journal of Political Power* 13 (1): 86–105.

Tong, R. (1994) *Feminist Thought.* London: Routledge.

Trines, S. (2017) https://wenr.wes.org/2017/11/education-in-vietnam. Accessed 17th November, 2021.

Tyler, T. (2005) "Introduction: Legitimating Ideologies." *Social Justice Research* 18: 210–215.

Tzanakou, C. and R. Pearce (2019) "Moderate Feminism within or Against the Neoliberal University? The Example of Athena SWAN." *Gender, Work and Organization,* 26: 1191–1211.

University College Union (UCU) (2021) *Eradicating Sexual Violence in Tertiary Education.* London: UCU.

United Nations (UN) (2021) *Transforming Our World: The 2030 Agenda for Sustainable Development.* | Department of Economic and Social Affairs. un.org

University of Leicester (2021) *Student Sex Work Toolkit.* https://le.ac.uk/-/media/uol/docs/offices/edi/student-sex-work-toolkit-final-december-2020.pdf

Upton, B. (2021) https://www.timeshighereducation.com/news/academics-reluctant-report-violent-online-threats-police?utm_source=newsletter&utm_medium=email&utm_campaign=editorial-daily&mc_cid=0d2ce502d0. Accessed 28th December, 2021.

USI. https://usi.ie/chatsforchange/. Accessed 14th January, 2022.

Valian, V. (2005) "Beyond Gender Schemas: Improving the Advancement of Women in Academia." *Hypatia* 20 (3): 198–213.

Van den Brink, M. (2015) "The Politics of Knowledge: The Responses to Feminist Research from Academic Leaders." *Equality, Diversity and Inclusion* 34 (6): 483–495.

Van den Brink, M. and Benschop, Y. (2012a) "Gender Practices in the Construction of Academic Excellence: Sheep with Five Legs." *Organization* 19 (4): 507–524.

Van den Brink, M. and Benschop, Y. (2012b) "Slaying the Seven-Headed Dragon: The Quest for Gender Change in Academia." *Gender, Work & Organization* 19 (1): 71–92.

Vettese, T. (2019) 'Sexism in the Academy' N +1, issue 34 Head case. https://www.nplusonemag.com/issue-34/essays/sexism-in-the-academy/

Webb (2008) "Re-mapping Power in Educational Micropolitics." *Critical Studies in Education* 49 (2): 127–143.

Wenneras, C. and Wold, A. (1997) "Nepotism and Sexism in Peer Review." *Nature* 387 (6631): 341–343. http://sciencethatmatters.com/wp,content/uploads/2007/04/wenneras97nepotism.pdf. Accessed 12th October 2011.

White, K. (2014) *Keeping Women in Science.* Melbourne: Melbourne University Press.

Whitehead, S. M. (2002) *Men and Masculinities.* Cambridge: Polity.

Whitehead, S. (2021a) *Toxic Masculinity.* Available online: https://www.amazon.co.uk/Toxic-Masculinity-Curing-smarterhealthier-ebook/dp/B0822YFNXL. Accessed 24th June, 2021.

Whitehead, S. (2021b) "That Sound You Hear is China Reversing Globalisation and Crashing International Schooling." *Educational Digest International,* 10th September.

Whitehead, S. (2022) *Total Inclusivity at Work.* London: Routledge.

Whitehead, S., Talahite, A., and Moodley, R. (2014) *Gender and Identity.* Oxford: Oxford University Press.

Woods, D. Y., Benshop, Y., and van den Brink, M. (2021) "What is Intersectional Inequality? A Definition and Goal of Equality in Organisations." *Gender, Work and Organization*, DOI:10.1111/gwao.12760.

Woolston, C. (2020) "The Precarity of Post Docs." *Nature* 587: 505–508.

Wynaden, D., McAllister, M., Tohotoa, J., Omari, Al O., Heslop, K., Duggan, R., Murray, S., Happell, B., and Byrne, L. (2014) "The Silence of Mental Health Issues Within University Environments: A Quantitative Study." *Archives of Psychiatric Nursing* 28 (5): 339–344.

Yen, J. W. 2019. "De-biasing the Evaluation Process of In-Person Review Panels for a Post Doctoral Fellowship." *Nature Astronomy* 3: 1014–1042.

Zheng, R. (2018) "Precarity is a Feminist Issue: Gender and Contingent Labor in the Academy." *Hypatia* 33 (2): 235–255.

Zippel, K. (2021) "#MeToo in Professional Associations: Harassment, Gender and Power." In P. O'Connor and K. White (eds.) *Gender, Power and Higher Education in a Globalised World: Where to Now?*, pp. 139–162. Cham, Switzerland: Palgrave Macmillan.

Zuckert, M. P. (2018) https://nationalaffairs.com/publications/detail/the-insoluble-problem-of-free-speech. Accessed 10th September, 2021.

For Product Safety Concerns and Information please contact our EU
representative GPSR@taylorandfrancis.com
Taylor & Francis Verlag GmbH, Kaufingerstraße 24, 80331 München, Germany

www.ingramcontent.com/pod-product-compliance
Ingram Content Group UK Ltd.
Pitfield, Milton Keynes, MK11 3LW, UK
UKHW021452080625
459435UK00012B/476